AF580680

MAD AS HELL

How *60 Minutes* Took on the Powerful and Made Television History

HARRY MOSES

PROSPECTA PRESS

Hardcover ISBN 978-1-63226-181-6
eBook ISBN 978-1-63226-182-3

PUBLISHED BY PROSPECTA PRESS
P.O. Box 3131
Westport, CT 06880
www.prospectapress.com

Book and cover design by Alexia Garaventa
Manufactured in the United States of America

CONTENTS

FOREWORD

Mad As Hell arrives at exactly the right moment. When forces of politics seek to undermine the best journalism in the world, Harry Moses's frank, honest memoir shines a light on a free press; its strengths, its weaknesses, and its indispensable role in democracy.

The First Amendment is forty-five words. It contains no asterisks, no exceptions, no fine print. It does not say the press shall be free except when the powerful find it inconvenient. It does not say the press shall be free unless its findings are embarrassing, expensive, or disruptive to the established order. The framers, who had just finished a war with a king, understood something we are in danger of forgetting: a republic without an aggressive, independent press is not a republic at all. It is a stage set.

Moses spent his life watching that stage. And when the powerful walked across it, he turned on the lights.

For nearly four decades, Moses produced stories at *60 Minutes*—a hundred of them, give or take—for Mike Wallace, Morley Safer, Dan Rather, Ed Bradley, Diane Sawyer, and me. The pages that follow are about how that work actually got done: not the polished twelve-minute miracle that landed on Sunday-night televisions across the country, but the months of reporting, the late-night editing sessions and more than a few screaming matches with executive producer and *60 Minutes* creator, Don Hewitt.

This is also a book about consequences. When Moses and Wallace sat across from the head of the Nuclear Regulatory Commission and revealed that one of his own engineers had just resigned over the safety of Indian Point 3, they changed the national conversation about nuclear power. When they exposed an internal Hooker Chemical memo that priced the deaths of the company's workers as a line item, they did not merely embarrass a corporation, they reminded the nation that progress and justice only flow from the truth.

Moses believes—as I do—that the scales of justice tilt toward the powerful. Journalism is one of the weights that bring democracy closer to balance. Not because reporters are heroes, and not because they are infallible. Moses is honest on both points.

What *60 Minutes* understood from the beginning, and what Harry Moses helped invent, is that journalism in America works best when it is built around a story we can recognize. A whistleblower. A grieving parent. A truck driver who is sure her thrift-shop painting is a Jackson Pollock. The *60 Minutes* audience has tuned in for nearly six decades to see whether someone will stick up for them when no one else will. "Nobody stuck up for us," people would tell Moses in town after town, "until you guys came along."

That sentence is the most important in this book. It is also a warning. There is no democracy without a free and independent press. James Madison once wrote that freedom of the press is the right that guarantees all the others. Harry Moses has captured that truth with the kind of compelling storytelling that makes American journalism the best in the world.

—Scott Pelley

PROLOGUE

I began my career in television when the medium was in its late adolescence and I was only a few years removed from mine. If the '50s were television's so-called golden age, the '70s were the golden age of television journalism. Leading the pack by a wide margin was CBS News, whose anchor, Walter Cronkite, was the most trusted man in America. He was joined by an all-star team of correspondents, among them Mike Wallace and Harry Reasoner. Mike and Harry signed on to host and report for a fledgling news magazine called *60 Minutes,* led by a creative force named Don Hewitt. The moment I saw the show's first broadcast on September 24, 1968, five days short of my thirty-second birthday, I knew I had to be part of it. The long and often comic journey that got me there, the impact that Mike had on my life, and what I learned about telling stories are in these pages.

What motivates me as a journalist and filmmaker stems from a deep-rooted obsession with life's injustices. A profound sense of moral outrage embraced me in utero, alerting me that my time on earth was going to be unfair and there wasn't one fucking thing I could do about it. Most of us emerge from the womb, accept this, and move on. I did not. The link between these feelings and the career I chose is obvious to me, although it took me decades to connect the dots. Ever since I can remember, I've had an overwhelming certainty that the scales of justice are tilted in favor of the powerful. This has led to certain lifelong behavioral problems, which in the spirit of full disclosure follow: I am not now, nor have I ever been, a team player. I root for the little guy, hold most Republicans suspect, and believe that large corporations are by habit and desire, corrupt. Although the business world doesn't regard these convictions as useful, journalism—which views skepticism as the first step toward enlightenment—differs. That is certainly the case at *60 Minutes,* where I was one of the show's earliest hires, producing almost a hundred stories for Mike Wallace, Morley Safer, Dan Rather, Ed Bradley, and Diane Sawyer. Almost every film I have made, at *60 Minutes* and everywhere else I worked, found its pulse from these core beliefs: A famous Black comedian who gave up a hugely successful career to fight racism. A female truckdriver who took on the art world over her thrift shop painting she thought was a Jackson Pollock. A renowned scientist who spent the last forty years of his adult life trying to prove that the enormous creature he saw rising from the waters of Loch Ness was, well, the real thing. I've spent a lifetime telling other people's stories, where the stakes are high and the outcomes are uncertain. Now it is time to tell my own.

CHAPTER 1

MAD AS HELL

The unique appeal of *60 Minutes* did not become clear to me until I began producing stories that took me away from big cities and I saw firsthand how the show was impacting average Americans. This almost always happened when someone would hear that we were in town and thank us profusely for taking on this crook, that evil corporation, or that wasteful government program. "Nobody stuck up for us," we were told time after time, "until you guys came along." That sentiment was perfectly articulated by Howard Beale, the mad prophet of the airwaves, in the totemic 1976 motion picture *Network*.

> BEALE
> I want you to get up right now and go to the window, open it and stick your head out and yell. "I'm mad as hell and I'm not going to take it anymore!![*]

* In 1974, two years before the last sentence of that speech entered the American zeitgeist, I got a call from a movie producer friend who asked me to share what I knew about tele-

Like the fictional Mr. Beale, *60 Minutes* was becoming a real-life proxy for the little guy. Almost every week it seemed, another pissed-off protagonist was rising up against injustice while millions at home cheered him on. Mike Wallace, who supplied most of the juice, got even more amped by the heartfelt response of ordinary folks everywhere. Mike loved the admiration, but he didn't leave it there. He wanted to know their names, what they did, what was happening to them. It wasn't bullshit either; it was curiosity. Mike was the most curious person I ever met, which is why the film crews and I always tried to spirit him away from the checkout counter before the motel clerk asked why *60 Minutes* was visiting East Podunk. The ensuing conversation usually led to something I didn't know about the story, which was followed by Mike berating me for my lousy research and insisting we stay on to pursue the lead. We only unpacked our bags once, but the threat was always lurking.

One of the most memorable stories Mike and I did used the now questionable technique of the so called ambush interview, in which the correspondent confronts the interview subject with information unknown to him until that moment. Although no one can be certain, it is probable that the first ambush interview in television history occurred in late January of 1973 on *60 Minutes*. Producer Barry Lando was preparing an admiring segment on multi-decorated Vietnam War hero Colonel Anthony Herbert, when he discovered that his premise was wrong. Lando's source was Army Major Jim Grimshaw, who told Lando that he was present during many of Herbert's supposed exploits and that they never took place. On the day of the Herbert interview, Lando placed Grimshaw in an anteroom wired for sound so that Grim-

vision news with a gruff, profane, cigar-chomping screenwriter named Paddy Chayefsky. Chayefsky wanted to know if there was anything the news business *wouldn't* do to get ratings. Since a story I'd recently produced for *60 Minutes* was on the local news scene in San Francisco, which exceeded even fictional anchorman Ron Burgundy's puffed-up witlessness, ("Stay classy, San Diego!"), I felt confident telling Chayefsky he could pretty much let his imagination run wild. I then put him in touch with some of the people I had found during the course of my research. Chayefsky ended up touring the country, talking to them all and eventually writing the script for *Network*.

shaw could listen to what Herbert was saying to Mike Wallace. When Herbert denied Grimshaw's allegations, Wallace summoned him into the room to confront a surprised Herbert directly.

60 Minutes used (many say overused) variations of this technique successfully throughout its first decade and beyond. The theory behind the ambush interview is that without it, the interview subject will (a) continue to obfuscate and/or, (b) knowing the true nature of the interview, decline the opportunity to be skewered by the show. My first ambush interview concerned an engineer named Bob Pollard, who was a safety inspector for the NRC, the Nuclear Regulatory Commission. As part of his job, Pollard had been asked to sign off on Indian Point 3, a Con Ed plant twenty-eight miles up the river from New York City. Pollard told his superiors that Indian Point did not meet the NRC's written safety standards and that he couldn't approve its license request. Pollard's bosses told him to keep his mouth shut. In anguish, Pollard sought out Ralph Nader, who sent Bob on to me. First, I checked out Pollard's background, which was superb. Then I had experts examine his concerns about Indian Point 3. I was told they were valid. Finally, I asked Pollard what he wanted to do. "I'm going to resign," he said. "I can't stay silent. If the plant goes, it could take New York with it."

"You know, Bob," I said, "if you *really* want to make an impact, don't resign now. Do it on *60 Minutes*." Pollard agreed, which left me in the difficult position of getting an interview with the NRC head, William Anders, without revealing its real subject matter: Bob Pollard. Instead, we told the NRC that we wanted to discuss the issue of nuclear safety with Anders, which was true as far as it went.

The NRC said yes, and on the day of the interview, Wallace, myself, two camera teams, and researcher Ellie Collyer appeared in Anders's office. As we were set to roll, Collyer excused herself to go to the bathroom. What she did instead was to call Pollard at work and tell him to resign *now*. Collyer returned and we began filming the interview. After tossing Anders a couple of softball questions about nuclear safety and receiving assurances that it was the NRC's primary concern, Mike told Anders about Indian Point 3 and Pollard. "He's resigned from your agency as an act of conscience," Mike said. Anders, a former astronaut, handled it well. He told Mike that he'd never heard of Pollard, but that it was not the habit of the NRC to stifle dissent, particularly when it came to matters of safety. At this point we ran out of film. While our cameras were changing magazines, Anders called Pollard's boss, Ben Ruschi, to find out more. Yes, Ruschi told him, Pollard resigned just ten minutes ago. Then Anders did something dumb. He put Ruschi on the speakerphone and introduced him to Mike. Mike alertly signaled the cameras to start rolling again as Ruschi proceeded to tell Anders that Pollard had this one little problem. "What problem is that?" asked Anders, counting on Ruschi to derail Wallace.

"He pays too much attention to detail," Ruschi said. Anders frantically reminded Ruschi that not only was *60 Minutes* in his office *but that they were recording every word Ruschi spoke* and that, in any case, attention to detail was *laudable.* It was too little too late. Mike licked his chops and moved in for the kill.

The story made front-page news from New York to Los Angeles and jump-started a national debate on the safety of nuclear power plants. Pollard left the NRC for a long and distinguished career with the Union of Concerned Scientists. However, *The New York Times* television critic John O'Connor was deeply troubled by our ambush of Anders, insisting that we had violated one of journalism's most sacrosanct codes by misrepresenting the story to the NRC. Five years later, I happened to learn that Anders—by then retired—was still furious at *60 Minutes* for gulling him into an interview that he would not have given had he known its real reason. I understand his anger and I also understand O'Connor's ethical concerns. But if we hadn't done what we did, which I firmly believe was in the public interest, Pollard's resignation wouldn't have made the slightest impact. Furthermore, Indian Point 3, the unsafe plant he cited, would almost certainly have begun operating without addressing the safety concerns that so worried Pollard and which his bosses at the NRC were ignoring. (Since 1977, when the story aired, Indian Point 3 was repeatedly shut down over safety issues. In 2021, more than forty years after the fact, it closed up shop for good.)

Although the Pollard story succeeded, sometimes the best-intentioned ambush interviews backfire. I learned this the hard way years later when I was in California researching a story on a pesticide that had polluted the local groundwater and was manufactured by Hooker Chemical. The pesticide, known as DBCP, was eventually banned by the Environmental Protection Administration when scientists determined its ingredients caused cancer. I was leaving the state courthouse in Sacramento when a man approached me and, in the best tradition of a John le Carré spy thriller, thrust a copy of *Life* magazine into my hand. "Page 52," he hissed in my ear as he sped away. When I got to my hotel room, I turned to the page and found his EPA business card paper-clipped to a memo on Hooker letterhead describing the company's plan to resume making the pesticide when the EPA ban expired. The memo, which was from the VP in charge of environmental health safety at Hooker's parent company, Occidental Chemical, was a bombshell. It proposed that the new manufacturing costs for DBCP include money to defend law suits from the families of the workers who might sicken or die from exposure to it. Although written in bland corporation-speak, the memo was implicitly sanctioning the deaths of Hooker's own employees in pursuit of profits—making our original story, the company's pollution of the local groundwater, look like a traffic violation. As a human being, I was appalled. As a producer, I was elated. All that remained was to brief my correspondent, Mike Wallace, for the interview with Hooker's new president, Don Baeder, who did not know we had the incriminating letter.

The night before our trip to Hooker's Houston, Texas headquarters, we met in my office to go over the material. Mike and I had previously ruled against contacting the memo's author, since we didn't want to take the chance of him alerting Baeder, who might then cancel the interview. (Baeder did know that we were going to talk to him about polluting the groundwater, which had already received a fair amount of press.) Mike and I normally prepared for a contentious interview by playing war games. He was the inquisitor, while I stood in for the interview subject and would attempt to parry his questions. Since the memo was indefensible, I saw no need for our usual rehearsal and said so. This was not what Mike wanted to hear. At that moment the door opened and the office cleaning man entered, presenting Mike with an unexpected target of opportunity. "Sit down!" Mike ordered, pointing to an empty chair. The cleaning man sat. "Isn't it a fact, Mr. Baeder," Mike said, "that your corporation plans to engage in murder?"

"No sir," the cleaning man protested, understandably confused and alarmed. "I don't know nothin' about no murder."

"Then what about this?" Mike said, pulling the smoking-gun memo from his pocket and proceeding to read it aloud in a voice worthy of the Sermon on the Mount. "This is an internal document stating that some of Hooker's own workers are going to die from making this pesticide. In all good conscience, sir, how can you allow this to happen?" The cleaning man shifted uncomfortably in his chair.

"I told you, I don't know nothin' about what you're sayin'," he protested. "I just clean up around here."

"You don't know anything about what I'm saying?" asked Mike incredulously, heeding some crazed inner muse. "I think you do, Mr. Baeder. I think you and your corporation are fucking killers!" Mike stormed out of my office in full fury, slamming the door so hard it shuddered. I took a deep breath and turned my head toward the cleaning man, who looked like he'd been ravaged by a Mongol horde.

I cleared my throat nervously. "Sorry," I said. "You can vacuum now."

Although I didn't act out my feelings as Mike had, the memo really impacted me. I wanted to get the bastards, and with Mike as my instrument I had no doubt we could. The interview with Don Baeder took place in one of those anonymous glass-enclosed structures that dot Houston's corporate landscape. When we arrived to set up our cameras, another crew was already there. Hooker's PR guy had hired them to record the interview and make sure that nothing his boss said was taken out of context. Although this happens from time to time, neither Mike nor I were bothered by it. It was simply further evidence that Hooker was nervous. As our own crew finished setting up, I pulled Mike aside. "Ready?" I asked. Mike nodded, his game face on. "Great!" I said. "Save the memo for last, and when we get there, don't hold back."

Mike began by quizzing Baeder on the polluted groundwater. Baeder was unfazed.

> BAEDER
> As soon as we found out it caused cancer, operations were shut.

> WALLACE
> All right. And you don't want to go into the business of making DBCP?

> BAEDER
> We are not going into the business of making DBCP.

This gave Mike the opening he needed to pull out the memo, which he first summarized and then read aloud its conclusion to Baeder.

> WALLACE
> "Assume that 50 percent of the normal rate for these people exposed may file claims of effects from the exposure. Determine the number of potential claims for sterility and cancer . . . Calculate the potential liability, including 50 percent for legal fees and other contingencies."

Mike paused before driving the nail into Baeder's coffin.

WALLACE
One gets the impression that profits are more important to the Hooker Chemical Company than care for human health.

BAEDER
We went out of DBCP as soon as we found out it presented any harm or exposure to . . . the workers.

WALLACE
And yet a year ago, you were . . . looking at the possibility of going back into the business.

BAEDER
People are looking at it, but we are not into it. And I—look, Mike, before I'm a president, I'm a human being . . . You're dealing with studies that people make. We make a lot of studies. Why do you hammer us on something that might have happened, but hasn't happened?

WALLACE
The only reason I'm hammering it is: Is this the way America does business?

Reading this I'd bet that most of you would come to the conclusion that Baeder got what was coming to him, and that Hooker Chemical deserved being exposed for its mendacity. But what you can't divine from a transcript are the personas of those in it. Because of my own sense of outrage, Mike became Mike squared: Bullying, judgmental, angered by Baeder's unwillingness to admit immoral corporate behavior. For his part, Baeder was calm, unruffled; a reasonable man who would never have countenanced the evil act raised in the memo; in short, Don Baeder was the epitome of a nice guy.

Mike, who was normally triumphant after a successful interview, came to my hotel room looking anything but. "Do you think I went at him too hard?" he asked, obviously concerned that he had.

"Absolutely not," I said self-righteously. "The memo's indefensible. It reflects the worst in corporate behavior and people ought to know it.

"Are you sure?" Mike said, pressing me.

"Absolutely! These people are evil incarnate. They deserve what they get!"

In the editing room, the reason for Mike's unease became apparent. Exuding decency from every pore, Don Baeder had fought Mike Wallace to a draw, perhaps even winning on points. What happened is that our biases—mine as much as Mike's—had allowed us to blow an extraordinary story. As I think about it forty-seven years later, I still squirm with embarrassment.

The day after the story ran, Don Hewitt walked into Mike's office, where Mike and I were talking. "We got three hundred letters on your Hooker piece," Hewitt said, depositing a stack of mail on Mike's desk. "Could be a record."

"Give me the headline," Mike said.

They're all pretty much the same," Hewitt answered. "How could Mike Wallace beat up on that nice man, Don Baeder?" He exited, a disgruntled look on his face.

Mike glared at me. "I won't say I told you so," he snapped, telling me in no uncertain terms exactly that.

CHAPTER 2

JOURNALISM 101

I didn't set out to become a journalist or a filmmaker. In fact, my first actual reporting experience was a total bust. I was one of the announcers on a nightly campus news show broadcasting from a classroom at Washington and Lee University in Lexington, Virginia, where I was a student. The program aired on the local NBC affiliate, WREL, whose call letters were the initials of famed civil war general Robert E. Lee. WREL promoted itself as the voice of Rockbridge County, which had tourist attractions like Natural Bridge, Virginia, "the eighth wonder of the world," and the crypts of General Lee and his horse, Traveler, but little else of note.

Then news broke out one night in the nearby town of Buena Vista. A local resident, John Smith (his actual name) was digging a sewer in his yard when it collapsed and he fell in. Smith was in the process of being rescued when I—who'd just gone off the air and was the only body available—was dispatched to his home. My journalism professor looked worried. I was not a star pupil, and this was my first experience in the field. "Remember, never ask questions that can be answered by 'yes' or 'no,'" he said, reciting the first commandment of interviewing.

It was raining heavily as I drove the six miles over the mountain to Buena Vista. In the passenger seat was my tape recorder, a reel-to-reel Stromberg-Carlson encased in mahogany, powered by twelve flashlight batteries and weighing in at fifty-two pounds. After several wrong turns, I pulled into Smith's driveway, passing the bulldozer that had just dug him out. I wrapped the cumbersome recorder in my raincoat to protect it from the downpour and staggered across the yard. Smith stood at the entrance to his house, a huge man covered in muck. "What y'all want?" he rumbled in the deepest voice I'd ever heard. Struggling to hold on to the bulky machine, I told him that I was from W&L and wanted to interview him about the accident.

"Didn't somebody call?" I asked.

"Dunno," he answered.

"Of course you don't," I said as I edged my way inside. "You were in the sewer."

"Ain't got a phone," said Smith, following me into the living room.

I took a deep breath. The smell was overpowering. "Okay if I ask you a few questions?" Smith scratched his buttocks. He took out a filthy handkerchief and blew his nose. Finally he grunted, which I interpreted as "yes." I set up the Stromberg-Carlson, making sure that all the batteries were in place and that the tape was threaded properly. I pressed the record button. "Testing one, two, three," I said. I stopped the machine and played it back.

"Testing one, two, three," it announced, startling the big man.

"Don't worry," I said, "it's just me." I held the microphone between us and began. "Mr. Smith, how did you wind up in the sewer?"

Long pause. "Fell," he said finally.

"I can see that," I said. "How?"

Another pause, this one even longer. "Hole." So far, the first commandment of interviewing wasn't performing as advertised. Dutifully, I continued.

"Can you tell me how the hole got there, Mr. Smith?" He shrugged his massive shoulders sadly, a telling gesture in the real world, but pretty much useless on radio. I pressed on. "You mean, you were digging and it just got . . ." There was a monumental pause while I waited for Smith to finish the sentence. He didn't. "Bigger!" I finally blurted out, my voice breaking.

Smith looked at me strangely. "You okay, son?" It was a legitimate query, which I realized upon seeing my reflection in a wall mirror. The odor of the sewer had turned my skin a pale shade of green and my face was a river of sweat. I decided to dump the first commandment of interviewing for another technique; one that my professor said would make even the most taciturn tell all.

"You were trapped in that sewer for a long time, Mr. Smith. *How did it feel*?" Smith paused to weigh the question, which would normally summon a response that, if not a complete sentence, was at least polysyllabic.

"Bad," he said.

After graduation (with a C in my journalism course) and six months in the army, I landed a job in the promotion department of WOR-TV in New York for seventy-five dollars a week. I was hired because my father was a close friend of the station's general manager and persuaded him that I was the next Ernest Hemingway. Hemingway I was not, nor did I need to be. My main assignment was to write print copy for the *Million Dollar Movie* program, which featured a bunch of black-and-white "B" motion pictures, (they would be called "films noir" today), from the old RKO Pictures library.

I spent two stultifying years at WOR-TV before moving on to the publicity department of Filmways, which produced commercials, television shows like *The Beverly Hillbillies,* and movies. The company was run by Martin Ransohoff, a balding, combustible man who dressed exclusively in velour sweat suits. The highlight of my year at

Filmways was a trip to Hollywood, where I had been summoned to help with a problem Ransohoff was having with actress Kim Novak. They were in the second half of a two-picture deal, in which Ransohoff was obligated to find an expensive property for her to star in. But the blonde bombshell had given him such a terrible time in the first film that he didn't want to spend the bucks. To solve the problem, I came up with what I perceived to be an ingenious solution: The classics. Since they were in the public domain, they would cost Ransohoff nothing. I bought a book of plot summaries, took voluminous notes, and drove over to Ransohoff's house. He sat by the pool, swaddled in lilac velour and surrounded by smoke from a big cigar. "What have you got?" he asked. I handed him my carefully typewritten notes, which he promptly waved away. "Pitch me," he said.

I began with the Bible and spent the next fifteen minutes working my way through Shakespeare. "Too talky," Ransohoff grumbled. I moved quickly on to the French, but having Mme. Novak play heroines from Flaubert or Stendhal were disbeliefs that Ransohoff was unwilling to suspend. "She's from Chicago," he pointed out. "Plus, she's a Polack." In a panic, I bypassed the rest of world literature and went to my ace in the hole.

"Are you familiar with Thomas Hardy?" I asked, my voice cracking under the strain of scholarship. Ransohoff shook his head. "Hardy wrote a book called *Tess of the d'Urbervilles*. Tess is a simple milkmaid. Tess barely talks at all!"

Ransohoff perked up. "What happens to her?"

"She falls in love with an aristocrat and then she's hanged."

"The guy doesn't rescue her?"

"He tries, but he's too late."

"We can change that," Ransohoff said. "Write me thirty pages." I did, Novak passed, and soon thereafter I left Filmways for another job opportunity.

On August 20, 1962, six weeks before my twenty-sixth birthday, I got in a used white Renault I had just purchased for $600, drove through the Lincoln Tunnel, and headed south to our nation's capital. I was to start work the next day as the promotion director of WTTG, an independent television station headquartered in the Hotel Raleigh on the corner of Twelfth and Pennsylvania, four blocks from the Kennedy White House. Although I was excited to get out of New York, this was not my idea of a dream job. I'd spent the last three years in promotion and publicity, of which I was not in the least enamored, and almost all the years before that in a prolonged state of frustration about my life. What Washington offered was change: An exciting young president, a large population of available young women, and a tiny basement apartment I'd rented in historic Georgetown that overlooked a weed-infested lot but was in the most charming section of the city.

There was nothing remotely charming about either the Hotel Raleigh, soon scheduled for demolition, or WTTG. The station's programming consisted of crummy science fiction movies like *Attack of the 50 Ft. Woman,* reruns of forgettable cowboy series—remember *Sugarfoot,* starring Will Hutchins? Probably not—and *Captain Tugg,* a daily children's show featuring a profane alcoholic named Lee Reynolds who lived below an American flag factory, studied Chinese calligraphy, and staggered his way through a daily hour of fun and games inside the patently fake tugboat set. Lee and his show's director, Dennis Kane, became my two closest friends, entwined by our disdain for the station, disenchantment with our jobs, and the distinct sense that things were not going to improve anytime soon. Lee was terminated after a show in which he ordered his permanently offstage first mate to "get his ass off the mizzenmast and bring the old captain his goddamn ration of rum." Dennis, a handsome Irishman, would leave the station for *National Geographic,* where he went on to produce the magazine's long-running documentary series. Having neither of these career distractions, I proceeded to fall in love with a thirty-four-year-old divorcee whose parents were friends with my parents. (More than friends, actually. To our mutual amusement, her father had a long affair with my mother.) After a year, our own affair ended when I asked her to marry me and she declined, citing the eight-year gap in our ages, her two children, and her view that the union would not last.

When bad stuff happens to me, I compensate by losing myself in work. At WTTG, however, this meant promoting further episodes of *Sugarfoot* ("Tonight at 9:00, Will Hutchins stars as a Vermont lawyer defending an Oklahoma Indian chief accused of murder!") or more colossally awful movies. This depressed me even further. Then one evening I turned on the TV and everything changed. What did it was a documentary called *Crisis: Behind a Presidential Commitment.* The film told how the Kennedy administration enrolled two Black students at the University of Alabama in defiance of Governor George Wallace, who parked himself at the schoolhouse door to literally bar them from entering. *Crisis,* which came from the cinema verité workshop of Drew Associates, had cameras everywhere: With President Kennedy; with his brother Bobby, the attorney general; with Wallace; with students Vivian Malone and James Hood; and with Deputy Attorney General Nicholas Katzenbach, who was Bobby's point man in Alabama. Produced by Bob Drew, a man I hadn't heard of, the documentary was so real and personal it took my breath away. When Bobby Kennedy and Katzenbach were talking long distance, you saw both ends of the phone conversation. When JFK was planning strategy inside the Oval Office, you were by his side. And when Katzenbach confronted Wallace with ten thousand federalized troops backing him up, you were wedged between them.

As the program ended, the epiphany hit me. What I had seen—the telling of a story that made you mad, made you proud, made you weep—was what I had been yearning to do with my life all along. Because I was twenty-six and didn't know any better, I decided to go for it.

The first step was to talk my way out of promotion and into production, which I did by moving back to New York and eventually landing a job with WNEW-TV as the producer of a new public affairs program. The show, called *Speak Out!,* had the then revolutionary idea of putting thirty teenagers in a studio and letting them talk about anything: Sex, drugs, the war in Vietnam, whatever they couldn't—or wouldn't—tell their parents. The talk was candid and refreshing, but getting it on camera was a technical challenge. Instead of zoom lenses, which in 1965 were new and costly toys, each studio camera had three different lenses mounted on a metal turret. As a result, no camera could go from wide shot to closeup without the operator manually rotating the turret to the necessary lens. Cutting to a second camera—sometimes the only other camera—did not necessarily avoid the problem since it was not always focused on the person talking. (Imagine peering through a viewfinder at a bunch of adolescents all trying to speak at the same time and guessing which one would prevail.)

Videotape editing, which was equally primitive, had a similar set of challenges. In those days, edits couldn't be done digitally, so the tape was cut with a razor blade, the splice was daubed with a cotton swab dipped in aluminum oxide, and the two ends were joined together with mylar. Since it was almost impossible to restore the edit without a jump in the picture, you needed to be certain about the consequences before you made the cut. No wonder that local studio shows like *Speak Out!* were done "live to tape," meaning that you recorded them to the predetermined program length and lived with the outcome—however unsatisfactory it was.

After a few weeks, I realized this was a lousy way to produce anything. Although the kids on the show were spirited, every broadcast had sections where the camera was on the wrong person, the speaker stumbled, or the conversation went off track. Watching at home, I could feel the viewer getting restless. Restlessness, I knew, was a bad thing. People would get a beer. Or take a leak. Or switch to another channel. Then more bad things would happen. The ratings would drop. The program would be canceled. I would lose my job. To avoid this, I over-taped each show by a third. Afterward, I would screen it, make detailed notes, and remove everything that didn't work.

Because *Speak Out!* was a public affairs show, it was low on the station's list of priorities. To give it pace and flow, I had to edit whenever there was machine time available—often in the middle of the night. I was a perfectionist, so the editors regarded me as a colossal pain in the ass. But trimming fifteen frames (about half a second) from a cut often made a big difference. The process was arduous in the extreme, but it taught me to be ruthless with the material, eliminating everything that didn't drive the discussion forward. *Speak Out!* ran for a year, was nominated for a local Emmy, and was promptly canceled.

My next assignment was associate producer of *The Mort Sahl Show*, a series featuring the legendary political satirist in a mixed bag of interviews and stand-up comedy. The producer was an ex-horn player and TV game show guy named Bob Bach, a decent but dour chap. Communicating with his notoriously difficult star made Bach gloomier than usual, so he had me assume the chore. After a couple of weeks, I understood why. Mort was an eccentric and irascible man. He wore three wristwatches; one set to New York time, the second to Los Angeles time, and a third—with Hebrew numerals—to the time in Tel Aviv. (We didn't ask. Mort didn't tell.) A control freak, Mort dictated everything on the show from what he wore (cashmere sweaters, pastel colors only) to newsmaker guests. When sex researchers Masters and Johnson announced the results of their groundbreaking study, in which they had filmed hundreds of people in the sexual act—including a husband and wife deep in their eighties—Mort told me to book them, or so I thought. It took days of constant calling, but I pulled it off. Even better, it was M&J's first TV interview. I thought Mort would be delighted at this coup. He was not. "I didn't want *them*," he said. "I wanted the old people that fucked."

Mort's predominant characteristic was paranoia, which he possessed in breathtaking abundance. The ramp on which he made his entrance was angled too steeply for his taste and Mort was sure it was only a matter of time before he would slip and fall into the audience. This triggered further complaints. Nobody appreciated him. Nobody was promoting the show. Nobody wanted him to succeed. Mort became convinced that top station management—two gentlemen named Korn and Fraiberg—were out to sabotage him. "The real problem with Hitler," he said to the audience after one show, "was that he killed the wrong Jews." The remark got rid of two more Jews, Mort and me.

With no job in sight, I joined the freelance world and managed to snag a producing assignment with a local public television series. The host was a hotheaded reporter named Al Goldman who was planning a show on the burgeoning (this was 1967) sexual revolution. At the pre-production meeting, Goldman informed me that we would be focusing on a children's book illustrator named Tomi Ungerer. When I asked what the connection was between the sexual revolution and Ungerer, whose books had bland titles like *George the Giraffe* and *Hector the Snake*, Goldman muttered something about artistic expression. I needed the gig so I dropped the subject, booked the film crew, and showed up.

Tomi Ungerer, who was tall, taciturn, and French, worked in a large, darkly lit studio. In the center of the room was an immense table covered with a brilliant red cloth. In the center of the cloth was a huge white circle. In the center of the circle was a big black swastika. Nervously, I told the cameraman to roll. Ungerer lifted the cloth, revealing a concentration camp in miniature, replete with machine gun towers and glistening barbed wire. Every detail was perfect.

When Ungerer switched on an overhead light, I saw how far his search for verisimilitude had taken him. The camp was populated with dozens of three-inch plastic figures. German army officers were meticulously dressed in Nazi garb, their leather boots polished to a high gloss. Some held whips and menaced inmates whose miniature armbands were stamped with yellow Stars of David. The women wore black-and-white-striped dresses that barely covered their buxom little bodies. Ungerer picked up one who was particularly top-heavy, delicately bent her knees and placed her on the ground in front of an officer he called "Cruel Hans." He then flipped a switch protruding from Cruel Hans's back. A motor whirred. The little Nazi moved his hips to and fro in the manner of Elvis before falling down. Ungerer now activated another officer poised behind the rear end of a horse whose tail was conveniently raised. More gyrations. Similar results. Spotlights swept over the concentration camp as the children's book illustrator madly energized the rest of his micro-militia. Wails of passion now blasted from wall speakers. Tiny people were moaning and thrusting and toppling everywhere.

Suddenly the soundtrack stopped. Silence filled the room as we viewed the carnage. "This is my portrait of war and sex," Ungerer announced to Goldman in an accent as gooey as camembert.

"Al, we may have a problem here," I said.

"You're the producer," Goldman snapped. "It's your problem."

I tried to fix it but I had no story. And when I showed my cut to the executive producer, I had no job. My mistake was breaking the second commandment of interviewing, (television section only): Never conduct an interview without meeting the subject beforehand. He could have a boil in the middle of his forehead, a speech impediment, or in the absolute worst-case scenario, an obsession with copulating toy Nazis.

I was on the beach for months and at the end of my unemployment benefits when the phone rang. On the other end was a three-hundred-pound talent agent named Gary Nardino. I had met Nardino on an actual beach at Fire Island in a pick-up touch football game. After knocking me down, falling on me, and pulling me groggily to my feet, conversation ensued. Nardino worked for the Ashley-Famous Agency, where he represented people in television. "I'll call you if something comes up," he told me. Now something had: A brief research assignment for a new client, Bob Drew. I asked if this was the Drew of Drew Associates, whose film on the Kennedys had so inspired me. It was. Drew wanted three or four ideas for a pilot he was researching on new developments in medicine. The stories had to be real, I had one day to find them, and the fee was a measly fifty dollars. I groaned as Nardino baited the hook. "I've just sold a series of Drew's to NBC. There's an associate producer's slot open. Knock yourself out. Maybe you'll impress him."

The *Guinness Book of World Records* does not have a category for most calls placed on a dial telephone within a twenty-four-hour period. If it did, I'm sure I'd hold it. When I met with Bob Drew the following day, I had talked to scores of hospitals, medical schools, and doctors, and had written up fifty-two separate stories. Drew, a large man with a flat Midwestern accent, listened politely and thanked me (perfunctorily, so I thought) for my efforts. Deeply depressed, I left a message for Nardino, told him I had killed myself metaphorically and would do so for real unless he got me the job. Then I went to bed. I was awakened sometime later by a typically terse phone call from my agent: "Associate producer. Five Bell Telephone Hours. Fourteen-five per annum. Start Monday."

CHAPTER 3

CINEMA VERITÉ

It was hard for me to believe that Bob Drew, the man whose documentary on the Kennedys had changed my life, was now my boss. Drew first came to prominence as a photo editor for *Life* magazine when he invented a revolutionary style of shooting still pictures that portrayed people and events with startling realism. Drew called the weekly back-page feature *Life Goes to a . . .*; for example, a pajama party for twelve-year-old girls whose giddy, gossipy excitement was captured by staying in the background, shooting lots of film, and never asking anyone to pose. Drew wanted to use this fly-on-the-wall technique with documentaries, but there were problems. To get sync sound, both film camera and tape recorder had to run at exactly the same speed. Prior to Drew, this task was performed by a six-foot power cable that linked the two machines together. But the connection made it impossible for a cameraman to move about freely without dragging his soundman along with him, a clumsy ballet that would eventually disrupt the proceedings. Drew's engineer solved the problem by inserting two tiny quartz crystals into camera and tape recorder. Their oscillating signals—one perfectly attuned to the other—eliminated the necessity of a cable and made cinema verité possible.

I knew none of this when I got off a tiny elevator that took me to the offices of Drew Associates, located on the top floor of a brownstone that had seen better days. (It has long since been replaced by a forty-nine-floor office building marked by an enormous red numeral 9 that perches in front of it.) Bob Drew sat me down to explain the year ahead. Four of the musical documentaries he would produce for Bell Telephone and NBC would focus on single personalities—Yehudi Menuhin, Duke Ellington, and the like. The fifth, would profile Louis Armstrong, Dave Brubeck, Charles Lloyd, and Dizzy Gillespie in a combined hour. My job would be to vet the characters in terms of interest, negotiate the deals, and assist the series producer on location. "How much do you know about making films?" Drew asked me.

"Not a great deal," I said, which was gilding the lily since I knew absolutely nothing.

Good," said Drew, clearly preferring a blank slate. "Start by learning the principles of editing. It's the last part of the process, but if you don't understand it, you can't do the rest. You'll be spending the week with one of our best cutters, Dee Nosworthy. Watch what she does. Ask questions. Take notes. I'll see you on Friday and we'll move on to the next step." Drew then led me to a rewind table on which sat dozens of reels of film. "You can make yourself useful until Dee gets here," he said. Drew placed a reel of film on a spindle. A couple of feet to its left was another spindle. On that Drew placed an empty reel. "The film is tails out and you want to get it heads up," he explained, "so you take the film and fasten it to the other reel. Turn the handle with your left hand. Put your right hand gently on top of the full reel to keep it steady." I watched as Drew demonstrated.

"Got it," I said.

"After you have the feel of it," he said, "try it this way." Drew pressed his foot on a floor pedal. The handles turned by themselves. Drew gave me a pair of white cotton gloves. "Wear these. They protect the film from the oil and acid on your skin."

Drew left. I put on the gloves and started rewinding. Since I'm mechanically challenged, I proceeded at a turtle-like pace. By the time I had rewound a half dozen reels, my left arm was ready to drop. Time to use the pedal. I pressed my foot down gingerly. The handles barely moved. I pressed harder. The film reel on the right began wobbling badly. I steadied it with my gloved hand and watched in horror as the white cotton turned a brilliant shade of red. The metal reel had slashed through the fabric and lacerated my palm. I removed the bloody glove and wrapped a handkerchief around the wound. Its thickness let me put more pressure on the reel. I pressed the pedal harder. Confidence surged through me as visions of D. W. Griffith, who surely must have started this way, danced in my head. Just as quickly, they danced out. My necktie was caught in the take-up reel. Instead of lifting my foot from the pedal, I lifted my head. No luck. The reel was devouring my tie, drawing me closer with each revolution. If I couldn't free myself, I would lose my nose. If I lost my nose, my brilliant career in film would be over. Suddenly my head bounced back. As I lurched away from the rewind table, I saw a woman holding a pair of scissors. "I'm Dee," she said. "Was it expensive?"

"Was what expensive?" I asked, gasping for breath.

"Your tie. I had to cut it off." I felt my collar. All that remained was the knot.

"Let's do some editing," Dee suggested. "It's less perilous."

By week's end I had learned the basic principles of editing, if not the skills to execute them. Drew then moved me on to the philosophy of cinema verité, which in Drewsian terms meant this: If you don't look like you're filming, the subject matter will forget about you, thus allowing you to get what would have happened if you were *not* filming. To help achieve this, Drew constructed an ironclad set of rules: no lights, no tripod, everything shot handheld. Taking sound was equally demanding. Drew did not permit headsets because they looked like, well, headsets. The only way to check levels was by watching a needle bounce around a meter on the tape recorder—which was like determining how hot it is by sticking your head out the window. When Drew saw a James Bond movie in which Agent 007 secretly taped a bad guy with a recorder concealed in a briefcase (a breathtaking concept back in 1967), things went from bad to worse. Drew built a similar contraption that prevented the soundman from knowing if something was actually being recorded.

Drew used this new invention early in the series while filming a practice session with violinist Joseph Fuchs. Fuchs was playing gorgeously that day but the "record" button (disguised as a lock on the briefcase) jammed, so there was no sound at all. Since opening the case to check on such things was verboten, we didn't discover this until Fuchs had gone home. The experience forced Drew to return to more conventional recording methods, although he insisted that with more time the device would have worked.

In spite of these burdens, I became a convert to cinema verité. The films Drew made in the early and mid '60s were unusually gripping, showing reality as it had never before been seen. Because there was no scripted story line, the drama was captured as it occurred. And since these occurrences were hard to anticipate, Drew's cameras seldom stopped rolling. One memorable documentary focused on the charismatic race car driver Eddie Sachs, who lost the Indianapolis 500 when his car broke down two laps from the finish. It was an electric moment that Drew caught by having one camera on Sachs, a second on his hysterical wife, and a third on the pit crew, which was trying unsuccessfully to get its driver back in the race. (The term "cinema verité" was coined by a French critic after a Drew camera crew followed Sachs into the bathroom when the race had ended and filmed him throwing up. "*Alors!*" the critic wrote. "The cinema of truth!")

All cinema verité films depend on stories with crises, which is the one time you can count on people truly forgetting the camera. Drew understood this, so he tried hard to make films that placed his characters in dramatic situations. This was easy enough to accomplish with race car drivers, less so with musicians and other performing artists. Dancer Edward Villella helped out by getting cramps in the middle of a ballet at Lincoln Center. Collapsing frequently offstage, but always in sight of the camera, Villella managed to recover seconds before his next entrance. Drew cut the sequence into a dazzling montage, which was the climax of the film. He was not so lucky with Count Basie, who preferred playing the ponies to playing the piano and was reluctant to have either activity recorded, forcing us to abort the profile.

Still, we managed to get through the season. The documentaries on Villella and Duke Ellington—both wonderful showmen with superb senses of drama—were memorable. An hour on violinist Yehudi Menuhin was as sweet-tempered as its subject matter, and the other films were better than average, mainly because of the access we got.

After the last film in the series, Drew was hired by Governor Nelson Rockefeller to produce commercials for his ultimately unsuccessful attempt to win the Republican nomination for president. The gig came to Drew through a gruff advertising executive and old friend of Rockefeller named Charlie Moore. Charlie had seen the Bell Telephone hours and became convinced that Drew could capture the real Rocky, someone who cared deeply about ordinary people, never mind his billions. Money being no object, the idea was to travel with Rockefeller for months, his every utterance documented by two film crews, each with its own producer. As the junior person on Drew's staff, my job was to capture the public Rockefeller, which essentially consisted of recording the same stump speech in whichever city his plane touched down. Drew's senior producer, Mike Jackson, was assigned the private Rockefeller. Mike's job was to shadow the candidate wherever he went and whatever he was doing, apart from the boring stump speeches. Moore promised Mike's crew total access to Rockefeller, saying it was worth tens of thousands of feet of film to get the uptight candidate to forget the camera, whereupon his warm, deeply caring persona would reveal itself and be turned into TV ads that would beat back the reprehensible Richard Nixon and win Rocky the Republican nomination. It was an interesting plan that might possibly have succeeded if (a) Rockefeller had cooperated, and (b) any warm, caring moments took place. Had they, Mike and his crew never got close enough to capture them. They were barred from meals, meetings, strategy sessions, and all human interactions between Rockefeller and his staff. The sole exception was what we came to call the Rockefeller ballet: The shirt-sleeved governor would walk out of his meeting, stride to the exit with eyes straight ahead and thrust his arms to the rear, knowing that a waiting lackey would guide the sleeves of Rocky's jacket through his outstretched limbs and place the garment gently over Rocky's shoulders. The performance, a tribute to split-second timing and indentured servitude, took place without a glitch. Mike's crew, which spent months waiting behind closed doors for Rockefeller to surface, captured dozens of these moments, unlikely as they were to win votes.

Having made a bundle on Rockefeller, but with no future projects in the hopper, Drew let everyone go. I, especially, was in a precarious position. I now had a network credit as associate producer on a prestigious series, but it wasn't the producer's credit necessary to get hired by a network news division, all of which were steadily churning out documentaries. So, I decided to strike out on my own. In retrospect, this was foolhardy. I had a wife, a child, a dwindling bank account, and no promise of work. But I had an idea I knew would jump-start my career.

CHAPTER 4

MURDER TRIAL

In 1968, only two states—Colorado and Texas—allowed cameras in the courtroom. Since this was a recent development, a murder trial had yet to be filmed. Realizing that few people had ever seen one, believing that a lot of people would want to, and hoping that the publicity might help free an innocent person, I decided to pursue the idea. But because I was just thirty-one and my producing credits were thin, I knew I had to get an attorney with star power to make the project irresistible. I then placed a cold call to F. Lee Bailey. Fresh from high-profile cases like the Boston Strangler, Bailey was the hottest criminal lawyer in America. If he agreed to be counsel for the defense, I thought I could raise the money to make my movie. Bailey eventually took my call and—lover of publicity that he was—signed on. He then sent me to a lawyer friend in Dallas to help me find a case. The friend dispatched me to San Antonio where the judges were friendlier and the murder statistics were more impressive. Since I didn't know anyone in San Antonio, I called the newspaper and spoke to its crime reporter, a nice guy named Joe Davenport, who agreed to let me pick his brain in return for picking up dinner.

Davenport, a large man wearing a large, black Stetson, met me at a local steakhouse that screamed Texas: sawdust on the floor, longhorns on the wall, and leather boots on every pair of feet but mine. After downing several Lone Stars and ordering the thirty-six-ounce T-bone special, Joe explained what lay ahead. "First you got to find a local defense lawyer who'll let Bailey run the show. There are no public defenders in San Antonio, so trial lawyers here take turns doing it." Joe then handed me a list with the names, phone numbers, and addresses of the attorneys with current murder clients. I tried to thank him but he waved me off. "That's the easy part. After you get your case, you got to convince the prosecutor and the judge that letting you film is a good idea. If they don't go for it, you can pack your bags and go back to Fun City."

"But I *can* talk them into it, right?" I asked anxiously.

Davenport speared a chunk of meat, stuck it in his mouth, and chewed thoughtfully for a while.

"You got desire. You got sincerity. You got enthusiasm. These are all fine qualities," he acknowledged, "but I'd say no."

Despite Davenport's gloomy prediction, I woke up the next morning raring to go. First on Davenport's list was attorney Tony Nicholas. Nicholas's client was accused of killing his wife with a crowbar. "Can't help you," Nicholas said.

"Why not?" I asked.

Nicholas looked at me in dismay. "'Cause he did it." I must have seemed crestfallen. "Let's see that list of yours," Nicholas said. "Maybe I can save you some time." He ran his fingers down it. "Henry won't do it . . . Neither will Albert . . . Gene might, but you don't want him."

"Why don't I want Gene?"

"Too fussy."

I was puzzled. "Fussy?"

Nicholas let his wrist go limp. "Like so. Fussy."

As candidate after candidate fell by the wayside, I wondered if I could check out of my hotel in time to avoid paying for another night in San Antonio. It was clear I was on a wild-goose chase with no chance of . . . "Found your man!" Nicholas said, shattering my reverie. "Name's Jack Leon. Represents some Mexican kid."

"Who did what?"

"Killed a cop . . ." Nicholas stopped in mid-sentence to amend himself. "So they say, anyway."

"This Leon fellow," I asked, anticipating a pitfall, "he's not 'fussy'?"

"Jack? Hell, no. Jack's a lady's man. Real gentleman, too."

"So, he'll cooperate?"

Nicholas smiled broadly. "Considering the case, it's a distinct possibility."

A few hours later, Jack Leon and I were having drinks at the Red Carpet, a dimly lit establishment that was one of several San Antonio private clubs he represented. Leon was a compact, darkly handsome man in his late thirties with a courtly manner and a fondness for Bloody Bulls, a lethal concoction made with tomato juice, beef bouillon, and considerable vodka. By his second Bloody Bull, Leon said he would be honored to have F. Lee Bailey serve as lead counsel on his little murder case.

"So, Jack," I asked, "is this Mexican kid innocent?"

"He says he is," Leon offered. "'Course they all say that."

"Do you believe him?"

Leon shifted in his seat and signaled for another round. "Until he tells me otherwise, I got no choice."

"What's his defense?"

"Here's the story," Leon said. "My client is getting out of his car when the cop comes up to him, spread-eagles him against the vehicle, and pats him down."

"How come?"

"Suspicion of robbery," Leon said. "Anyway, the kid resists. The cop pulls his gun. There's struggle. The gun goes off. The cop is dead."

"Any witnesses?"

"The cop's partner, who arrested the kid."

"And the partner says what?"

"That the kid wrestled the gun away, aimed it at the cop, and pulled the trigger."

"Where did the bullet go?" I asked.

"Here," Leon replied, drawing an imaginary bull's-eye on his forehead. "Got him dead center."

"Was your client alone?"

"No. He had a friend in the car. Another Mexican."

"What happened to the friend?"

"Drove away. Still at large."

I drained my Bloody Bull, the effect of which—if not the taste—was growing on me. "I'm not an expert, Jack, but it doesn't sound great."

"You play the hand you're dealt," Leon said. "I just got dealt F. Lee Bailey, so my hand's looking better. Get him down here and we'll see if we can find you a friendly judge."

As it happened, Bailey was in St. Louis, just a hop, skip, and jump from San Antonio if you happened to own a Lear jet, which Bailey did. Jack Leon and I got to the airport in time to watch Bailey stride smartly across the tarmac, a short, barrel-chested man with the aura of a movie star—hopefully *my* movie star. Leon briefed him as we drove to the Bexar County courthouse to meet with prosecutor Jim McDaniels, a beefy Texan who took an immediate dislike to Bailey. "So, you think you can win this case?" McDaniels asked Bailey, over whom he towered.

"The odds are slim," Bailey replied in a gravelly Boston accent, sounding as humble as he could, considering the huge ego he was toting around. "It's a Mexican kid's word against a cop's. That can't play big around these parts."

"Correct," said McDaniels, "but now we got something better. They found the second kid. He says his friend yanked the gun away and shot the cop in cold blood. He'll testify to that."

"Let me guess," Bailey said. "In return for immunity?"

McDaniels allowed himself a small smile. "It seemed like the sensible thing to do."

"These Mexican lads," asked Bailey, "do they have records?"

"Long as a donkey's dick," said McDaniels. "Armed robbery. Felonious assault. You name it, they done it."

Bailey gazed mournfully at me. "The odds just got worse," he sighed. I glanced at my watch to see if I could make the last flight out, as Bailey continued. "What the hell, Jim. If you don't mind letting a bunch of moviegoers see justice at work, it's okay with me."

McDaniels eyed Leon suspiciously. "You withholding some vital piece of information, Jack? Your client tell you something I don't know?"

Leon, who had been driven into a severe slouch by all the bad news, straightened up. "I'm not withholding anything, Jim. I'm the court-appointed attorney here. I got no dog in this fight."

"How 'bout you, Mr. Bailey?" McDaniels asked. "You got a dog in this fight?"

"Only the public's right to know," Bailey answered, looking positively noble.

McDaniels paused to calculate his chances, which I had been doing, too. It struck me that this was a case Clarence Darrow couldn't win. McDaniels had evidently come to the same conclusion. "Count me in," he said. "Let's go see Archie."

Archie was Archibald Brown, the judge assigned to the case. He received us in the living room of his house with coffee, pastries, and deep suspicion. After the usual pleasantries, the judge cut to the chase. "I've followed your career, Mr. Bailey, and there is one thing that concerns me. Circuses."

"Circuses?" Bailey asked, pretending to look mystified.

"Circuses, Mr. Bailey. I will not have my courtroom turned into a three-ring circus. Not by you. Not by anyone. There will be no grand-standing during this trial. Is that clear?"

Bailey looked mortally wounded. "Perfectly clear, Judge. I would have it no other way."

"As for you, Mr. Leon," the judge said to Jack, "do I have your word that you will conduct yourself in a manner that does honor to your profession, to the city of San Antonio, and to the state of Texas?"

Jack stared down at his boots. "You do, Judge Brown."

"And as for you, Mr. Moses," the judge continued, "your camera is to remain stationary, glued to the ground, fixed in place. No running around. No jumping about. No activity that will disrupt the dignity of my courtroom. Understood?"

"Yes sir," I said, my heart pounding in anticipation of a deal.

"There is one further demand," the judge said sternly. "Without it I will not proceed."

"Christ," I thought. "There goes the ballgame."

"Your autograph, Mr. Bailey," smiled the judge.

"Delighted to oblige, Judge," said Bailey, reaching into his brief-case for an eight-by-ten glossy of himself that happened to be lodged there. The judge handed him a pen. "To Archibald Brown," Bailey intoned as he wrote, "Judge, colleague, friend." Bailey handed the picture to the beaming jurist as we headed for the exit. My God, I had actually pulled it off!

The rest of the day was pretty much a blur. We celebrated at the bar in the Hilton Hotel, consumed an enormous amount of alcohol, and closed the joint. Bailey had offered to fly me back east in his Lear jet, so I went to the airport the next morning nursing a horrible hangover. Bailey was already in the plane. So was the nineteen-year-old cocktail waitress from the night before. "Jessica expressed a desire to see Boston," Bailey said as the plane sped down the runway. When we reached cruising altitude, Bailey suggested that I might enjoy riding in front with the pilot, a weather-beaten man from Lubbock. I opened the door to the cockpit and sat down.

"Ever fly one of these, son?" the pilot asked.

"Not exactly," I said.

"Practically steers itself. Put your hands here," he said, placing them on the controls. "Push forward to go down. Pull toward you to go up. Nothing to it. Okay?"

"I think so," I said uncertainly.

"Good. You take over now. Just look straight ahead and make sure we don't hit anything." He then stood up.

"Where are you going?" I asked.

"Got the shits. Be back as soon as I can."

The pilot left. I squeezed the controls for dear life and peered anxiously through the cockpit window to a thankfully empty horizon. As I began to relax, a horrible shaking commenced. The plane was bumping up and down. "I must have done something awful," I thought, "but what?" The bumping continued. I opened the cockpit and knocked on the bathroom door.

"Can't rush these things," said the pilot. I returned to the controls and pushed down ever so slightly to try to counter the bumping. No luck. I pulled the controls toward me, which seemed to exacerbate matters. I knocked on the door again. "Montezuma's revenge," the pilot's voice boomed. "Goddamn Aztecs can't be trusted." The god of all things Mexican must have been listening because the little jet commenced bumping more violently than ever. I hadn't wanted to bother my celebrity attorney, but there was no choice. I poked my head through the curtain that separated the plane's front compartment from the back.

"Close that thing," Bailey growled, peering over the shoulder of the cocktail waitress who was bouncing like a jackhammer on his lap.

"Sorry," I said, slinking back toward the cockpit where—to my great relief—the pilot had returned. We landed in Boston without further incident. Two weeks later, my real troubles began.

After several stops at several places that could have financed my murder film, but didn't since they thought the producer/director (me) was too inexperienced for their comfort level, I called Gary Nardino, my agent. "No problem," Nardino said. "Your film will be a David Frost production. David has megabucks behind him."

"How come David Frost?" I asked, since an affiliation with the popular British-born talk show host, who wouldn't recognize me if he fell over me, seemed an odd choice.

"Because I represent his production company," my agent said, "and he's looking for interesting projects. His US guy, Marc Merson, will call you. Don't screw it up."

Pretty soon, Merson and I were sitting at the offices of Warner Bros., where a bearded, heavy-set man named Fred Weintraub, who had just produced the fabulously successful documentary *Woodstock*, was listening to our pitch. "I like it," he said, "but is it a story?"

"Well," I said, "it's about life and death. That's pretty good for starters."

Merson interrupted before I could carry this line of reasoning any further. "What Fred means is, where is the arc of the drama?"

"Exactly," said Weintraub. "Which is what we have to find out."

"Look," I replied. "You've got F. Lee Bailey, the most famous criminal attorney in America, representing a Mexican kid who's going to be executed unless Bailey gets him off. Plus, it's the first-ever film of a murder trial. Isn't that enough?"

"No," said Weintraub. "What we need is a professional writer with true crime experience to assess the situation. If *he* likes it, I'll recommend that we go forward." Weintraub stood up, indicating that the meeting was over. "Get me a list of writers and we'll choose one," he said to Merson. "We'll pick up the expenses."

Two weeks later, Merson, a writer named William Bradford Huie, and I were in the Mexican kid's jail cell. Huie, the author of *Three Lives for Mississippi,* a true crime book about the unsolved murder of three civil rights workers in the Deep South, seemed to be the ideal choice for the assignment. He reeked with authority and had a strong opinion on just about everything. Unbeknownst to me and Merson, he had also been harboring a desire to star in a major motion picture. Huie sat down next to the Mexican kid. "Son," he drawled, looking the youth squarely in the eye. "The time for bullshitting is over. Do you promise to tell me the truth?" The kid nodded his head. "I don't hear you," Huie said.

"I promise," the kid said softly.

"Good. Then I only have one question for you. Did you kill that cop intentionally?" The kid shook his head.

"I don't *hear* you," Huie said disapprovingly.

"No," answered the kid.

"And if I were to give advice to you during the trial, would you follow it?"

"Yes," said the kid, who by this time had caught on to Huie's ways.

"Let's go," Huie said, apparently finished with his examination of the drama's principal character. We had flown half way across the country and spent less than five minutes with him.

At the hotel bar, Huie made clear where things stood. "Hell of a story, boys. I am prepared to tell Warner Bros. that this is a great project. I just have a few minor suggestions. During the trial, I'll be sitting next to Bailey and his client, feeding lines to them both." I started to protest but Huie had anticipated my objection. "They don't have to memorize them or anything like that, they just have to follow the general storyline as I see it. You direct the film, Harry. I'll worry about the dramatic arc." He smiled as though he'd just done me a tremendous favor.

"But you can't do that," I said more loudly than I had intended. "This is a trial."

Huie signaled for another drink. "This ain't a trial, son. This here's a movie." The following then ensued: I went to my room and threw up. I got Merson on the phone and made him promise to talk Huie out of his insane idea. Merson told me that he had scheduled a meeting with Warner Bros. for the next day.

At the studio's New York headquarters, Merson, Huie, and I sat waiting to see Weintraub and his boss, Ted Ashley, who ran Warner Bros. Clenching my sphincter, I pulled Merson aside. "Marc, you talked to Huie, right?"

"Yeah, yeah," Merson assured me. "No problemo. The cat's in the bag."

"Meaning he'll recommend the story but he won't talk about feeding lines to people?"

"Uh-huh," Merson said. "Don't worry. I can smell a deal."

At this point we were ushered into Ashley's office. He was a diminutive, bearded man with a permanent look of ennui etched on his face.

"Ted has been briefed on everything," Weintraub announced before directing his gaze at Huie. "Bill, what do you think? Is it a movie?"

"It's not a movie," said Huie. "It's a cinematic masterpiece."

I unclenched my sphincter. Weintraub was beaming and Ashley actually was looking interested.

"So, the story's there?" asked Weintraub.

"I'd stake my journalistic reputation on it," said Huie.

"Tell us how you see the arc unfolding," Weintraub said, still looking at Huie. Clearly I was the forgotten man here.

Huie stood up. "It is noon in the courtroom," he began dramatically. "We know that by the clock on the wall and the ominous tolling of church bells in the distance. The jury foreman has begun to announce the verdict when the sound dims and the camera pans to the defense table. Sitting there is F. Lee Bailey, the Mexican kid, and me. I turn to the camera and say something like this: 'The life of an eighteen-year-old Mexican youth hangs in the balance. Is he a cold-blooded cop killer or an innocent victim? For the first time ever, you will be taken inside a murder trial to see how justice in America works.'" Huie sat down, looking enormously pleased with himself. I reclenched my aching sphincter again.

"Then you flashback to the actual crime?" Weintraub said.

"Exactly," Huie answered. "Recreated so that what happened is ambiguous. Cut to the courtroom where I'm sitting at the defense table. Throughout the trial you see Bailey conferring with me. You see me going over testimony with the kid. When things go badly, I'm there with ideas for a new course of action, suggesting lines of dialogue, shaping the drama."

I leaned over to Merson and hissed in his ear. "Marc, you said you'd talk to him. You *promised* me you talked to him." Merson moved away from me like I had leprosy. Huie droned on, explaining how Warner Bros. had little to risk since he, Huie, acknowledged master storyteller and true crime expert, would be controlling the dramatic arc. Ashley, who was looking bored again, turned to me.

"Mr. Moses, do you have anything to add?" I rose to my full height, which happened to be several inches more than Huie's.

"This is a very simple story, Mr. Ashley. A Mexican kid is going to live or die depending on what happens in the courtroom. The drama is inherent. So is the fucking dramatic arc. What isn't is the narcissistic asshole controlling the action. This film doesn't need any help. It's great all by itself and you *must* let me make it that way." Whereupon, like Jimmy Stewart in *Mr. Smith Goes to Washington,* I collapsed from exhaustion and fainted dead away.

Actually, none of the events described in the previous paragraph occurred. Hoping we might still have a chance and figuring that I could deal with the Huie problem later, I mumbled something about camera lenses and remained seated. "Thanks, guys," Ashley said. "I'll let you know tomorrow," which he did. The answer was no, the murder trial went on without me, and I've been kicking myself ever since for not making the speech you just read—except for maybe the fainting part.

CHAPTER 5

DICK GREGORY

60 Minutes premiered on September 24, 1968, five days before my thirty-second birthday, immediately filling me with envy. For years I had pined for a job with CBS or another of the network news divisions, for whom producing documentaries was my ultimate goal. But they weren't hiring anyone without the network credit I didn't have and couldn't get. It was the ultimate catch-22; impossible to escape without the aid of some magical genie. Suddenly, in the fall of 1969, he appeared in the unlikely guise of a brilliantly talented Black comedian and civil rights activist named Dick Gregory.

In the '60s, Dick Gregory had made the considerable leap from performing for mostly Black audiences to establishment nightclubs whose patrons were largely white. Gregory's material was driven by social issues that few other comics were touching, and his witty, acerbic act had made him the hottest comedian in America. But as the decade was ending, he gave it all up to embark upon a new career where he believed his humor could actually effect change: lecturing to college students about the civil rights movement.

I had seen Gregory perform and admired him greatly. Then one night when I was having drinks with one of his writers, an irreverent gay minister named Jim McGraw who'd been a guest on *Speak Out!*, Gregory unexpectedly appeared. I'd heard about his college tour, so I asked Greg, as everybody called him, where he'd be lecturing that fall. He named a whole bunch of schools, one of which was the University of Alabama, which had been memorialized by the Bob Drew documentary that caused me to become a filmmaker. "They're letting *you* speak *there*?" I asked.

"They got a whole lot of Black folks now," he said. "Even got some playing for Bear Bryant." (Bryant was the notoriously bigoted Alabama football coach who had once vowed publicly that he would never allow a Negro on his team.) "Last year, one of them gained over a thousand yards. Made All-American, too. I do believe that old racist bear done been converted. Not only is he *recruitin'* us, he even makin' *house* calls." Greg then lapsed into a deep-voiced Bear Bryant drawl. "Son, how'd you like to attend the University of Alabama? . . . Hell, no, we ain't prejudiced. We *love* niggers now . . . especially them *fast* ones . . . No, you don't have to worry about your SATs. That shit's for white folks. You here to play football, boy, not to get an education."

"Will you do that kind of material?" I asked Greg after I stopped laughing.

"Sho 'nuff," he drawled, grinning mischievously.

"How about if I tagged along and filmed it?"

"Okay by me," Greg said. "Who would you do it for?"

"Probably public television," I answered. "I'll find out."

I found out the next day when I proposed the idea to Don Dixon, who headed the prestigious Public TV documentary series *NET Journal*. My pitch consisted of seven words: "Dick Gregory at the University of Alabama."

"I've got $17,000 available," Dixon said without missing a beat. "Can you do it for that?" I had no idea if I could do it for that since I hadn't done a budget. But I quickly decided this was no time to be chicken.

"You bet," I said, swallowing hard.

"Okay," Dixon replied. "Go to it."

Two weeks later, I found myself in Chicago, where the film crew and I spent a day getting B-roll of Gregory and his wife and ten kids. Then we flew with him into Birmingham, the city where Sheriff Bull Connor had aimed those huge water hoses at Black demonstrators during the height of the civil rights movement and where Gregory had put his own life on the line. We arrived an hour later in Tuscaloosa, where we barely had time to set up before Greg walked on stage. I gazed nervously out at the audience, which was predominantly white and looked pretty hostile to me. I crossed my fingers and hoped for the best.

Greg began by attacking some American shibboleths. "I read your white history and it tells me that you came to these shores and discovered a country that was already occupied. *Who* the criminal? How you going to discover something that's not only occupied but being *used* at the time. That's like me and my old lady walking out of here today and you and your old lady sitting in your brand-new automobile, and my lady say, 'Gee, honey, that's a beautiful automobile. I sure wish it was ours!' And I say, 'Well let's *discover* it!'"

After Greg saw that the students were enjoying themselves, he began to bring in the heavy artillery. "Let me ask you young people to do me a favor. One day this week, stop off in the library and copy down the Declaration of Independence. Don't read it. Just copy it. And when you copy down the Declaration of Independence, keep it with you twenty-four hours a day, never be caught without that Declaration.

"Now here's my favor. When the riot season open up again—oh yeah, this system even gives us a riot season, July through August.

This season we didn't show and the whole establishment got upset: 'Where were you? We had the tanks waiting for you.' They asked George Wallace, 'How come you think they didn't riot?' He said, 'Oh you know those niggers are lazy and shiftless. They just got tired.'"

Greg paused for the laughter, which was coming at him in waves. "Now here's the favor I want you to do for me. When the riot season open up again, I want you to run home and take your television set and put it in the middle of the room. When they show them Black folks rioting and burning the town, at that point I want you to go upstairs and get your parents and bring 'em down and put 'em right in front of that television set. Then listen to them—you've heard 'em before—just listen to 'em good. And after you've heard 'em talkin' enough, I'd like for you to take out that Declaration of Independence, get way back *behind* them parents, and while they lookin' at them niggers riot, I'd like for you to read the Declaration of Independence as loud as you can, and maybe for the first time them fools will understand what they lookin' at."

Greg's conversational cadence suddenly changed. Now he was a minister speaking in a booming voice to his flock. "WE HOLD THESE TRUTHS TO BE SELF-EVIDENT: THAT ALL MEN ARE CREATED EQUAL AND ENDOWED BY THE CREATOR WITH CERTAIN INALIENABLE RIGHTS. AND WHEN THESE RIGHTS ARE DESTROYED OVER LONG PERIODS OF TIME, IT IS YOUR DUTY TO DESTROY OR ABOLISH THAT GOVERNMENT."

Dead silence. The audience acted as if it had been punched in the solar plexus. Then came applause; a smattering at first, soon building steadily to a crescendo that refused to stop. The white students were on their feet now. They had boarded Greg's train and weren't getting off. Greg let the applause die down before speaking to them quietly, personally, reaching out to every young person there. "I'm sure that with a minimum amount of persuasion, you'll be able to teach your parents that that was their beloved Declaration of Independence—

that one with the mistake on it; that one where y'all forgot to write 'for whites only.' And you know when Black folks read it, we dumb enough to believe it was for *all* Americans."

When I looked at the dailies back in New York, I realized that the film was less about Gregory himself than about the profound effect his words had on the white students, which was mirrored in their eyes. There was one girl in particular, blonde and beautiful, whose remarkably expressive face illustrated the epiphany most of the audience seemed to be experiencing. In fact, the reaction shots of the students were so powerful that I decided to stay on their faces almost half the time. The documentary got terrific reviews, including one from the powerful television critic of *The New York Times.* Now that I had managed to get the network producing credit I so desperately needed, there would be no stopping me. Sadly (for me, anyway), I was wrong.

Not only would the news divisions not hire me, I couldn't get a foot in their respective doors. My carefully crafted letters went unread. My constant phone calls went unanswered. And the Gregory film, which I sent to every important news executive, went unwatched. I was back where I began, and my anxiety was rising.

CHAPTER 6

THE ROAD TO *60 MINUTES*

In 1972, a couple of years after I'd made *Dick Gregory Is Alive and Well,* I was hired by the division of Motorola that manufactures walkie-talkies for police departments to make a documentary on an unusual aspect of police work. I spent a week in the public library going through stacks of newspapers and magazines for possible stories. On the last day I found something interesting. In Oakland, California, a progressive police chief named Charles Gain was having the cops in his family crisis unit audiotape the interventions they made, then gather once a week to critique their performances. I telephoned Gain, who took my call (probably because he always answered his own phone), and told him that I wanted to document the experiment. Gain readily agreed, so cameraman Vic Losick and I flew out to Oakland to spend a week with the unit. This would be real cinema verité. Vic would shoot handheld, using available light, buttressed by a five-hundred-watt photoflood we could plug in when needed. Since the budget was tight, I took sound myself.

When we arrived, I learned that intervening in a family crisis (the police call it a "415-F") was the most consistently dangerous area of police work. Statistics at the time—and they haven't changed all that much since—showed that 80 percent of all homicides occur between people who know each other, most often members of the same family. When the Oakland cops responded to a 415-F, they did so in a stage of high alert. Within that parameter was the dreaded "5150," police code for a person or situation that is out of control.

It only took one night with officers Marty Burnett and Jimmy Galvin, two large, beefy cops in their thirties who had been partners for eight years, to fill Vic and me with respect. The first 415-F—which, in order to get our feet wet, we were allowed only to observe—was from one Richard Forman, who said he was being threatened by his son. When we responded, a very tall, very beautiful young Black woman wearing six-inch heels and a glittering evening dress came to the door. In a husky voice, she told us to go away. "Not until we talk to Mr. Forman," Burnett said. The woman opened the door a crack.

"He's not here now," she said.

Burnett shouldered his way into the house. "We're in no hurry," he said. "We'll wait."

No sooner had we come inside than Forman, an older Black man, raced down the stairs. "Took you long enough to get here," he said testily. "My son hit me. I want you to arrest him."

"Where's your son?" Galvin said.

"In front of you," Forman answered. "You blind?"

It took me a few seconds to realize that the glamorous woman standing before us was a man. Neither Burnett nor Galvin seemed all that surprised. "So, did you hit your father?" Burnett asked.

"Slapped him, maybe. Got tired of him tellin' me where I can go, what I can do, when I need to be home."

"What's your name?" Galvin asked.

"Michele," he said.

"It's Michael!" Forman shouted.

Michele/Michael ignored the outburst. "I'm eighteen. Old enough to do what I want."

"Not in that outfit!" said Forman.

"Ain't no law saying I can't dress like this," Michele/Michael responded.

"Let's get a few things straight here," said Burnett. "Mr. Forman, is your son eighteen?"

"Yes, but . . ."

Burnett cut him off. "Then he's of age. He can come and go as he pleases."

"In *those* clothes?" shouted Forman.

"Mr. Forman," said Burnett politely, "there's nothing in the Oakland statutes about style of dress."

"Told him that already," said Michele/Michael."

"Now as for you, Michele," Burnett said, "no more slapping, is that clear?"

"Wasn't no slap," Forman said. "Was a punch. Almost knocked me down."

"No more slapping and no more punching," said Burnett wearily. "If this happens again, Michele, we'll have to arrest you. Behave yourself and have a pleasant evening."

Later, I asked Burnett and Galvin if this sort of bizarre encounter was typical. "There is no typical," Galvin said. "There are so many weird things out there, you become cynical very quickly. Spend a week with us and you'll be just like us."

"So, can we start filming?" I asked.

"Now that you've seen how we work, sure. Just stay in back of us and be . . ." Galvin was interrupted by the squawk of his police radio, instructing them to respond to a 5150 in one of Oakland's toughest neighborhoods.

"What did they tell you about the call?" I asked Galvin, as we were speeding toward the destination in the squad car.

"Not much," he said. "A woman called. Lydia Washington. Told the operator her husband has a weapon. Then she hung up. That's all we know."

The squad car parked at a dimly lit corner. Galvin and Burnett had removed their guns from their holsters. Holding them loosely at their sides, they approached the first-floor apartment in a ratty-looking project. "Stay in back of us," Burnett said. Heart pounding, I hit the Record button on my Nagra tape recorder, stuck out my shotgun microphone, motioned for Vic to roll, and hoped for the best. Burnett knocked at the door. Eventually a young Black woman appeared, holding an infant in her arms.

"What seems to be the trouble?" Burnett asked her.

"My husband . . ." she said breathlessly. She was hyperventilating so much that she couldn't complete the sentence.

"Please relax, Lydia," Burnett said. "We're here to help you." Positioned to the left of Burnett and Galvin, I was able to look beyond Lydia and into the shadowy apartment. Standing several feet from her was a highly agitated Black man in his twenties. He was pointing a huge revolver at his wife and child. I tried whispering this to Burnett but he elbowed me away. "Mr. Washington," he said, "please come out where we can see you."

"Put your guns back in your holsters first," Washington said. To my surprise, Burnett and Galvin did. Washington moved closer to the dimly lit doorway. Now he was pointing his revolver at the cops.

"What seems to be the trouble, Mr. Washington?" Burnett asked calmly.

"Goin' back to Vietnam tomorrow. Don't want to."

"You got to," Lydia said. "If you don't, the army'll throw you in jail. Then what'll happen to us?"

"Same as if I come back in a body bag."

"You'll come back, honey," Lydia cried. "We need you to come back."

"To what? Grease monkey? Fry cook? Some dead-end job?" Washington was now pointing the gun at himself.

"Mr. Washington," Burnett said, "I'll make a deal with you. Give me the gun and we're out of here. No report. No arrest. This never happened."

"Give him the gun," Lydia wailed. "Please!" The baby began to cry. Reflexively, she handed it to her husband. Washington took the child and lowered his gun. I was sure Burnett was going to jump him, but he didn't move. Sobbing convulsively, Lydia reached out for her husband and held him close. He let the gun slip to the floor. Burnett opened the door and took it.

"Any more weapons in the house, Lydia?" he asked. She shook her head. Washington cradled his wife and child in his arms as he wept.

"Okay," Burnett said, "we'll be leaving now." Vic and I followed Burnett and Galvin down the block and into a coffee shop where we all collapsed into a booth.

"Why didn't you jump him when he lowered the gun?" I asked Burnett.

"Thought of it," he said. "Didn't like the odds."

"Wife could have been killed. Baby could have been killed. Marty could have been killed," Galvin explained. "Anyway, Marty knew I had him covered."

"You mean while the two of them were arguing, you drew your gun again?"

Galvin nodded his head.

"But how could Marty know that?" I asked. "You were behind him."

"You partner with someone for a while, you get to know certain things," said Burnett.

"Then after you picked up the gun, how come you didn't arrest him?"

Burnett smiled. "No point to it. He's got enough trouble as it is, and the situation was defused."

I then had a horrifying thought. "Vic, you were rolling the whole time, right?"

"Yeah, but you won't see anything. Not enough light for an exposure."

"Shit," I said, allowing my producer's zeal to obliterate the human tragedy I had just witnessed. Burnett saw my frustration.

"Relax," he smiled. "We have four more days."

The rest of the week was mildly productive. We managed to film four interventions from top to bottom. Although some were interesting, they lacked the drama I needed to make a compelling film. It was now Friday night and we were down to the last hour of Burnett and Galvin's shift. A woman had called complaining that her husband was drunk and had thrown a punch at her. When we responded, my heart sank. The man was so inebriated he could barely put two words together. Burnett cut to the chase. "Mr. Jones," he said, "you have an alcohol problem."

"Don't drink," Jones said.

"Yes, you do," Burnett insisted. "This is the third time we've responded in the last six months. You know what that means, don't you?"

Jones, a large, fat man in his fifties, suddenly sobered up. "You can't take my driver's license. If I can't drive, I can't get to work."

"Show me where you keep the booze," Burnett said.

"This way," said Jones, staggering down a flight of stairs to a kitchen containing two refrigerators. "In there," he said, pointing to the smaller of the two. Burnett opened it. There were a lot of TV frozen dinners and a solitary bottle of cheap wine.

"Open the other fridge," Burnett told him.

"Nothing in there," Jones insisted.

"Have it your way," said Burnett. He pulled open the door, revealing an aluminum army of Budweisers. "You want to keep your driver's license, Mr. Jones, you get rid of this beer." Jones looked like he'd been hit with a two by four.

"Okay," he said, swallowing hard, "I'll do it tomorrow."

"Now," Burnett ordered. "In the sink."

Jones gazed at him in disbelief. "You want me to empty them . . ."

"In the sink," said Burnett. "All of them."

Mournfully, Jones took a can, popped it open, and slowly poured its contents down the drain. Burnett glanced at his watch. "You got thirty minutes, Mr. Jones. If you're not through, I'm taking your driver's license. Permanently." Jones's jaw dropped as he stared at Burnett. "You just lost ten seconds," Burnett said. "Pick up the pace." Jones began moving like a demon. After getting some shots of him shuttling back and forth between the refrigerator and the sink, I told Vic to concentrate on Jones's face, whose expression told the story of a loss so unimaginable words could not express it. By the time Jones finished, he had emptied 132 cans of beer and I had the sequence I so desperately needed.

The film turned out so well that I persuaded Motorola to let me try to sell it to *60 Minutes,* thereby recouping some of the cost and benefiting from the exposure on network television. Unmentioned was my hope that the show's executive producer, Don Hewitt, would be so impressed with my work he would hire me. It took more than a dozen phone calls before I got through to Hewitt. But when he screened the film, he loved it and ran it immediately. I pitched him for work. "Keep calling," he said. I did.

Months went by. When my phone calls continued to go unanswered, I screwed up my courage and decided to try Mike Wallace, who had narrated my story but whom I hadn't met. Much to my surprise, he answered the phone. "Mr. Wallace," I said, "I'm the guy who produced the piece on the family crisis intervent . . ."

"I know who you are," he interrupted. "What can I do for you?"

Haltingly, because I was anxious, I explained that I wanted a job producing for *60 Minutes* but that I wasn't having much success getting through to Hewitt.

"I'll talk to him," Mike said. "How do I reach you?" I gave him my number and the conversation ended. As I reflected on the unlikely possibility of ever hearing back from him again, the phone rang.

"It's Mike," he said.

"That was quick," I gasped.

Mike ignored my reaction. "I talked to Don. He says there's nothing now, but there could be an opening soon."

"So what should I do?" I asked.

"Call me every two weeks. My secretary's name is Merri. If I'm out of town, she'll find me."

Before I could thank him, he'd hung up the phone. I sat there dazed. Why was America's most famous television correspondent taking a personal interest in my career? Since I couldn't figure it out, I decided to put it out of my mind until the next phone conversation—if there was one.

Two weeks later, I dialed Mike again. This time he was on assignment. I left word that I had called and prepared myself for the long and painful wait of never hearing from him. Once again, the phone interrupted my thoughts. Mike was calling from London, where it was eleven o'clock at night. "There's been some progress," he reported. "Don says he's sure there's going to be a slot open and you're a leading candidate. I'll keep you posted."

I was rapidly becoming a charter member of the Mike Wallace fan club. Producing for *60 Minutes* was the most sought-after position in broadcasting. Thanks to this man I'd never met, I had a shot at it. In the space of the next several months, during which Mike and I were now conversing once a week, I learned that my competition for the job was a producer named Craig Leake, who had produced a film called *Hair Comes to Memphis*. Leake's documentary told the story of that city's shocked reaction to this quintessential '60s musical, some of whose cast members took their curtain calls in the buff. In our last phone conversation, Mike told me that he didn't regard the film as a serious piece of work (it sounded pretty good to me) but that Hewitt loved it, hoped to run it on *60 Minutes,* and now wanted to hire Leake. In despair, I asked Mike if he thought Hewitt could be turned around.

"Unclench your sphincter," he said. "I'll see what I can do."

Whatever he did worked. Leake's film never aired, the threat of Leake vanished, and Hewitt offered me the job. I accepted immediately and asked to meet Mike. Don walked me down the hall to his office, which was cluttered and surprisingly small. After introducing us, he left me alone with my unlikely benefactor. I had seen Mike on the tube hundreds of times over the years, but I was not prepared for the intensity of his presence. At fifty-four, he was startlingly youthful. His hair was jet black—black enough to have come from a bottle—although I later learned it was untouched by dye until later in life. Mike's eyes, an otherwise ordinary brown, were strikingly intelligent, and when he focused on you, it made an impact. A bad case of acne as a child had left his skin heavily pockmarked, which added to his generally intimidating aura. Most of all there was his voice, that famous weapon of a voice: deep, insistent, knowing—demanding that attention must be paid. The thought of fooling someone like this would have been out of the question; the thought of getting on his bad side, terrifying.

"There's something I have to ask you," I blurted. "You didn't know me from Adam. How come you helped me?"

Mike glanced up at me from behind his desk. "I liked your work, kid. Keep it up."

Relationships between people like me and people like Mike are invariably one-sided. They wield the power. You do not. They have an ego that you must serve. They are in the public eye, while you remain anonymous. All of this was fine with me. Because of Mike, I had been transported from the teeth-grinding uncertainty of a freelance existence to the best producing job on the planet. In a world where merit counts for little, Mike had recognized mine and gone to bat for me. In a system where political connections are everything and I had none, Mike supplied them. And for the best of reasons—the *only* reason as far as I was concerned: He liked my work.

CHAPTER 7

ORIGINS

That *60 Minutes* happened at all was largely dumb luck. Don Hewitt said so himself in an interview I did for this book shortly before his death. Don told me that he and his boss, CBS News president Fred Friendly, had a relationship that verged from dicey to downright antagonistic. Friendly, who was portrayed winningly but inaccurately by George Clooney in the movie *Good Night, and Good Luck,*** was a large man, ponderous in manner and devoid of humor. Friendly fired Hewitt as the executive producer of the *CBS Evening News* in 1965 and gave him his own unit to produce documentaries, which in Don's mind was like winning a contest where the grand prize was a week in Philadelphia. Hewitt was temperamentally and philosophically opposed to Friendly's fondness for these programs, in which the news was administered to an audience the way a mother forces medicine down a child's throat, never mind the taste. Hewitt was

**In the recent theatrical version, Clooney played Murrow, a much better fit.

convinced that if the news were less Fred Friendly and more viewer friendly, the audience wouldn't be as reluctant to swallow it.

Don spent his time in exile dreaming up new ways to attract viewers. He'd seen a weekly Canadian Broadcasting Company series called *This Hour Has Seven Days,* which took several hard news stories from the events of the past week and produced mini-documentaries on them. He was also an admirer of *Omnibus,* a defunct magazine program on the arts that featured the urbane British journalist Alistair Cooke as host. Hewitt thought a show that blended serious and light within the same hour would be infinitely more appealing and a whole lot zippier than the vision imposed on him by Friendly. Each program would have three items (i.e. stories), just like the menu for a Chinese restaurant back then. The viewer could choose one from column A, one from column B, and one from column C. If they didn't care for the appetizer, the entree might appeal to them. If that wasn't to their satisfaction, there was always dessert. The stories would be brief, none lasting more than fifteen minutes. Viewers would leave the program feeling both satisfied and hungry for more.

Hewitt took his idea to Friendly, who wanted no part of it. Then Friendly suddenly resigned as president of CBS News after the network refused to preempt a rerun of *I Love Lucy* to air a US Senate hearing on Vietnam. Friendly was replaced by Richard S. Salant, who had been Friendly's predecessor until Friendly overthrew him in a palace coup. After Salant had settled back in, Hewitt pitched him his new magazine show. Knowing that Salant, a Harvard-trained lawyer and a serious man, was also prejudiced against anything that dared to stray from hard news, Hewitt began by saying that he had presented the very same idea to Friendly, who hated it. That was all Salant needed to hear. It took Hewitt three years, but *60 Minutes* had its green light.

I arrived there as a staff producer on January 2, 1973, full of nervous energy at having landed my dream job at the advanced age of thirty-six. I knew little more about the show than what had been written. *60 Minutes* made its television debut in September of 1968 and finished the season in last place, seventy-second out of seventy-two prime-time programs. Since then, it had switched from time slot to time slot, producing stories that were talked about within the industry but whose ratings were merely mediocre. Nothing about the show back then foretold the legend it would become.

The show's twelve other producers and I toiled in a warren of ratty offices, deep in the bowels of CBS News. The building, a converted dairy barn, stretched almost the entire length of Fifty-Seventh Street from Tenth to Eleventh Avenues, one of Manhattan's least distinguished locales. Because *60 Minutes* was part of CBS News, I expected a buttoned-down, corporate environment. What I got, to quote the intro to *Monty Python,* was something completely different. Richman, the maintenance guy, roamed the halls hustling items of dubious provenance (furs, pearls, rings, watches) that he sold for bargain-basement prices. There was a weekly high-stakes poker game that executive producer Don Hewitt held in his office, a permanent floating backgammon game that was going on when I arrived and still going when I left, and a Monday morning doubles game whose outcome Mike Wallace scrawled in 72-point chalk on the office blackboard—if he won. Almost everything about *60 Minutes* was boom-box loud, especially the story screenings. To get through them, I resorted to valium, the anxiety drug du jour, while Don Hewitt and Mike Wallace yelled at each other and largely ignored me. The Tiffany Network's weekly news magazine, offspring of the classiest news operation on television, had the gravitas of a children's sandbox.

When I joined *60 Minutes,* the show was ensconced at 6:00 p.m. on Sunday, except for being preempted in the fall by football, in the winter and spring by local programming, and in the summer by a schedule change that moved it to the time slot of Fridays at 8:00 p.m., when people did everything except watch television. It would be wrong, however, to paint an overly bleak picture. *60 Minutes* was comparatively cheap to produce and was much too useful to CBS to cancel. Although it wasn't always prime time, it was still the big time, and its impresario, Don Hewitt, acted that way. Hewitt, a compact man with the élan of an Energizer Bunny and the bravura of a Barnum, was the show's ringmaster. There was this line of copy he'd just written, this joke he'd just heard, this fabulous party he'd just been to—all needing communication *right now.* So long as Don could satisfy this requirement, little else mattered. The broadcast's standard of excellence was high; its standard of civility scraped bottom. Underneath lay a Darwinian struggle between the correspondents to field the best possible team of producers. At the end of every season, they met behind closed doors to decide our fate. Star players were untouchable, journeymen were traded to other teams without being asked, and those with bad seasons were banished to the minors (i.e., somewhere else at CBS News).

Along with Don Hewitt, the person most responsible for the success of *60 Minutes* was Mike Wallace, the show's alpha male and my self-appointed mentor and father figure. Mike gave me the approval that my real dad never did, before adding items no one in his right mind would want: a racing pulse, recurring nightmares, and anxiety that gripped me like the Death Star. Then, when all appeared lost, enough love—measured in micrograms—to keep me from self-destructing entirely.

Mike had a spellbinding presence and an uncanny ability to get people to say things on camera they wouldn't have told their wives, husbands, or lovers. He was also a provocateur, once famously goading volatile tough guy Burt Lancaster into walking out on him during a live broadcast. No one denied Mike's talent, but his critics accused him of being a muckraker, a yellow journalist, and a son of a bitch—all of which in varying degrees were true. As he would later tell me,

Mike felt the need to change his image. At the age of forty-five, he took a dramatic cut in income to join CBS News and refurbish a somewhat questionable job history (for a serious journalist) that included hosting game shows, shilling for a tobacco company, appearing in a failed Broadway comedy, and humiliating scores of people on camera. Ten years later, which was when I met him, the transformation was complete. With the exception of Walter Cronkite, Mike Wallace was now the most famous television newsman in broadcast journalism. He was by any measure the most feared.

The show's other correspondent was a forty-one-year-old Canadian transplant named Morley Safer, master of the offbeat yarn. When Safer took a ride from Paris to Istanbul for a story on the Orient Express, the passengers he profiled included two wealthy Syrians on their way to Turkey to hunt swans with machine guns. Exotic run-ins like this happened more or less regularly to Safer, who relied on his writing skills and eccentric sensibilities to do pieces in which the story was not immediately apparent. Although he would rightly have rejected the notion of being a one-note Morley, he will be remembered for bringing an engaging and literate quirkiness to television. In a sense, Safer was the anti-Wallace: diffident, detached, and largely devoid of charisma. But Morley made up for this in other ways. He gave off a certain air of sophistication on camera that was aided by his choice of apparel. As a result of spending years in London, Safer had adopted the dress code of a Mayfair dandy: boldly patterned shirt, severely clashing necktie, and brightly hued silk square that complemented neither and drooped from the breast pocket of his jacket like a flag on a windless day. The look was buttressed by other distinctive qualities: a gravelly voice sustained by a three-pack-a-day habit, a gift for turning a phrase, and a clever wit. These attributes and his sterling work in Vietnam separated Safer from the scrum of reporters auditioning for the job and landed him at *60 Minutes*.

When I came on board, Safer had begun his third season on the show and was highly competitive with Wallace. Although their styles were totally different, Safer loathed playing backseat to his elder colleague, who wielded the real power and made no secret of it. Even more irritating, the man on the street recognized Wallace on sight while almost no one knew who Morley was. Many of the people he interviewed would actually refer to him using the wrong name. (Morley Safer invariably became Maury Schaefer.) Safer knew that if the error wasn't corrected on the spot it would present problems in editing, yet he refused to say anything. As a result, the embarrassing task of stopping the interview to make the revision fell to me and his other producers, which irritated Safer even more than the pesky name recognition problem.

Although I would do the majority of my stories with Mike, my first three pieces were with Morley. The initial one focused on an eighth-grade teacher named Joe Acanfora, who had been given the boot by the Maryland public school system because he was gay. This enraged me, but even though the story got on the air, it had major problems. Acanfora was only an okay character, not nearly compelling enough to carry the story by himself. And considering that the school system refused to be interviewed and wouldn't let us film in his classroom, and that no parent would talk to us, I should have dropped the story. (Remember, this was fifty or so years ago, when a schoolteacher who came out of the closet was a very big deal.)

Knowing I could do better, I decided that the quickest way to make my mark was to produce a story about a subject that TV had never before tackled: pimps. That I did not know any pimps was beside the point. I was resourceful. I would find them. And my reputation at *60 Minutes* would be made. (I had yet to learn that the subject matter of a story does not in and of itself make a story.)

First, I had to convince Hewitt that the idea had merit. Because he knew even less about pimps than I did, it was an easy sell: "Mile-high afros, fabulous outfits, private polo ponies," all of which I promised to deliver. My first stop was Ohio, where a source had set me up with the Babe Ruth of pimpdom, a legendary Cleveland native with the *nom de guerre* of Silky. Silky, the source assured me, would cooperate if convinced of the seriousness of my venture. "Also," said the source, "bring champagne."

I arrived in Cleveland on a cold and snowy evening clutching a bottle of Dom Perignon ("Silky doesn't drink the cheap stuff," the source said), and took a taxi to the hotel ("Get a suite, it will impress him") where Silky was to meet me at precisely 8:00 p.m.. The appointed time came and went, as did 9:00 p.m. and 10:00 p.m., which I filled by plumping the pillows on the living room sofa and ordering a bucket of ice for the champagne. At 10:45 p.m. there was a knock on my door. I leapt from my chair to welcome my guest, a thirty-something Black man wearing a sensible tan coat, a Brooks Brothers shirt and blue jeans. Attributing his less-than-flamboyant outfit to the weather, I popped open the champagne and offered him a glass of the bubbly, which he sipped and shoved aside somewhat disdainfully, I thought, although this might have been due to my rising paranoia. I then launched into my sales pitch, which consisted of explaining that *60 Minutes* wanted to achieve an understanding of what pimps did and how they went about it.

"How you gonna do that?" he asked. Silky's voice was surprisingly high-pitched. Also, I thought I detected a lisp. I told him that we'd like to spend a couple of days following him around with a film crew, but that I'd know better once I'd hung out with him tonight, which my source had prearranged.

"Tonight'th not tho good," he said, rising from his chair. I was right about the lisp. I reminded him that I'd come all the way from New York and that we didn't need to make it the whole night, that a couple of hours would do. "Maybe thome other time," he said. "Got to thee my mom." Whereupon Silky exited.

Aware that the story was more problematic than I'd thought, I called the NYPD and talked them into letting me film their pimp patrol, which consisted of two officers in a squad car combing the streets for likely suspects. Three nights with them yielded a lot of dialogue about the perils of the job, but zero pimps. Down but not quite out, I flew to San Francisco where, to my great good fortune, a married pair of sociologists were holding a book party at an outdoor café for the publication of their three-year study on pimps in the Bay Area. The husband, Richard Milner, had told me that every pimp in town would be attending, tricked-out in their fanciest duds and driving their flashiest cars. We hit the café and waited. And waited. At 2:00 a.m., with no pimps in sight, I made an impassioned plea to Milner, the gist of which was that if he didn't find me a real live pimp, my career was headed for the toilet. Impressed by the gravity of my plight and the realization that his book would go unplugged on *60 Minutes,* Milner excused himself to make some phone calls. An hour later, he returned. "You're all set," he said. "I got you the biggest pimp in San Francisco. This guy's the real deal, right out of central casting. And he loves publicity." Milner gave me his address and told me to meet him there for breakfast. "If he likes you, you can film him to your heart's content."

As it turns out, breakfast for pimps means 1:00 p.m., so with my film crew waiting in the van, I broke bread with Mr. Johnson, as he preferred to be called. Mr. Johnson was indeed straight from central casting. He had the look, he had the wardrobe, he had the swagger. Better yet, he spoke in a manly baritone that sailed easily past any lurking sibilants. I listened raptly as he described his plans for the day. "First, I visits my tailor. Then I checks on my women. Later on, I plays golf or polo, depending on the weather."

"That's some life!" I said in genuine awe. "Are you the exception to the rule or is it like that for every pimp?"

Mr. Johnson bolted upright in his chair. "Don't use that word," he said.

"What word is that?" I asked. "You mean, 'pimp'?"

"I told you not to say that word," he said, glaring at me. "I don't like it."

"So, in the story, you don't want me to say 'pimp'?"

Mr. Johnson was visibly upset. "You said it again, son. How many times I got to tell you? Don't use that word. That word an ugly-sounding word."

After swearing that the *P* word would never cross my lips, Mr. Johnson agreed to let me accompany him throughout the day, filming whatever and wherever I wanted. The crew and I followed his midnight-blue Cadillac to the first location, Mr. Johnson's tailor, where a double-breasted, fire-engine red outfit awaited its final fitting. The assistant cameraman held up the slate, the final step before filming. "Camera roll one, sound roll one, take one," he announced as he dropped the clapstick. "Pimps."

Dead silence. I looked at Mr. Johnson. Mr. Johnson looked at me. I had neglected to inform the crew that the title of the story had been changed. "Sorry," I said. Mr. Johnson's hand dropped down to his pants pocket, where there was a prominent bulge. For some reason, the classic Mae West line popped into my head: "Are you happy to see me, or is that a gun?" Since the answers to both questions were obvious, they called for a change of plans. "Pack up," I said to my mystified film crew. "It's a wrap."

I finally managed to wrangle enough pimps to get it on the air, but it was not one of *60 Minutes*' finest stories, nor one of mine.

CHAPTER 8

MIKE

Mike Wallace and I began our long professional relationship with a profile of former tennis champion Bobby Riggs. In the spring of 1973, Riggs had irritated feminists the world over by issuing a sexist challenge to Margaret Court Smith, the number one women's player in the world. Riggs, who was twenty-five years her senior and had long ceased playing competitively, trounced Smith by feeding her junk until she self-destructed. Thrilled at the chance to work with Mike, I headed to Las Vegas, where the match had been held at Caesar's Palace and where Riggs was currently holed up, enjoying the avalanche of press from his victory.

I had driven to McCarran (now Harry Reid International) Airport to pick up Mike and was pacing nervously as I waited for his plane to land. It wasn't that I was ill-prepared for his arrival. To the contrary, I was overprepared. I had spent a couple of days with Riggs, taking copious notes on his life and times and supplementing those with reading material I had brought with me from New York. I then compiled a briefing paper for Mike, wrote a series of interview questions, set up some other interviews, wrote background and questions for those, scouted possible film locations, and arranged for permission for our camera crew to trail Riggs, a notorious gambler, as he rolled the dice in various casinos on the strip. In short, I had it covered. Because it was my first story with Wallace, I was determined to leave no stone unturned and no question unasked to reveal the essence of Bobby Riggs and show Mike that I knew what I was doing.

Mike walked off the plane. His California trip had gone well and he was in a good mood. On the car ride back to the hotel, I reviewed everything with him and gave him the material I had prepared. "Tell me about Riggs," he said. "What's he like?" I explained that Riggs was a real character: never shuts up, high energy, even more anti-feminist than advertised. The only problem would be getting him to be as outrageous on camera as he was in person.

"He's a little apprehensive about the interview," I told Mike.

"Don't worry," he said. "I'll handle it. Anything else going on in his life? How does he support himself?"

"He used to work for some brokerage company, but now it's mostly through gambling. He's a hustler. He'll bet on anything."

"How do we show that?" Mike asked.

I said we had permission from various hotels to film him playing craps, and that we could watch him play high-stakes backgammon with a friend.

"Not dynamic enough," Mike said. "Backgammon's a bore. Craps is an improvement, but how long can you watch somebody throw dice? Let's do better." I assured him I'd get on it. "Where are we doing the interview?" Mike asked.

"I thought we'd do it in his hotel room. It's a nice size, and . . ."

Mike interrupted me. "Kid, this guy has just knocked off the number one women's player in the world and you want to interview him in a hotel room? Don't they have tennis courts here?"

I allowed that they did.

"Let's do it on the one where he whipped Smith's ass. Set it up"

Thankfully, the taxi had pulled into Caesar's Palace. Mike went up to his room to read the material for tomorrow's shoot and I went anxiously to mine. Although Mike had been surprisingly pleasant about everything, I had obviously flunked the preparation test, which I couldn't do anything about until the morning. I turned off the light and prayed for sleep.

The next day came, and with it my increasing admiration for Mike. As I was to see so many times over the years, he had a facility for relaxing people (unless it was not in his interest to do so) and making long-planned interviews appear spontaneous through the sheer force of his personality. Here was this guy, this really famous guy, who knew everything about you, was interested in everything you said, and listened to your story in a way you always had longed for. For the person being interviewed, it was heady stuff.

Bobby Riggs was no exception. Mike charmed him out of his initial wariness and got Bobby to say everything we had hoped for, barely pausing to breathe. As for Riggs the hustler, I put together a series of sequences in which Bobby bet on various activities in which the odds seemed heavily against him. He won big money playing golf with ex-heavyweight champion and four-handicap golfer Joe Louis, who was a front man for Caesar's Palace. (Bobby was a scratch golfer, news that he kept from the champ.) He held a foul-shooting contest with two visiting NBA all-stars, in which Bobby got twenty-to-one odds because he would be blindfolded. (Shooting underhanded, Bobby sank eighteen out of twenty baskets, winning handily.) And he played tennis against singers Paul Anka and Steve Lawrence, evening the odds by placing six chairs on his side of the court and carrying a shoulder bag that held a yapping toy poodle. (The dog urinated frequently, but Bobby still won 6–0.)

Although the Riggs story didn't need a lot of heavy lifting, working with Mike usually came with an enormous amount of baggage. Mike couldn't bear the thought of going into an interview without knowing everything there was to know about the story and the person he'd be talking to. But when you briefed him personally on it—in addition to the scrupulously researched white paper you had prepared—he would unerringly ask you the one question you hadn't thought of. Because of Mike's fear of being caught flat-footed, this was seldom done kindly and made me more anxious than usual. This, of course, delighted him.

Mike's well-publicized battle with depression was not known until he went public with it in the early '90s. I never asked him whether he identified it as such beforehand, but it clearly had an effect on his behavior. When Mike was "up," he was high-spirited, charming, and incredibly fun to be with. When low, he was—to use a Dan Rather-ism—rattlesnake mean. I tried to read Mike's moods, but I didn't always succeed. One day I showed him the cut of a story I had worked hard on and thought was pretty good. After the first five seconds he stopped the film to deliver his opinion. "Kid," he said, "this is shit."

"That's not fair!" I protested, hitting the Play button before he could elaborate further. "You need to watch the whole thing." Mike squinted at the film for another five seconds before stopping it again.

"It's worse than that," he said. "It's baby shit."

I endured the punishment because of Mike's extraordinary skills. Simply put, he made your stories better than they had any right to be. He understood that interviewing was more than a matter of getting information. If the subject lacked verve, the interview lacked impact, so Mike wouldn't stop until he got the best out of everyone he talked to. I always tried to choose interesting characters for him to interview, but occasionally I was stuck with someone who had to be included in the story but was tedious. Even Mike could not transform a dud to a dude, but he could raise the performance an entire level. Mike was equally gifted at penetrating the protective carapace of the super famous. Whether persuading a reluctant Vladimir Horowitz to play *Stars and Stripes Forever*, or getting the Shah of Iran to say that God spoke directly to him, Mike knew exactly what buttons to push. The problem was, he pushed everyone else's whenever he felt like it. He certainly knew how to push mine, often doing it for the sheer enjoyment of seeing my pained reaction.

I never met anyone with less impulse control. If Mike wanted to talk to you, he would call with total disregard for the lateness of the hour. It got to the point where my wife would answer the phone and say "Hold on, Mike," without bothering to ask who was calling. This irritated Mike no end.

"Why does *she* always pick up the goddamn phone?" he asked me after one midnight call.

"Because it's on her side of the bed, Mike," a truthful answer that failed to mollify my impatient correspondent.

Mike was very savvy about getting out of any situation he didn't want to be in. This included his annual summer respite in Haiti, a place that his third wife, Lorraine, adored and that Mike barely tolerated. Before he left, Mike would ask me to call him on a specific date and time so he could make sure that he and Lorraine were together. My mission was to identify myself, remain on the line, and shut up. What follows is a typical "conversation," a word I put in quotes as Mike did all the talking:

> "I thought we were supposed to shoot the interview in September, Harry." (Pause) "What do you mean, the guy won't be available then?" (Pause) "Harry, in case you're not aware, I'm in Haiti. I can't come running back to New York every time there's a crisis." (Pause) "Then you tell Don I just won't do it. If we lose the story, then we . . ." (Pause) "Don's leading the season with it? The publicity's gone out? Jesus H. Christ! Why didn't somebody tell me this?" (Pause) "By when do you need me?" (Pause) "Tomorrow? I can't possibly do that, Harry!" (Long pause) "Okay, okay! Make the reservation and meet me at home

> to go over the material." (Pause) "Yes, I'm having a wonderful time, Harry. Thank you for fucking up my vacation!"

Dealing with Mike was like navigating one of those obstacle courses where impediments keep popping up. Until I got smarter, I would show him a first cut in which I had recorded the narration—called a "scratch track" because it's intended to be temporary. Although I have a better-than-average delivery, the timbre of my voice (or the absence of his) irritated Mike no end. Then everything became fair game. If Mike thought the film was in trouble, he would grab the transcript book to search for better interview material. When finding a passage he liked, he would read it aloud theatrically, making the words sound as though they had been uttered by Sir Laurence Olivier. "Why didn't you use that?" he would ask, conveniently forgetting that the person who actually spoke the words was so boring he would have been booed off the stage.

Mike loved needling people. Whenever he found me lacking, he would invariably use the same sarcastic putdown: "Good luck to you, Harry, in whatever career you choose to pursue." Mike employed the phrase so frequently that I would recite the words along with him the moment they emerged from his mouth. This actually made him smile. After a year or so of working with Mike, I learned that you needed to give as good as you got or you were a victim forever.

I confess that I found many of Mike's shticks amusing; delivered with such obvious gusto it was difficult to take them personally. Less amusing was the way Mike treated women on the staff. Each morning, he strode briskly down the hall, snapping the bra straps and pinching the bottoms of any female unfortunate enough to be in his path. Today, he'd be sacked.

Mike thrived on other people's inadequacies—real or perceived. He was a stickler for correct grammar. If, for instance, you said something like, "I don't know who this belongs to," Mike would look at you sternly and say, "*Whom,* object of the preposition *to.*" He was equally obsessed with the performance of his bowels. On the road, the first exchange of the day invariably began with Mike declaring he was either (a) stopped up, or (b) that the hot water and lemon he swore by had worked and that he'd had a glorious movement. Then Mike would inquire about the state of *your* colon. At first I didn't know what to do with this, but after a while I got into it, complaining even longer than he about my constipated condition, which I said was the legacy of being toilet trained at nine months. (My mother insisted this was a true story. I was less certain, but it came in handy.)

Lunch on the road with Mike was also an experience. Although he understood that the film crew had a contractual hour lunch break, Mike considered the meal an unnecessary interruption of the workday and connived to get through it as quickly as possible. This almost always meant fast food. Mike would make a show of taking down everyone's order, darting into a local McDonalds and reappearing with a tray piled high with burgers, soft drinks, and fries. He would proceed to spread them out on the hood of the camera car, distribute napkins and utensils and make a great show of refusing payment. The meal seldom cost more than ten bucks and never took more than ten minutes, which was nine minutes too long for Mike.

Then there was driving. Mike always drove. Not because he didn't like the way I handled the wheel, (although he didn't) but because he was certain we would get there faster. One day we were on a shoot in Florida. Mike was traveling at an excessive rate of speed when we heard the wail of a police siren. Mike glanced in the rearview mirror. A cop car was gaining ground on us. We pulled over to the side of the road as the officer got out of his vehicle and started walking toward us. "Give me your driver's license," Mike commanded. I was in the process of handing it over when I realized this was not a good idea.

"Why do you want it?" I asked.

"Because I left mine at the hotel," he said, trying to tug the then pictureless license from my grasp. I held on tight.

"Mike, it has my name on it. As soon as the cop sees you, he'll know you're not Harry Moses." Mike kept his grip on the edge of the license.

"Give it to me, damn it! I'll put my finger over the name."

"No!" I said, tugging back. "Haven't you ever had a speeding ticket? They always take the license." Mike won the tug of war—sort of—winding up with three-fifths of the torn license. He glared at me as the cop stuck his head through the window.

"Good afternoon, sir," the cop said.

"Good afternoon, officer," Mike replied innocently, stuffing his portion of the driver's license in his pocket. "Anything wrong?"

"Your left brake light is out," said the cop. And in the future, please take it a little easier. You were going fifty in a thirty-five-mile-an-hour zone." He paused for a moment before heading back to his vehicle. "Love your show, Mr. Wallace. Keep sticking it to the bad guys."

CHAPTER 9

IDIOT SAVANT

The bar for accuracy at *60 Minutes* has always been extremely high. Yes, there have been some embarrassing mistakes: the Benghazi story and the Bush draft evasion debacle come readily to mind. But since its inception in 1968, the show's track record has been amazingly good. In large part it's because of the checks and balances along the way, requiring the producer to defend a series of hard questions about the facts in each and every piece. Producers are expected to get the story right, but telling it right is every bit as important. The typical *60 Minutes* segment takes eight weeks from start to finish and can go through upward of five cuts before the producer thinks enough of it to show the correspondent. After the inevitable rewrite, there are several additional cuts, in which the structure of the story is reexamined and every nut and bolt is tightened so no loose elements remain. The result should have pace, flow, conflict, drama, and be populated with compelling characters. It should also be a model of clarity, understood equally well by PhD candidates and those who never made it past the eighth grade. *60 Minutes* never dumbed itself down nor became a smart aleck in its approach. It continues to pride itself on respecting the audience's intelligence and fulfilling the universal desire for a good yarn.

For its first thirty-six years, this process culminated in the all-important Hewitt screening. (In 2004, eighty-one-year-old Don Hewitt was replaced by the show's second executive producer, Jeff Fager. In 2018, Fager was replaced by Bill Owens, and in 2025 Owens resigned and was succeeded by his second in command, Tanya Simon.) Hewitt looked at stories in a room reminiscent of the old Thalia movie theatre in New York. It had a dozen overstuffed red lounge chairs that sat on a threadbare carpet marred by coffee spills, cigarette burns, and countless food stains. In the rear was a console with volume controls for the various soundtracks and a speaker that let you talk to the projectionist. The producer sat behind the console with his editor, who would mix the sound on the fly. In the audience were Hewitt, the correspondent attached to the piece (in my case, usually Wallace), the show's senior producer, and the senior editor, who had the unenviable task of reading the raw interview transcripts and deciding whether we had played fair in cutting the story. I attended more than fifty screenings with Hewitt, all of them as painful to the eardrum as they were to the psyche. As the lights came on, something like the following took place: "Harry, you've told it wrong," Hewitt says. "Your real beginning is about four minutes in, where the whistleblower is telling Mike why he was fired. Start there, then go to the place about three minutes later where his coworker is talking to Mike in the car, then go back to where you began. And take out that stuff about the family. It doesn't have anything to do with the story."

"Don, you can't take that out," Wallace says. "It's important information."

"Then put it in a line of narration," says Hewitt, his voice getting louder.

"We tried that, Don," I say, raising my voice to his level, which was the only way to be heard. "It was too long."

"Okay, okay," he says. "I've got a better idea. Leave in the stuff about the family. Put it after Mike's interview with the expert."

"Don, if you do that, we'll have to write a bridge to the last sound bite," Mike says. The way it is now, you don't need narration!"

"The way it is now doesn't work," says Hewitt, raising the decibel level further.

"Everyone else thinks it works," Mike shouts, ignoring that no one else had said a word.

"I have an idea," I say. "Suppose we . . ."

"Got it!" interrupts Hewitt. "Have Mike do a standup that takes you from the family and sets up that last bite, which needs punching up anyway."

"Let me recap," I say, wanting to get the hell out of there before any more changes were made. "Begin with the whistleblower being fired, go to the coworker in the car, then back to the beginning, move the interview with the expert before the family sequence and do a standup that sets up the end of the piece."

"That's it," Hewitt says. "Now it'll work."

What's more, it usually did. When it came to critiquing a story, Hewitt's skill was as uncanny and mysterious as an idiot savant's, a term he used himself when asked to describe his particular talent. Don Hewitt, who died in 2011, was no intellectual. Except for newspapers he was not especially well read, but he had a genius for storytelling. If Don heard somebody use the term "nonlinear," he probably would have been puzzled, yet it's exactly the way *60 Minutes* stories were structured. Typically they would begin in the middle, circle back to the beginning, jump forward in time, go someplace else, and zigzag their way to the finish line. The idea was to keep the viewer wondering what was going to happen next.

Stories also were fast-paced. They had to be. Like the peripatetic organ in *Deep Throat,* Hewitt's attention deficit disorder had migrated from its customary place of residence in the brain to a more southerly location. In a screening, Hewitt's twitching posterior was an early-warning system against stories that lagged, prose that confused, or characters that put you to sleep. "Boring" was a word you didn't want to hear from Hewitt. "Boring" meant you had lost the viewer. "Boring" was the ultimate *60 Minutes* sin.

CHAPTER 10

WHO KILLED MARILYN MONROE?

The first investigative story I did for *60 Minutes* took on an icon of American writing, Norman Mailer, whose riveting account of the 1968 political conventions had won him a National Book Award and a Pulitzer Prize. It happened, as many stories do, through a combination of curiosity and luck. I had finished filming the Bobby Riggs story and was flying back to New York when I struck up a conversation with my seatmate. The guy mentioned that he was doing publicity for an upcoming book on Marilyn Monroe, which combined never-before-seen photographs of the late film star with a lengthy text by Norman Mailer. In it, Mailer theorized that Monroe had not died by her own hand but was done in by right-wing elements of the FBI and CIA to embarrass President Kennedy and his brother Bobby, the attorney general, both of whom were rumored to have had affairs with her. By the time we landed, I had persuaded the guy to give *60 Minutes* an exclusive on the book.

Mike and I began filming at the Beverly Hills Hotel in Los Angeles, where the publisher was throwing a press party to hype the book. Mike talked to Jack Lemmon and several other movie stars who had worked with Monroe, but he didn't get much useful information.

Back in New York, I looked at the rushes of what we'd shot thus far. Upon doing so I immediately recognized the problem. Aside from a few serviceable anecdotes about Monroe (with the real gossipy stuff still to come from Mailer), the story was little more than a puff piece for the book, which itself was full of conjecture. I was in despair. I had pitched Mike hard and now I had a mess on my hands. I was trying to script my way out of it when I heard my words being recited in an all-too-familiar baritone: "'Marilyn Monroe was the epitome of glamour, and when she died, a little of us died with her.'" Startled, I turned around. Mike had crept into my office and was standing in back of me, reading aloud what I had just typed. I tried to snatch the paper from the roller, but Mike was too quick. Grabbing it, he continued to declaim my dreadful copy, his voice dripping with sarcasm. "'Here among the mountain of hors d'oeuvres, the cigar smoke and the wine, we spoke to some who knew her well.'"

"Mike," I said defensively, "it's a first draft. It's not ready to be looked at." I snatched the paper back from him, crumpled it up, and stuck it in my pocket before he could read any more.

"Come into my office, kid," he commanded. "We need to talk." Dutifully, I followed him. He closed the door behind us, not a good sign. "Sit down," he said.

I deposited myself on a chair, feeling like a first grader with a dunce cap. "Mike, it's unfair of you to judge this on the basis of . . ."

"It's not the writing I'm concerned about," he interrupted, "although the writing isn't much. It's the story." I knew what he was talking about, of course, but I didn't know what to do about it. "I just reread the book," he said. "Mailer's full of shit."

"About what?" I asked.

"Monroe's so-called murder. It's bullshit. I'd bet anything on it."

"What if it is?" I asked. "Where does that get us?"

"Where it gets us is a story," Mike said, "which at the moment we don't have. Let me spell it out for you. How long did Mailer take to research and write the book? Two months, wasn't it?"

"That's what the publisher told us," I said warily. "So . . ."

"*So* . . ." Mike said, somehow making the monosyllable sound like a summation to a jury. "In sixty days, Mailer came to the conclusion that Marilyn Monroe's suicide—the most thoroughly investigated suicide of the century—wasn't a suicide at all and that the CIA or FBI murdered her to get back at the Kennedys, particularly Bobby, who was fucking her at the time." I opened my mouth to respond, but Mike wasn't through. "*And*," he finished, "conveniently for Mailer, no one was home that night to contradict his version of events. Or so Mailer says."

"Where are you going with this?" I asked.

Mike looked at me (to use one of his favorite expressions) like I was a hair in his soup. "Suppose there was someone home that night? Like Monroe's housekeeper? What would that do to Mailer's theory?"

"It wouldn't help," I offered.

"Wouldn't *help*?" Mike said, his voice dripping with sarcasm. "It would sink it."

I waited for him to cool down. "Mike, how are we going to prove that?"

"Find the housekeeper. See what she knows. See what she told Mailer." Mike stood up and shooed me out of his office. "Let me know as soon as you reach her," he said, his lip curling somewhere between a smile and a threat. "It's your ass if you don't."

Back in my office, I considered the difficulty of my task. It had been eleven years since Monroe's death. God knows where her housekeeper was now. She could have an unlisted phone number. She could have moved from Los Angeles. She could be dead. To make matters worse, Mailer's book had only referred to the woman by her last name: Mrs. Murray. My anxiety, which I had attempted to hide from Mike (no doubt unsuccessfully), was now in full throttle. I picked up the phone and dialed Los Angeles information. "Could you tell me how many Murrays there are in Los Angeles?" I asked. The answer did nothing to quell my incipient panic. There was an entire page of Murrays, about six hundred names. At an estimated five minutes per call, allowing for no answers, busy signals, callbacks, and the briefest possible explanation of why I was looking for Marilyn Monroe's housekeeper, it would take fifty hours to accomplish the task with no guarantee of success. Surely there was a better way. I lit a cigarette to calm my nerves and inhaled deeply. Suddenly it dawned on me that any one of Monroe's biographers would also have talked to Mrs. Murray and, unlike Mailer, used her full name. A call to the CBS News library confirmed that I was right. The mysterious Mrs. Murray now had a first name: Eunice. Excited, I called Los Angeles information again. No Eunice Murray. "Are there any E. Murrays?" I asked the operator. Indeed, there were. Thirteen of them. I took down the numbers and began to dial.

Happily, Eunice Murray was still among us. When we talked, she proved Mike right: telling me, and later Mike on camera, that she never left Monroe's house; that Monroe's death was a suicide, not a murder; and that neither Bobby Kennedy nor anyone else had visited that night. What's more, Mailer had never spoken to her, even though she was listed in the Los Angeles telephone directory, the same place I had found her.

After our session with Mrs. Murray, we went to interview Mailer at his loft in Brooklyn Heights. Mike threw him a few softball questions before cutting to the chase.

> WALLACE
> It was as though you didn't want too many of the facts, but were more anxious for the mystery that could have been very quickly solved by the simple expedient of picking up a telephone and calling Eunice Murray.

MAILER
I vetoed [calling her] because I hate telephone interviews. As a writer, I hate them. I hate that way of getting facts. And I just don't like to work that way. I don't believe in fact gathering.

WALLACE
Then you get on a plane and go to Los Angeles.

MAILER
I was coming down to a deadline. I had something like 20,000 words to finish in the last week—

WALLACE
But facts, Norman!

MAILER
What I knew was I was sailing into a sea of trouble and I said, "Fine, that's what we're going to sail into." Because the alternative was this: I did not have the time to do both.

It was a classic Mike Wallace moment. Mailer later claimed he'd been blind-sided and announced that he was going to punch Mike out the next time he saw him. But when the interview ended, he seemed more chagrined than anything else, so I asked him to sign his book. Mailer smiled ruefully, picked up a pen, and said, "What shall I put? 'To my executioner'?"

CHAPTER 11

WELCOME TO CORPORATE AMERICA

My years at *60 Minutes* taught me that corporations by and large will sacrifice their mission for profits just about all of the time. A case in point was the story Mike and I did on our own business: how television reports the news. Starting in the '70s and continuing even today was a local news format then known as "Happy Talk," in which anchors and reporters seemed determined to prove that everyone on the show was one big happy family. In addition to creating absurd promos for their shows, like having anchormen dressed as cowboys riding off into the sunset, these so-called news broadcasts did almost no news, choosing instead to cover subjects that were silly, salacious, or otherwise sensational—the TV equivalent of a tabloid newspaper. After visiting several local news markets, I wound up in San Francisco. There, the NBC affiliate had published a full-page ad in the *Chronicle* showing its reporters wearing floppy-eared dog costumes, because—as the headline said—they were "news hounds."

The ABC affiliate, KGO, which was the highest-rated local news station in town, was much worse, as became apparent when Mike interviewed its slick co-anchor, Van Amburg.

WALLACE
One of your colleagues says that what [you're doing] is exactly what KGO's call letters stand for: Kickers, Guts, Orgasms.

AMBURG
I wouldn't have won the Press Club Award the last two years in a row because of very in-depth stories that I've done, Broadcast Journalist of the Year, if all I was doing is coming on with kickers, guts, orgasms. Let me tell you something. I led with a story one night on the eleven o'clock show. I don't know if you know this. It was about a human male sexual organ that was lying beside a local railroad track.

WALLACE
I remember there was a tease that went ahead of it: "Male genital found on railroad track—stay tuned."

AMBURG
We weren't trying to grab an audience.

WALLACE
You weren't trying to grab an audience?

AMBURG
No, we were trying to inform an audience . . . To me

> there was a victim somewhere; something had happened. We didn't cut that thing off and put it over there.

Although the San Francisco stations seemed like easy marks, we had taken them seriously. I commissioned a graduate class in journalism at UC Berkeley to tape every station's local newscast for a week and track what percentage of stories were newsworthy as opposed to tabloid. The statistics were far worse than we'd imagined, the prime offender being KPIX, the CBS affiliate in San Francisco, doubtlessly because it was last in the ratings and was desperately trying to attract an audience. Wallace's interview with its news director, who denied he'd gone tabloid, resulted in one of those "gotcha" moments.

> WALLACE
> You did sixty-five seconds on the Nashville Stomper [who had a fetish about stepping on women's feet]. A Horneyville, North Carolina, massage parlor where the masseurs tickled everything including the fancy of the subject—that was fifty-five seconds. Would you agree that's tabloid?
>
> NEWS DIRECTOR
> You don't save souls in an empty church.

The day after the show aired, I was called into Richard Salant's office, the president of CBS News. This was a very big deal for a lowly producer who'd only been with the news division for a year and had yet to meet its leader. Looking grim, Salant informed me that KPIX's owner, Westinghouse Broadcasting, was so incensed by my story it was threatening to switch the San Francisco station's affiliation to NBC. He added that Westinghouse was prepared to do the same thing with its CBS affiliates in Pittsburgh, Boston, Philadelphia, and Cleveland, all of which were first in their market. Should this happen,

Salant explained, CBS's present status as America's number one television network would go down the tubes. It got worse. Westinghouse's director of research was insisting that our tabulations were in error and that KPIX was actually doing a good job of reporting the news. I tried unsuccessfully to look unconcerned, but I could read the tea leaves. If I had screwed up, my career at *60 Minutes* was kaput. "Harry, how sure are you that your statistics were accurate?" Salant asked.

"Positive," I answered, sounding a lot more certain than I felt.

"Do me a favor," he said. "Check them again."

Although Salant had been civil, I was quite concerned. I had gone over the raw data with the journalism class in detail but hadn't looked at it since we did the KPIX interview. So, I reviewed the tapes of KPIX's local news broadcasts for the week they were monitored to see if any of their hard news stories had been incorrectly identified as tabloid. I did find an error, but to my great relief it made KPIX's tabloid take on the news even worse. I dutifully reported this to Salant. "Are you sure?" he asked.

"Yes," I said, handing him the data. "I checked it three times."

Salant laughed. "I'll send it on to Westinghouse. Maybe it'll get the bastards to do something about their newscast."

"But aren't you worried they'll leave CBS?"

"Not anymore," he said. "They're big boys. They'll get over it." Which, of course, they did.

Eventually I got to know the personal side of Salant, who among other things was a tennis enthusiast. When he heard through the grapevine that I was a decent player, I was invited to join his weekly indoor doubles game at Midtown Tennis, a bubble on West Twenty-Seventh Street, where Salant enlisted me as his partner. Since our opponents were not terrifically talented, Salant and I won most of the time and "Mr. Salant" soon became "Dick." What's more, I grew to like him. He was smart, dedicated, and really, really cared about the news division producing a serious, uncompromising product . . . something that has become less common in today's digital age.

I never saw in Salant the kind of corporate posturing I've observed in other news executives. His goal was excellence and I admired him for it, particularly since the other stuff—the phony glibness that passes for competence in so many companies—was totally lacking in the man. Another news executive, for example, would probably have fired me for an incident that took place during the production of a story Mike and I were doing on J. P. Stevens, the giant textile manufacturer. Stevens' draconian treatment of its workers was memorialized in the 1979 film *Norma Rae*, in which Sally Field won an Oscar for her portrayal of a worker trying to unionize a Stevens plant. A couple of years before the movie was made, we took a look at the highly charged conflict between Stevens and the Amalgamated Clothing and Textile Workers Union, which had been trying to unionize the company's eighty or so mills, most of them scattered throughout the South. We started filming in rural Georgia, where we followed two union reps through a series of clandestine meetings with workers who wanted to join the union but knew Stevens would fire them if the vote in their plant went the wrong way. Then we went to Roanoke Rapids, North Carolina, where Crystal Lee Sutton, the real Norma Rae, had defied J. P. Stevens by giving a fiery pro-union speech before being dragged from the mill by J. P. Stevens' goons. Although the Roanoke Rapids plant had since voted to join the union, its members told us that their conditions and pay had seen only incremental improvements. In short, J. P. Stevens was still a classic corporate bully.

All that was left was an interview with J. P. Stevens' top executive, James Finley, who had been with the company for thirty-four years, the last fourteen as CEO. Mike and I had sent several written invitations to Finley requesting an interview. They went unanswered, as did a series of Wallace's phone calls to Finley's office, which never got further than one of his secretaries. Before giving up, I decided to attend the Stevens annual meeting in New York, hoping that I would somehow be able to have a word with Finley and persuade him to talk to us on camera. I sat there, surrounded by stockholders, and listened to Finley report on corporate earnings, prospects for the coming year, and his pledge to keep the Stevens plants union free. Cheered by the thunderous applause, which was led by a phalanx of corporate executives seated in the first two rows, Finley announced that he would take questions from those in the audience. "Ask anything you like," he said. My original plan was to try to speak with Finley after the meeting ended, but this was too good an opportunity to pass up. Finley surveyed the room, saw my hand, and recognized me.

"Thank you, Mr. Finley," I said. My name is Harry Moses. I'm not a shareholder, but I hope you'll consider taking a question from me." The phalanx of executives swiveled in their seats. All were dressed in dark-blue suits.

Finley looked at me suspiciously. "Go ahead," he said.

"I'm from CBS News," I said. "Specifically, I'm a producer with *60 Minutes*. As you may be aware . . ."

I was startled by an uproar of boos from the executives. I looked at Finley, who looked back at me. "As you may be aware, Mr. Finley," I continued, "we're doing a story on J. P. Stevens and we've been trying unsuccessfully to get an interview with you." More boos from the executives, some of whom were waving their identical gray fedoras vigorously in my direction.

"I know nothing about this," Finley lied. "Who is the correspondent?"

"It's Mike Wallace," I said. The mention of Mike's name triggered a tsunami of boos. The executives were now standing and shaking their headgear at me in unison. I counted twenty-four of them before Finley held up his hand. They immediately sat down.

"Send me a formal invitation and I'll respond," said Finley. That was when I perhaps did something unwise.

"With all due respect, Mr. Finley, we have sent you several formal invitations and you have not responded." The executives shot up from their seats to voice heartfelt sentiments of dismay: "No! No! No!" "God damn crooks and liars!" "Don't do it!" Then, in a spontaneous display of corporate fealty, several moved toward me, waving their matching fedoras with increased vigor. I looked at their flushed white faces and promptly sat down. As Finley took another question, I took the opportunity to exit.

Having failed to get an interview with Finley, the story aired that Sunday with the usual disclaimer: "J. P. Stevens declined our request for an interview." The next day, Salant called me into his office. Wasting no time with pleasantries, he said he'd received a phone call from Finley, who had complained about my question and was threatening to withdraw advertising for any product manufactured in J. P. Stevens mills—a list of brand names that at the time included Ralph Lauren and Laura Ashley. I explained to Salant how I came to confront Finley, assuring him that I did not represent myself falsely and was responding to an open invitation from the CEO for questions. Salant arched his substantial eyebrows.

"I guess you had to be there," he said finally.

"Probably," I answered.

"Get out of here," he laughed, "and don't let it happen again."

"I won't," I said, scurrying out the door before he changed his mind.

In five frantic years, Mike and I did every conceivable manner of story, from investigating unscrupulous debt collectors to profiling the little country of Norway. It was exhilarating and emotionally exhausting. I ended up with an ulcer I named Myron (Mike's given name) and a therapist with whom I spent hundreds of costly hours complaining about Mike. Eventually I understood I had to sever the relationship. Citing my ulcer, I begged Hewitt to assign me to another correspondent. Don, who was as fearful of Mike as I was, preferred a different strategy: the guilt trip. He would tell Mike that job pressures (caused by you know who) had sent me to the hospital for exploratory stomach surgery and an uncertain return. This would give him time to effect a change without confronting Mike head on. Although the plan had undeniable flair, it lacked practicality. Instead, I screwed up my courage, walked into Mike's office, and asked for a divorce. "No problem," Mike said, managing to look surprised, betrayed, wounded, and noble at the same time. "We can probably use a break from each other. Why don't you leave after the next story?"

"Mike," I said, my voice rising several octaves, "I need to leave *now.*"

"It's a story we've been planning for a year," he said, lying through his teeth.

"Mike, *60 Minutes* doesn't have community property. The story's yours. Do it with someone else."

Mike realized I meant business. "Okay, kid," he said, flashing his most dazzling smile. "You'll be back."

He was right. Although it took a while, I was.

CHAPTER 12

VERY FAMOUS PEOPLE

Woody Allen, Neil Simon, Arthur Miller, Calvin Klein

"Let me tell you about the very rich," wrote F. Scott Fitzgerald. "They are different from you and me." I believe the same rule of thumb applies to those who have achieved genuine celebrity. But unlike Fitzgerald's ultra-wealthy, many of whom popped out of the womb with trust funds in place, real fame is achieved.

Over the years I've profiled some very famous people. A couple of playwrights. Some politicians. An athlete or two, and so on. Although their personalities were completely different, they all shared the indefinable something that made them famous and allowed them to behave in ways different from you and me. Or, to use another word, badly. This set me to thinking about the internal qualities that catapult a person from routine to rare, from humility to entitlement. What makes a person famous? Character? Talent? Drive? We all know people who possess those traits in abundance and are successful but not famous. My former psychotherapist, for example, has all of the above and then some. He graduated summa cum laude from a top Ivy League school, was chief of psychiatry at the medical school of a major university, and is esteemed by his patients and peers. But fame has eluded him; or, to put it more accurately, he has eluded it. Whereas the TV shrink, Dr. Phil, a former clinical psychologist with an undistinguished professional career, a history of ethical violations, and a penchant for dishing out questionable advice to those he has just met, has his own syndicated talk show with an audience and income in the millions.

Then there's the case of Roger Maris. A solid professional outfielder, Maris was never a star until he broke Babe Ruth's record of hitting sixty homeruns in a year. It put him on the front page of every newspaper, but the fame accompanying the feat didn't sit well with Maris, who eschewed the spotlight and was miserable when it was thrust upon him. Fans of baseball will recall Roger Maris with alacrity, but those with only tepid interest in the game will not.

Lastly, there's Donald Trump, famous long before he became president, and even—some would argue—before *The Apprentice* turned the simple phrase "You're fired" into a national mantra. Trump's unbridled id and unfettered self-regard transported him from the wealthy offspring of a Queens real estate developer to one of the world's best-known citizens. None of the celebrities I either profiled or worked with were Trump-like, but almost everyone had no compunctions about being imperious, unreasonable, or weird whenever they felt like it. Years ago, I got to spend some time with Woody Allen, a notoriously shy man who is uncomfortable with his celebrity—or so his fans are encouraged to think. Woody may indeed be shy, but he has turned diffidence into a suit of armor that protects him from anything he does not wish to face. In the middle of the profile I was doing on Woody for *60 Minutes,* we happened to be attending the same movie preview, a little-remembered film called *Someone Is Killing the Great Chefs of Europe.* As I passed him on the way to my seat, I said, “Hi, Woody.” No slowing of step. No pausing for chitchat. Nothing. The next day at the office, a female researcher angrily confronted me, “What did you do to that poor man?” she asked. After establishing that she had been sitting next to Woody, I asked her what she meant. “You embarrassed him,” she said, then telling me that as the lights dimmed and the movie began, Woody became increasingly anxious, whispering the words “I'm having a panic attack” throughout the opening credits and the first quarter of the film, until he exited, perhaps believing that whoever was killing the great chefs of Europe was about to cause his own demise.

Was Woody's implosion triggered by my acknowledgment of his presence or was it a way of inspiring sympathy through suffering? I saw the same thing happen again during the final day of filming. Woody, a competent clarinetist, was in New Orleans to record the score to his movie with the legendary Preservation Hall Jazz Band, a group of elderly Black musicians who were unlikely to be familiar with Mr. Allen or his oeuvre. But as my film crew and I were in Woody's hotel to film his limo ride to Preservation Hall, the same thing happened. Surrounded by an entourage of agents, managers, and hangers-on, Woody plunged into full panic mode, insisting that he simply wasn't good enough to play with the jazz band that was waiting for him to show up, and the full house that was there to witness the occasion. The panic attack would have made a terrific sequence, but I felt that shooting it would have been an intrusion on Woody, so I decided to do nothing. Only in retrospect did it occur to me that Woody might have wanted it on film, since it perfectly captured the image he had painstakingly curated. If this sounds cynical, fast-forward some years later to Woody's Oscar-winning film *Annie Hall*. Because of it, Don Hewitt decided to repeat my profile, but he wanted to update it with a brief opening sequence of Woody walking by the theater whose marquee advertised the movie. Considering that it was a terrific plug, I thought that Allen would comply. Thereupon, the following phone conversation ensued:

WOODY
I can't do it. Someone might recognize me.

ME
What if we filmed it at night?

WOODY
No. Someone might recognize me.

ME
Okay. No walking by the theater. But we still need an up-to-date shot of you. How about walking in Central Park? The entrance is across the street from your apartment.

WOODY
Too many people there.

ME
Are you an early riser?

WOODY
Pretty much.

ME
We can do it at sunrise. There's no one around except squirrels.

WOODY
I can't take the chance.

We finally settled on a shot of Woody playing the clarinet on his balcony, where the sole spectator was a disinterested pigeon. As I was leaving, Woody asked me to tell his driver that he'd be down in five minutes. His apartment building had an entranceway in which several cars were parked. Since Woody hadn't described the vehicle, I knocked on the window of each car and asked the occupant if he was waiting for Mr. Allen. Three negative answers took me to a final car, which had just pulled in. Behind the wheel sat a liveried chauffeur wearing a tan cap with a leather bill, and jacket and pants cut from the same expensive gabardine. The outfit was topped off, or in this case bottomed off, by a pair of highly polished leather boots. I tapped on the window, which slid down silently. Except for the absence of a monocle, the driver was a dead ringer for the legendary Austrian-born actor Erich von Stroheim. In a disappointing New York accent, the man affirmed that he was there to pick up Woody.

"He'll be down in a minute," I said, stepping back to admire the modest Mr. Allen's transport of choice—an eye-popping, white Rolls-Royce convertible.

I had always wanted to follow a play from it's first day of rehearsal, to out-of-town tryout, to opening night on Broadway; the thought being that the process of mounting a Broadway production had so much inherent drama it would be riveting. I was not the first filmmaker to come up with this idea. A decade earlier, Bob Drew had made a transfixing documentary on just such a subject. His film was called *Jane,* the first Broadway-starring vehicle for twenty-five-year-old Jane Fonda, who was the principal actress in a long-forgotten comedy called *The Fun Couple,* which was anything but fun. Fonda, already exhibiting the temperament of a diva, fell under the spell of her oily Greek director, Andreas Voutsinas, with whom she clearly was having an affair. *The Fun Couple* was so definitively dreadful that Drew filmed critic Walter Kerr calling it "one of the five worst plays he'd ever seen."

I certainly was not looking for another turkey when I pitched the idea to Mike Wallace and Don Hewitt. The vehicle I hoped to track was the latest effort from Broadway's most celebrated creator of comedies, Neil Simon, whose cavalcade of hits—*Plaza Suite, The Odd Couple, The Sunshine Boys*—kept on coming. Simon's play *God's Favorite* was a modern retelling of the Old Testament's Book of Job, in which God enlists Satan to test Job's faith by taking away everything the pious merchant values. In Simon's version, Job is successful businessman Joe Benjamin; while Satan's emissary is one Sidney Leonard Lipton, a zany messenger from God, who enters wearing a varsity sweater with a huge letter G.

Before he agreed to let us film, Simon wanted to meet. So, Mike and I made our way to the Eugene O'Neill Theatre where *God's Favorite* had just begun rehearsals. Mike explained to Simon (who, like Woody Allen, was serious in person) that we were not out to do a hatchet job—a fear that most people have when they see Mike Wallace. "We simply want to memorialize the experience of bringing a play to Broadway," said Mike, adding that he was personally curious how Simon could make something as somber as the Book of Job, whose main character was beset by everything from the loss of his fortune to the loss of his wife, get laughs.

"I'm curious too," Simon said, smiling faintly. "That's what we're going to find out."

By the end of our meeting, Simon and his producer, Manny Azenberg, had agreed to let us tag along for the ride, also agreeing that we would have total access to the cast, to Simon, and to the opening-night party as they awaited the reviews.

We returned to film a couple of days of rehearsals and to do a preliminary interview with Simon, who said that the play was running long, but he didn't want to cut anything until a theater audience saw it in New Haven. "I would rather have [them] tell me what I should cut," he said. "And they'll tell me."

So far (which was not very far), so good. My film crew and I boarded a chartered bus to New Haven with everybody present except Simon, who had opted to make the journey in less egalitarian fashion. We filmed another day of rehearsals there and recorded a dinner with the director and cast, but again without Simon, who was holed up in his hotel room. I asked Manny Azenberg if he could arrange a brief interview to get Simon's feelings on the play's progress, which was met with a firm no. A request to get a shot of him at his typewriter, with no questions asked, got the same response. This was not a good sign. I had been promised total access to everyone involved, and now my main character was having second thoughts. I chose not to push it, but I could see trouble looming.

Opening night at the Shubert Theater in New Haven. Our camera position allowed us to film what was happening on stage and then pan to get the audience's reaction. The first act was very funny, with comedian Charles Nelson Reilly getting huge laughs as the satanic messenger dispatched by God to test Joe Benjamin's faith. The second act told a different story. Actor Vincent Gardenia as Joe Benjamin did his best to wring laughs from the caravan of woes besetting his character, but there were few to be had. In the lobby of the Shubert, Mike interviewed the departing theatergoers, whose reaction to the play they had just seen was uniformly negative: First act, funny. Second act, not. Mike went home to the hotel, and as the crew was starting to pack up, I noticed that Simon had appeared on the stage and was staring forlornly at the now empty theater. This was clearly not the time to talk to him, but it spoke volumes about his mood and the problems that lay ahead. Then, Manny Azenberg and a tall, elderly man I'd not seen before entered from the wings. Azenberg introduced him to Simon as Maurice Bailey, the longtime owner of the theater where *God's Favorite* had just premiered. I signaled the crew to join me on the stage and asked the sound man if we could get decent audio where we were, which was about thirty feet from them. "Not without booming them," he said, meaning that we'd have to get close enough to hold a boom mike over their heads. Knowing that in Simon's present frame of mind he could easily throw us out and cancel the story, I decided it was not worth the risk; so, I inched myself closer to hear what I was going to miss. Although I did not take notes, and the dialogue took place almost fifty years ago, it is still in my head.

BAILEY
I enjoyed your play, Mr. Simon.

SIMON
I wish I could say the same.

BAILEY
Are you referring to the second act?

SIMON
It was a disaster.

BAILEY
There were problems, but . . .

SIMON
I can't fix them. We'll finish our run here, but that's it. I'm not taking it to Broadway.

BAILEY
Isn't that premature?

SIMON
I don't think so. Now if you'll excuse me.

BAILEY
Mr. Simon, I'm an old man, but I know something about the theater. I've been at opening night of every play here since 1941 . . . *Oklahoma!,* with an explana-

> tion point, yet. Except it wasn't called that. It had some silly name like *Away We Go,* and Oscar Hammerstein was in despair about it . . . *Streetcar Named Desire.* Tennessee Williams was so sure he'd written a lemon that he went out and got drunk. It took until morning to find him. But the worst was *My Fair Lady.* Rex Harrison was so convinced he couldn't sing, couldn't even remember his lines, that he refused to go on. No one could persuade him otherwise. I finally got his press agent to talk some sense into him . . . I believe you know the rest of the story.

Bailey put his hand on Simon's shoulder and gave it a gentle squeeze. "You'll be okay," he said, "and so will your play." He exited, leaving Simon to his demons. For me it was another opportunity missed, another moment lost.

Although we would cover the same ground when Mike interviewed Simon the next day—who by then had come out of his funk and begun to fix what was broken—it didn't begin to match what I'd witnessed last night. We finished the story without any further cooperation from Simon, who even shut us out of filming the opening-night party by saying that there wasn't going to be one. (There was.) Needing a finish for the story, I borrowed a page from Drew and accompanied Clive Barnes, the drama critic for *The New York Times,* back to the newspaper, where he let us look at his review before it was printed and gave Mike a brief interview. Barnes found *God's Favorite* lacking the laughs of Simon's other comedies. He didn't pan it, nor did he praise it; pretty much the way I felt about our own story when it aired a couple of weeks later.

Arthur Miller had barely turned thirty when he wrote *Death of a Salesman,* a play that changed modern dramaturgy by demonstrating that Willy Loman, purveyor of ladies' hosiery, could lead a life as tragic as Shakespeare's emperors and kings. I had seen *Salesman* shortly after it debuted on Broadway at the Morosco Theatre in 1947. I was eleven years old, but the pain of Willy's failures tore me up. Another thirty-seven years passed before I would meet its author in the flesh. Miller lived in a sprawling eighteenth-century house in Roxbury, Connecticut, overlooking an apple orchard whose heady, pungent aroma (Miller didn't spray his trees) induced a mild dizziness when first inhaled. His large living room was dotted with pieces of sturdy, well-crafted furniture that Miller had designed and made. The occasion of our meeting concerned Miller's intention to direct the first production of his most famous play in Beijing, where the Chinese government had—for reasons known only to them—extended an invitation. The play was going to be performed in Mandarin, a language with which Miller's familiarity went no further than the Chinese restaurant near his New York apartment.

None of this seemed to perturb Arthur Miller, a tall, gangly man whose speech blended the nasality of a Brooklyn cabbie with the self-assurance of an Oxford don. I had come to persuade him to let CBS News document his China adventure for a series that Bill Moyers was doing for the network. I told Miller that the story I had in mind was to see if a devoutly communist audience could be moved by the singular presence of Willy Loman: lousy dad, unfaithful husband, true believer in the capitalist dream. Miller airily dismissed my premise, assuring me that Willy's predicament was so universal that identifying with him would not be a problem, no matter one's political persuasion. Nor, Miller added, would directing the cast in a language he did not speak be a handicap. He knew the play, after all, pretty well, and the actor playing Willy Loman, who had also done the translation into Mandarin, spoke fluent English. But if you want to come along for the ride, Miller said, you can. So, we did.

In 1983, Beijing was not the booming metropolis it is today—choked with automobiles and pedestrians. Most of the main thoroughfares were yet to be paved, the preferred mode of transportation being bicycle or foot. And when the wind gusted, it blew a gritty substance of dust and dirt into one's face, inducing shortness of breath and temporary blindness. Still, matters like these, or the supposedly grand hotel at which the Chinese government installed us—an establishment called the Wa Du that was inconvenient to all locations—were minor annoyances. With its bustling multitudes, its incomprehensible language, and the huge, vaguely unsettling portraits of Mao, Lenin, Stalin, and Engels in and around Tiananmen Square, China was exotic as hell. I had real doubts that *Death of a Salesman,* the author's supreme confidence notwithstanding, could make this alien culture relate to its unlikable protagonist, Willy Loman.

We spent much of our time in Beijing filming Miller rehearsing the play. The actors had already memorized their lines, but in the Chinese theatrical tradition their performances were over the top—too big, too emotive, a soap opera on steroids. Miller, who communicated with his cast through the play's translator and star, Ying Ruocheng, kept trying to pull them back, to give him less when their instinct was more. Then there were the play's "Americanisms"—such as the tossing of a football between father and helmeted sons—which Miller did not want to alter into a pastime more familiar to the Chinese. "They'll get it," he said. "It's a lighthearted scene. That's all they need to know."

So far, Arthur Miller was giving us the access that Neil Simon had denied us. Even better, the sequences of him directing his all-Asian cast were highly visual, with Miller acting out key scenes while Ying simultaneously translated his remarks. Then it was time to move from the rehearsal hall to the People's Art Theatre, a cavernous space that had room for an audience of almost two thousand. Because another play had just left the premises, Miller was forced to combine the afternoon dress rehearsal with the tech rehearsal (an opportunity for sound and lighting to smooth out the rough spots) before the next day's opening night. We took our position in the second row, using the performance to film the two scenes from the play I had decided to cover. It would mark the first of four days shooting those same scenes from different angles so they could be edited into a seamless whole. Directly in front of us and filling the entire first row was a phalanx of photographers dispatched from newspapers across the length and breadth of China. Each of them was armed with a noisy Speed Graflex, an old-fashioned press camera from the '50s. The curtain rose. All remained hushed until Ying Ruocheng stepped out of the dark and onto center stage, his tired face and sagging posture perfectly capturing the worn-out Willy Loman. As Ying was about to deliver his first line, the photographers jumped to their feet, pointed their cameras at him and clicked madly away, triggering a tsunami of exploding flashbulbs. Ying stood silently until they finished, then spoke his line and entered a shabby living room, where his long-suffering wife, played by a famous Chinese actress, greeted him. The photographers bounced from their seats and repeated the whole jarring routine. I glanced at Arthur Miller, who was in the middle of the orchestra, alongside the technicians operating the soundboard. Arthur rose and in his Brooklyn cabbie voice, yelled "Siddown!" The photographers kept at it, not knowing who was shouting or what he was saying; their grasp of English equal to the playwright's command of Mandarin. Seeing Miller's distress, Ying stepped to the footlights and gently told him it was a long-standing custom for photographers to interrupt the dress rehearsal in the service of their newspapers and that the actors were accustomed to it. "Well, I'm not!" Miller shouted back. "This is my one and only chance to see a tech run-through before we open. Tell them to knock it off and take their seats. Now!" Ying complied. Although his instructions lasted far longer than Miller's outburst—either due to the longwindedness of the language or the tactfulness of his translation—the photographers ceased what they were doing and took their seats. All but one, that is. Either out of loyalty to his newspaper or fear of being sacked if he didn't complete the assignment, he kept clicking his shutter and detonating flashbulbs. "Stop!" Miller yelled. "Tell him that the author of the play is very angry, that it's not the way we do it in America, and that if he doesn't stop interfering with my play, there won't be a play." Even I, with a minimal knowledge of Chinese sensibilities, understood that this was not the best way to win friends and influence people. This time, Ying did not waste words. Whatever he said to the photographer was over in seconds. The man sprinted toward the exit sign and vanished.

In case you're wondering if I filmed this unique interchange, I did not. Miller himself had determined our camera placement, and with his rage in full and frightening display, I knew that if he saw it pointing at him, I could kiss China goodbye. This would mean returning to CBS News without filming the actual play, and quite possibly without a job.

Later that afternoon, the crew and I attended a party for Miller at the American Embassy, bringing the camera to shoot some B-roll. Arthur saw us and approached. "I thought you were done," he said, looking displeased at our presence. I said that, yes, we were, except for filming the play. "Isn't that what you were doing earlier?" he asked. I explained that we needed to cover the same scenes from other locations to give us choices in the editing. Miller, who had a surprisingly limited understanding of how films are made, was having none of it. He extended a long, bony finger, which he used to jab me in the chest. "You're just covering your ass, Moses. No more going inside the theater. No more filming of the play. It's over. That's it."

After a sleepless night, I sought out Miller's wife, Inge Morath, who had traveled with him to China. My hope was that Morath, a famous Magnum photographer, knew more about the editing process than her husband and could explain that banning us from the theater was not in his best interest. Although Morath understood my plight, she was unmoved. "You know Arthur," she said, speaking in a thick Austrian accent. "When he's like this, one must leave him alone."

"Is there a chance he'll change is mind?"

A tiny, tinkling laugh escaped her lips. "No," she said.

Over a morose lunch, I consulted with our translator Cecilia, an American graduate student enrolled at Beijing University. Halfway through the sea cucumber main course (a titanic error), an idea hit me. I'd read somewhere that the Chinese were not beyond taking bribes and asked if it was true. "Absolutely," she said. The workmen here don't get paid a lot, so any extra income is welcome."

"Would the stage manager take a bribe?" I wondered.

"He's pretty high up," she said, "but we could try."

I paid the check and we hurried off to the theater, where we found the stage manager asleep in his chair. We had hit upon a payoff of seventy-five dollars, which Cecilia told me was on the high side. As she finished explaining our predicament, he launched into a speech that lasted several minutes, looking unhappier with each sentence. Cecilia gave me the gist of it. "He has a wife and children. If he is caught, he will be sent to prison and never see them again." I asked if she thought this was true.

"Probably not," she said.

"Never mind. Triple the amount."

Cecilia looked at me aghast. "That's too much!"

"See what he says."

Cecilia made the offer. "Not enough," the stage manager replied, evidently having picked up some English during the negotiation.

"Make it a flat hundred per night. Tell him we'll be here for three nights. All he has to do is let us into the theater, take us backstage so we can film what we need, and let us know when Miller is around so we can stay out of sight."

Cecilia complied. The stage manager smiled for the first time. "Pay in dollars," he said. I pulled out my wallet and handed him three one-hundred-dollar bills—everything I had on me. Our filming went off as scheduled, and except for a sudden Miller appearance that forced all five of us to take refuge in a broom closet, we got everything we needed. The story aired without incident and even won the Directors Guild Award for best documentary, which pleased me—although a Purple Heart would have been more appropriate. Arthur Miller liked it too, but in his 395-page book about bringing *Death of a Salesman* to Beijing, the encounter with the photographers—a theatrical moment, if ever one existed—was conspicuously absent.

In a way, profiles are more difficult to do successfully than traditional investigative pieces about, say, nuclear power or corporate malfeasance in which the research is time-consuming but the story is clear. That's because the structure is less apparent when you're looking at someone's life because of their star power. Additionally, there's the worry about access. How much will you be allowed to hang around, waiting for those unpredictable, unguarded moments that make a film come alive; knowing that if you pull the trigger—as I chose not to do with Woody Allen, Neil Simon, and Arthur Miller—you will likely be given the boot. Most famous people, especially those in the arts, are guarded about their personal lives and touchy about letting you see how they actually live. Mike Wallace was one of the few who could break through this veneer, a combination of his skill as an interviewer and his own fame, which put him on equal footing with the person we were profiling. But I didn't have Mike as my correspondent when I profiled Calvin Klein. I had Diane Sawyer, who for all her dazzling looks and considerable wile, was not always able to connect with a resistant interview subject in a useful way. About some things, Diane could be downright stubborn. We set about profiling Klein in 1985 during the height of the AIDS crisis, and years before he publicly came out. Even before we began, Diane made it plain she wished to ask Klein about his sexuality; especially about a rumor in which he had every drop of contaminated blood drained and replaced with HIV-negative plasma. I thought the tale was as absurd as it was impractical, and in any case irrelevant to our subject matter. Yes, Calvin Klein was gay, and yes, a lot of people knew it; but we were profiling him because of the fashion empire that this grocer's son from the Bronx had built from scratch. His line included not just high-priced designer outfits but sunglasses, socks, shoes, watches, perfume, jeans, and underwear—all promoted in elegant ads with obvious sensual overtones. Diane agreed to put the issue of Klein's gayness on the back burner, but I knew it would surface again.

Klein, who had a fashion show coming up for the fall season, saw the advantage in a *60 Minutes* profile and agreed to it, but he wanted to talk to me before we began filming. We did so one Saturday morning in his offices in New York City's Garment District. Normally, meetings with heavyweights like Calvin Klein do not take place without a publicist being present, so I was surprised when I rang the bell and Klein opened the door himself. He escorted me through the empty workrooms to his small, cluttered office. "How are you for time?" he asked.

"Fine," I said.

Klein took out a notebook. "In order for me to give you what you want, I need to know how your show works. You're producing the story, correct?" I nodded yes. "And exactly what does that mean?" I explained that the producer is responsible for the overall content: directing the film crew, picking the locations, briefing the correspondent, coming up with questions for the interview, supervising the editing, and writing the script. After Calvin dutifully took this down, he asked what he could do to make this story come alive, make it the best possible profile. No celebrity, in fact no other person I ever profiled, was interested or savvy enough to ask these questions. Klein continue taking notes while I explained that the most important thing was access.

"Because you're a designer, I need to see you working with your staff. I have no idea how a dress is made and where the idea comes from, but it would be great to see it in progress," I explained.

Calvin looked up from his notepad and circled the last entry he had made. "Done," he said. We went through a few more sequences that I had thought of and some that he suggested himself: selecting products displaying his name but that his company didn't make. "We have a guy coming to the office next week showing me frames for sunglasses. I will try them on and eventually pick one. I'm decisive, so the whole thing doesn't take more than five minutes. Would that work for you?" By the end of our meeting we had every sequence in the show planned, including a preview of his fall collection to a fashion editor, which top designers frequently do. "I've got the perfect candidate," Calvin said. "Polly Mellen is the fashion editor for *Vogue*. She loves special treatment and she's flamboyant. I know exactly what you want and I'll make it happen. (The sequence, in which Mellen and Klein sat in a room for an hour while a stunning model paraded in and out wearing various outfits, was hilarious.)

POLLY MELLEN
Exquisite! Oh, Calvin, why did you show it to me in white?

CALVIN KLEIN
Because I *love* white.

POLLY MELLEN
Chills, Calvin! Chills!

Sequences like this take time to surface, so Calvin kept working his audience of one until he got what I needed. In this case, the moment was not lost.

After two hours, and Calvin having filled his notebook, we were done. Almost. "What about the interview with Diane?" he asked.

"What can you tell me? How should I prepare myself??" I decided to be honest.

"Nothing you don't know or can't handle," I said, "but Diane seems intent on raising the topic of your sexuality." Calvin started to respond and I waved him off. "Honestly, it's not something I care about, and if I have anything to do with it, which I most certainly do, it's not going to be part of the piece. I give Diane questions. She adds some of her own. But I exert a good deal of control over what's in the story, and when Diane and I disagree—which isn't often—we duke it out." I made eye contact and smiled reassuringly. "I'm not worried, Calvin, and you shouldn't be either."

"Fair enough," he said. "Thanks for your time. I'll do my best to give you what you want."

Three weeks later, everything we discussed was in the can. We had been given extraordinary access and Klein and his staff bent over backwards to cooperate; the usual ubiquitous publicist nowhere to be seen. Then it was time for the interview. After filming a trainer-supervised workout with Klein in his home gym, he went upstairs to change. While we were waiting, Diane pulled me aside. "I want to ask him about that rumor, the one about the blood."

"Diane, it's not part of the story."

"People know about it," she said. "We're journalists. It's our role to ask uncomfortable questions.

"Jesus, Diane, it doesn't have anything to do with the story, or with journalism."

"Yes, it does," she insisted. "He's never acknowledged that he's gay, and . . .

"Diane," I said, beginning to lose it. "This is a story about the billion-dollar fashion business Calvin Klein built from scratch. It's about his name being a household word. It's not about who he fucks or his fear of contracting AIDS. We don't need to go there."

"I disagree," she said, pausing as Klein entered the room. "Calvin, come back upstairs with me. We have to talk." Diane looked at me as if to say, "Are you coming?" which I wasn't about to do.

"You go ahead, Diane. I've got some stuff to go over with the crew."

Diane and Calvin came back about fifteen minutes later and we began the interview. Halfway through it, Diane asked him a question alluding to his homosexuality. Although I no longer recall what she said, the discussion went nowhere and she went on to the next question. When I omitted it from the cut, Diane said nothing. Hewitt loved the story and it ran the next week. The day after it aired, I got a phone call from Calvin's assistant. "Mr. Klein would like to take you and your wife to dinner."

"We'd be delighted," I said, hiding my surprise. A week later, my wife and I met Calvin (who had arrived early and was alone) at Lusardi's, an unpretentious Italian restaurant with excellent food. The evening was easy and fun, and Calvin thanked me for doing a professional job. I thanked him for delivering on everything he promised—and then some. In a world where the famous are regularly excused for churlish acts, Calvin Klein gave me and *60 Minutes* the access we needed and the best possible version of himself. Behaving badly was not in his lexicon or his interest.

CHAPTER 13

THE THORNWELL FILE

I produced this story for *60 Minutes* way back in 1979. It continues to resonate with me almost fifty years later; not just because of the story's sheer force but because it's about an act of moral outrage committed by a major institution against a powerless person, a little guy.

The first thing I noticed about Jim Thornwell was his left thumbnail, which he had painted purple. The second was that he was always cold. I met Thornwell in February of 1979 at a law office in Oakland, California, where he sat shivering in its overheated confines as his attorney, Harvey Kletz, recounted what the US Army had done to his client. Thornwell's story began seventeen years earlier in Orleans, France, where he served as the only Black in his intelligence unit. When some classified documents went missing, his superiors charged Thornwell with the crime, although there was no evidence to support it. Thornwell was imprisoned and brutally interrogated for three months. When that didn't work, the army put LSD in his drinking water and drove him in a staged, high-speed car chase to an old mill. There, his captors told Thornwell that if he didn't confess, he would be made permanently crazy. When he did not, the threat became a reality. Since his discharge from the army, Thornwell, who was forty-one when I met him, suffered from seizures, had been through two marriages, held a variety of increasingly menial jobs, and was relying on the kindness of friends for food and shelter. "There's a lot more, but those are the broad strokes," Kletz told me. I glanced at Thornwell, who had pulled his wool cap down over his forehead and was rubbing his hands together to ward off the non-existent chill.

"Jim, how did you learn about the LSD?" I asked. I knew the answer, but I wanted to hear him speak and thus far he hadn't opened his mouth.

"I got this letter from the g-government. It said that I'd been in a m-medical testing program and that the surgeon general wanted to r-reach me." Thornwell's stutter amplified the impression of a man who was lost in the world. "I always thought that the army had done s-something to me, but I didn't know what."

"Jim came to me with the letter," Kletz said. "It said that the testing had taken place at Edgewood Arsenal in Maryland. I did some research and found out that Edgewood was the place where the army conducted various LSD experiments on volunteers in the late '50s and early '60s. But Jim said he'd never been stationed there. So, I contacted the army. When it stonewalled me, I filed a Freedom of Information Act request and got these." Kletz picked up three fat binders from his desk and handed them to me. "It's more than a thousand pages. It happened in France, not in the US, but Jim was the only person in the armed forces to have been given LSD without his knowledge or consent. Everything they did to him is in here."

"I'll read them on the plane back to New York," I said, stuffing them in my briefcase. "Jim, are you okay with *60 Minutes* doing this story?"

"I had a lot of p-potential," he said. "I was a troop l-leader for the Boy Scouts. I won a trip to Washington. I was on my way to being s-somebody." It was not an answer to my question, so I shook his hand and left it at that.

"I'm glad we met, Jim," I told him. "I'll be in touch."

The binders contained a litany of horrors: Thornwell was put in isolation, interrogated daily, abused both mentally and physically, was denied food, water, and bathroom privileges for sustained periods of time and endured repeated threats to his life. It was a classic *60 Minutes* story. Thornwell was the little guy oppressed by the establishment, a David confronting the Goliath of the US government. What's more, there was no doubt that Thornwell had been wronged by the army—its own account revealed this in exhaustive detail. Better still (not for Thornwell but for *60 Minutes*), the army was refusing to compensate him for its actions, saying it had no legal obligation to do so. The stumbling block, as I learned from Thornwell's Washington, DC, attorney Terry Lenzner, whose law firm had taken the case on a pro bono basis and was suing the government for $10 million, was an obscure law known as the Feres doctrine, which is worth going into as an example of military justice gone awry.

In 1947, an army lieutenant named Rudolph Feres died in a barracks fire caused by a defective heating system. Feres's widow filed a claim against the army, saying that her husband's death was a direct result of the army's malfeasance. The case went to the US Supreme Court, which concluded that "the army could not be held liable for Lt. Feres's demise because it [coincided with] his service." In other words, the court found no distinction between a death on the battlefield, in which the military is immune from litigation, and Feres's death in the fire. The Feres doctrine was the legal albatross that hung around Thornwell's neck. While his attorney, Terry Lenzner, would try to establish an argument against it, my *60 Minutes* piece would focus on the laundry list of injustices suffered by Thornwell.

Although the army's treatment of Thornwell was beyond the pale, telling his story had problems. To begin with, I had only fifteen minutes. That meant distilling those three fat US army binders to their essence without using actors in dramatic recreations, which *60 Minutes* did not (and does not) allow and which I do not believe in. Then there was Thornwell himself, who initially appeared more odd than sympathetic. Although it was clear there was something wrong with him, he did not come across as a person you immediately cared about, which was crucial if the story was to have impact. Finally, the cast of supporting characters was thin. There was no reason to interview Harvey Kletz, Thornwell's California lawyer, whose involvement in the case could be covered by a few lines of narration. This left Thornwell's psychologist, Dr. Paul Berg, who would explain how the LSD had affected his patient, and Terry Lenzner, his Washington, DC, attorney, who would use the platform of *60 Minutes* to frame his argument against the army. Because my correspondent, Dan Rather, was not available, I did the Lenzner interview myself.

> LENZNER
> This is not just break-ins of people's homes. It's not just invasions of privacy by illegal wiretapping. This is an invasion of a person's mind, a physical invasion of a person's mind. And that is about as profound an injury, except for loss of life, that the government can impose.

After Lenzner, I flew to California, where Rather would meet me to interview Thornwell and Dr. Berg. I had also persuaded Berg to let us film a therapy session with Thornwell, although Berg told me there was little chance that anything useful would come out of it since Thornwell rarely talked about his time in the military. Because I needed footage of Thornwell to narrate over, I began by following him throughout a typical day—which mostly consisted of walking the streets, waiting for buses and riding around on them. The next stop was Dr. Berg's office, where we set up for the therapy session. I had decided to film unobtrusively by shooting handheld and using available light. The office was relatively dim but cameraman Greg Cooke assured me that his new prime lens was fast enough to get a decent image. Because I wanted Cooke to be the only *60 Minutes* person in the room, we put lapel microphones on Thornwell and Berg and ran wires to an office down the hall where Rather and I would be listening on a speaker. Before we started, I took Berg aside and asked once more if there was any chance Thornwell might talk about what happened to him at the old mill. "I doubt it," he said. "In the year I've been seeing him, it's only come up once."

"How do you feel about raising the subject?" I asked. "Dan's obviously going to ask him about it in the interview, but if we could get something here it would help."

"I'd be uncomfortable," he said. "I don't like setting an agenda."

"Fair enough," I said. Because film stock was expensive, I instructed Cooke, with whom I would not be able to communicate during the session, to shoot sparingly. "They'll be talking for about an hour," I said. "Once you get the pictures you need, turn off. His shrink says that nothing much is going to happen."

"Will do," he said. The therapy session had gone on all of five minutes when I realized that my instructions to Cooke were a terrible mistake. Thornwell, whose previous demeanor was characterized by an absence of emotion, had become a different person.

THORNWELL (crying)
Seventeen years. Can't even talk about it. I can't even talk about it.

DR. BERG
Do you want to talk about it, Jim?

THORNWELL
You know, I had to—all these years I had to keep fighting to tell myself that I wasn't crazy, and everybody was telling me that I was crazy.

DR. BERG
Anybody that would have gone through what you went through would have come out some terrible way, Jim. Do you understand that it's not you, it's what happened to you?

THORNWELL
Why is it so painful?

It went on like this for the rest of the hour as Thornwell walked Berg through the corridors of his past. Although the contents of those army binders were chilling, Thornwell's tortured, first-person account was a hundred times more powerful. I sat in a back room, transfixed by Thornwell's devastating narrative, as I raged against my own stupidity. Greg Cooke was a smart guy, but he didn't know the story as well as I did. Suppose he'd taken me literally and had stopped filming? Or what if he hadn't brought enough film into the room to keep shooting? I thought about checking on him and decided against it, knowing that if I opened the door, it would almost certainly break the session's spell. This left me listening anxiously as Thornwell began to describe the effect the LSD was having on his mind.

THORNWELL
I was at a table. I was with one of the agents. This man looked quite grotesque. It looked like he had probably been dead for two hundred years. "James," he says, "you're in a lot of trouble. I have to know, do you have the documents?" I said, "No." He said, "If you have them, you must turn them over to me so they won't

> fall into the wrong hands." I said, "I don't have the documents." He says, "Where did you put them?" I said, "I didn't put them anywhere." Then all of a sudden I just stiffened. It was like I was in an electric chair and somebody turned the juice on. And I just sort of froze and my skin began to raise up on my bone, and I looked down to see if I was growing larger, because it felt like I had just gained a hundred pounds.

Thornwell went on this way for another few minutes, building toward a climax that ended with an unearthly scream. I raced to Dr. Berg's office, where I waited for the door to open. Eventually Berg and Thornwell exited, looking as wrung out as I felt. I rushed inside. "Did you get it?" I asked Cooke, who didn't look any better.

"I got it," he said.

"All of it?"

"All of it. Never stopped shooting."

"Thank God," I said. "How did it look?"

"Like it sounded. Horrifying." My anxiety began seeping out of me. Cooke, who'd been a combat photographer in Vietnam, had seen his share of horrifying stuff.

"Were you on Thornwell for the scream at the end?" I asked. "Were you rolling for that?"

"Harry, relax, will you? It's all there."

I wondered, of course, if Thornwell had been doing this for our benefit, until I realized that it would take the talent of an Olivier to deliver the performance I'd just heard. I do think that our presence in some way prompted Thornwell's reliving of his LSD-fueled interrogation in the old mill, but I had no doubt that his torment was genuine. Furthermore, what I had on celluloid (although I'd yet to screen it) completely changed my approach to the story. The sequence in Dr. Berg's office was so compelling it would dominate the film. It also alleviated the concerns I had about Thornwell being sympathetic.

Unless our viewers were misanthropes, their hearts could not help but reach out to him.

After a break, Rather interviewed Dr. Berg, who spoke in perfect sound bites.

> BERG
> Mr. Thornwell is a man who, by appearances, looks like every other man. But if you examine him, you'd find out that he's missing—missing a lot of things that most people have. He's missing memories, he's missing interest, he's missing ambition. He misses feelings.

We then went on to Thornwell. Before the therapy session, I had thought his interview would go for at least an hour, with most of it focusing on his treatment at the hands of the army. Considering what we already had in the can, Rather would need only to flesh out the details of his life prior to the army.

> THORNWELL
> I was voted most popular when I finished high school. I was not an introverted kid. I was into everything. Oh, I was very c-confident. When they didn't vote me the most likely to succeed, it almost broke my heart.

> BERG
> He was a person who was a high achiever, who was excelling; a scholarship student, a young Black man who was on the verge of working his way out of being a young Black man in the South of the 1950s. That kind of background, those kinds of traits, do not lead to the decimated person you see now, unless something happened.

What did happen—Thornwell's horrific treatment by the army—would be told in exposition. I would need to have Dan Rather steer the audience through the labyrinthine plot by putting him on camera at various locations in Orleans, France—most importantly, the old mill. But how to find it? Thornwell, who had been drugged and blindfolded, was no help. The only clue the army binders gave was that he'd been spirited by car across a bridge and taken to "an old mill where two American army officers, were living." The route, the names of the officers and the site of the mill had been redacted. I would have to start from scratch.

My London-based cameraman, Mike Edwards, met me in Paris for the hour and a half drive to Orleans, which got its fifteen minutes of fame almost six centuries ago when a teenage girl in armor drove the English from the city and restored the monarchy to France. At the Orleans tourist information center, which overlooked a statue of its heroic rescuer, Joan of Arc, we were told that Olivet, a hamlet on the other side of the Loire River, had a section that was known for its watermills. Originally built by monks in the tenth century, they were now private residences, twenty in all. We got in our car and drove across the bridge to Olivet, which perched prettily on the banks of the Loiret, a tributary of the main river. We parked at a local restaurant and began our walk around the mill area, which was dotted with houses—some modest, some grand. Our first stop was a magnificent watermill overlooking a pond where several swans were paddling. A huge iron gate guarded a stone courtyard from which a padlocked door barred the entrance to the house. We swung open the gate and knocked on the door. No answer. "This may not be the place they took him, but it *ought* to be," Edwards said. "The pictures would be fantastic."

"We'll come back," I said. "Maybe there'll be someone home later." The next stop was a house with a far more unassuming mill. Its owner met us at the door. In halting high school French, I asked if some US Army officers had rented from her in 1961. "*Non,*" she said, closing the door in our face. The day went by in a blur of houses with mills, houses that once had mills, owners that didn't want to talk to us, and those who wouldn't stop talking. In the end, we had struck out. All that remained was our original mill, which we returned to as the sun was setting on the Loiret and the temperature had dropped to near freezing. We swung open the gate and knocked on the door, whose padlock was now removed. Soon enough, an elderly man greeted us. As I explained our predicament, I peered inside. The room was high-ceilinged, stone-walled, and enormous. Protruding from the far wall was the inner machinery of the mill, a sinister-looking iron wheel that was easily twenty feet in circumference. The man, who spoke some English, told us that he and his wife were in the process of turning the ground floor of the mill into a café, which in the summer would serve meals in the courtyard. But things were going slowly, he said, and they hadn't done very much. By now we were inside the bare room. In the middle was its only furniture, a table with two wooden chairs facing each other. I explained our mission to the owner, asking him if by chance he had rented the property to a couple of American army officers in 1961.

"Let me ask my wife," he said. "I'll be right back." I looked slowly around the room, taking it all in. I could visualize Thornwell at the table, being questioned under the influence of LSD as he sat under shadows cast by the giant wheel. So, it seems, could my cameraman, who was looking at the surroundings through a lens he had fished out of his pocket.

"Two lights," he said. "One on that wall and the other on the table. That's all you'd need. It's like something out of the Spanish Inquisition."

"Wrong century," I said, "but I get your point."

The man had now returned with his wife in tow. Her English was better. "We let the army stay here for that year," she said. "I remember because your President Kennedy had come to Paris *avec sa jolie femme*, Jacqueline. Such an elegant couple."

"Do you remember who lived here then?" I asked.

"Their names? *Non.*"

"But were they officers?"

"Of course. *Il etait une question de classe.* We would not have allowed ordinary soldiers to stay."

So, we had found the old mill. And with the promise of a location fee, the couple agreed to let us film there. The story was falling into place.

Back in Paris, I spent the day writing the copy that Dan Rather would deliver on camera. In addition to a standup at the old mill, he would do another one outside the garret where Thornwell had been given LSD. Finally, we would recreate the staged car chase that preceded Thornwell's interrogation with Dan traveling the same route. At least that was the plan until Rather flew in from Malta, where he'd been doing another story. In a foul mood because his luggage had not made the flight, Dan decided that he wanted no part of the standups. "I'm a reporter," he said. "My job is interviewing people, not talking to the camera. That's what actors do. Or models." Because I had worked with Rather before, I was used to a certain amount of unpredictable behavior, although getting one's face on the tube is not something correspondents normally turn down. I reminded him that we had an enormous amount of exposition to get through and that the most effective way to deal with it was to put him on camera at the same locations the army had taken Thornwell. Rather was adamant. "You don't need me for this, Harry. Go get yourself an actor." At this point I would have done so gladly, but since this was not a realistic option, I had to find a way to make things work.

"Dan, telling a story is part of what we do. It's another aspect of reporting. Agreed?" Rather glared at me, not giving an inch. I continued, taking care to sound calm and reasonable, although what I wanted was to throw him in the Seine. "So just because a print reporter writes up the facts, it doesn't mean that he abdicates his responsibility to tell the story well. We've established the facts. Now we have to make the story lucid, and that means putting you on camera. Furthermore," I said, hating myself for what was coming next, "an actor wouldn't have your conviction. You've interviewed Thornwell. You've done the reporting. That's going to show up in these standups. Okay?"

A long silence ensued. "Let's see how it goes," he said. "I'll see you tomorrow."

Tomorrow, which as Scarlett O'Hara correctly observed, is another day, found Rather, me, and our three-man film crew outside the building where Thornwell had been imprisoned in a fifth-floor garret. Finding the place was easy enough, as Thornwell had remembered the name of the street. Getting inside it was another story. The landlady, who remembered Thornwell quite well, had a tenant who wouldn't let us film there. So, I placed the camera on the roof of our car, which would track Rather walking down the street toward the building as he said these words:

> RATHER
> For the first month, Thornwell insisted he was innocent. Then, unable to take any more of the intense interrogation, he made up a confession, admitting he stole the documents and supposedly telling how he did it. The army checked his story out; it didn't hold up, not at all. So, they continued to interrogate Thornwell and Thornwell continued to confess; continued, in fact, to say anything that would stop his torture. It was then that the army hit upon a bizarre solution, a plan combining terror and LSD.

At this point, the camera tilted up from Rather to the garret window, over which he voiced the following lines.

> RATHER (V.O.)
> On June 12, 1961, in this room, after twenty-four

> hours of continuous interrogation, Thornwell was given LSD without his knowledge or consent.

It was a complicated setup. The car had to move at exactly the same pace as Rather, while the camera assistant had to track him with a handheld light. And because we had no one controlling traffic, we had to wait for a stoplight up the street to turn red, so cars and trucks would not whiz by us and interfere with the shot. After a couple of false starts, we managed to get a good take. Or so we thought. But when Mike Edwards tilted his camera up to the garret, its tenant was standing at the window, thumbs in his ears, fingers wiggling and tongue sticking out. We waited until he left and did a second take. But the guy was on to us. As soon as he saw the camera start its move, he resumed his position and repeated the lunatic gesture. Three more takes yielded the same horrific results. And now Rather announced that if we didn't get it in one more take, he was out of there. Then Edwards had a brilliant idea. "If we wait a couple of minutes," he said, "the sun will be shining directly on the window and you won't be able to see our little friend." He was right. The sun did what it was supposed to do, the take was perfect, and I had a happy correspondent. Then my real troubles began.

As we were packing up to go to the next location, the man in the window came running toward us, screaming in French and carrying a tattered law book, which he was madly waving. With him were two uniformed policemen, who looked considerably graver than I thought the situation warranted. Our translator, an Orleans girl about the same age as Joan of Arc, but lacking her leadership qualities, explained that he was accusing us of violating his privacy. I told her to apologize and to say that we would gladly compensate him for any inconvenience our presence may have caused. She was about to translate this when Rather stopped her. "Ask if he knows who I am," he said. She did and was met by a stream of invective, which in French sounded quite impressive. "What's he saying?" Rather asked.

"He says that he doesn't know who you are and he doesn't care. He says that you invaded his privacy and he wants all of you arrested."

Rather drew himself up to his full height, which was a foot taller than his bearded antagonist. "Tell him that I am an American news correspondent, that I am a personal friend of the American ambassador to France, and that he will be in great trouble if he doesn't get back to his garret now."

"Dan," I said, "perhaps a little diplomacy might work better here." But there was no stopping the Rather locomotive, which was barreling down the track on a full head of steam.

"And tell him that if I call the ambassador, he will call the president of France, and *you*," Rather said, pointing at his diminutive accuser, "will be the one going to jail." Our translator looked at me strangely, which was understandable as I was violently shaking my head from side to side, signaling her *not* to translate, which she then proceeded to do. Rather's remarks certainly had an effect, although not their intended one. The two gendarmes grabbed him by both arms and hustled him down the street, with the film crew, the translator, and me following in their wake. We entered a police station and were all pushed into a jail cell, the door slamming shut behind us. I glanced at Rather, who was fuming. Now would be a perfect time for him to call his buddy, the American ambassador, I thought, as I settled in for a long afternoon behind bars. After a few minutes, one of the gendarmes appeared and unlocked the cell. "Now that you are calmer," he said to Rather in delightfully accented English, "you may leave. But if I see you in Orleans again, your stay here will not be as brief." We exited and checked into our hotel. Tomorrow would be yet another day, and hopefully a better one.

I was woken up the next morning by a phone call from my editor, Tony Baldo, who had finished screening the footage I had shot of Thornwell's therapy session, which I still had not seen. "It's terrific stuff," he said, "except for one thing. You know the part at the end where Thornwell loses it?"

"Yes," I said warily, "is there a problem?"

"You could say that. When Thornwell starts screaming, the camera is on the other guy, the shrink."

This was horrible news. I was going to end the story on the scream and now I couldn't. "Tony, that's impossible. I even asked Greg if he was on Thornwell and he said he was. Are you sure?"

"Positive. I screened it twice."

"There goes our ending," I said. "What the hell am I going to do now?"

"I don't know," Baldo said. "You'll think of something."

At the moment, the only thought that came to mind was not to share this piece of news with my correspondent, who probably would have bolted if he'd heard it. The rest of the day, however, went better than the start. Using the army's own account as a template, I'd written a long piece of copy for Rather, which we filmed in sections. It began with a tilt down from the garret to the street, where Rather's voice-over would tell us that army officers burst inside and ran Thornwell down four flights of stairs. Rather continued the story on camera, saying that Thornwell was handcuffed, blindfolded, and forced into a waiting car. Rather got in the car and after it pulled away, we cut to him inside it.

> RATHER
> As Thornwell was sped out of Orleans, he was told that the French police were following and would kill him if they caught him. Thornwell had reason to believe this, as he had previously been threatened with death by these same police—a staged threat, although Thornwell didn't know that.

After filming shots of the car speeding through the streets of Orleans, we set up on the bridge that connected Orleans to Olivet and panned with the vehicle as it crossed the Loire and disappeared into the countryside. Over these shots, Rather would explain that the police were gaining on Thornwell, which in actual fact they had been, all of this having been prearranged with the local authorities to terrify him. Then the car squealed to a stop. Rather exited and—as he told the camera—matters worsened for Thornwell.

> RATHER
> He was pulled out the door and as his blindfold was removed, Thornwell saw the French police approaching with drawn pistols. Thornwell was ordered into their car and the French police drove him away.

Inside this car was an American army officer who, as Rather explained, told Thornwell he could stop the police from seizing him if he were to reveal what he'd done with the documents. At this point the car had reached the gates to the old mill. As they swung open, we followed Rather as he walked into the courtyard.

> RATHER
> Thornwell was dizzy; dizzy from the LSD that had been slipped into a glass of water he'd been given earlier. With his head reeling, Thornwell was led through this door and into the old mill.

The camera glided past Rather and went inside. I knew that I would be cutting from the interior of the mill to the footage of Thornwell in his therapy session as he described the final moments of his interrogation.

> THORNWELL
> He says, "Just tell me where the documents are." I said, "I don't know where they are." And he says, "Yes, you do." And my head went over on the desk, and my head began to swell. And I felt my face, and I couldn't even feel my face. And I grabbed my head

> and I hold it. And he said, "Crawl over here." And I find myself crawling across the floor. And he says, "Sit in the chair." And I felt like my mind had left my body, that my mind was sitting out there in space and I was sitting there looking at my own brain. And I just reached for it. [*Crying*] And I kept reaching for it. And I found myself up against a table, and he was there, "Where are the documents?" And then I was reaching for my mind, and it was just—it was just . . .

Thornwell had now become incoherent and was starting to scream. But with the camera panning to Dr. Berg instead of staying on Thornwell, the picture was of no use. In order to retain the sound of Thornwell's agonized cry, which I absolutely needed to do, I would have to replace the shot of Berg with a more suitable image. Mike Edwards and I walked around the periphery of the old mill, trying to come up with a solution to the predicament. Nothing occurred to either of us until I glanced down at the pond, which the mill overlooked. In it were the two swans we'd first seen a few days ago. "Suppose," I said, "we startle them so that they fly away, making it seem as though the scream had caused it. It's poetic license, of course, because the interrogation took place seventeen years ago, but I think it would be effective."

"What about CBS News standards?" Edwards asked, referring to the bible that all CBS News employees were sworn to observe, a long list of "don'ts" that included the staging of events. "You'll never get away with it."

"It doesn't say anything about getting swans to fly. I think we should go for it." Not knowing exactly how to startle a swan, I clapped my hands. The swans didn't budge. I picked up a stone and threw it in the general vicinity of the birds. The larger one glanced up at me, obviously annoyed. I let loose another stone. This time I got an irritated honk, but no significant movement. "The fuckers won't take off," I said. "We need a bigger noise. Like a gunshot. You don't happen to be carrying a pistol, do you?"

Edwards, the very model of British resourcefulness, pulled out a shiny weapon from his equipment bag. "It's a cap pistol," he said, handing it to me, "but it makes a nice loud bang." The pistol had six caps in its barrel, all that Edwards had left. He put his camera on the tripod and focused on the swans. "I'm rolling, Harry. Fire when ready." I pulled the trigger but there was no sound. "The caps may be waterlogged," he said. "Try again." I did. Same result. "One more time," he said. "If it goes off, keep firing." The swans were now swimming directly underneath me. I aimed the cap pistol at the larger one, whom I had begun to detest, and squeezed the trigger. The noise startled both me and the swans, who were now paddling about furiously and honking madly. I fired off my last three shots and watched my feathered nemesis flap his wings, rise from the water, and fly.

Back in New York, my editor, Tony Baldo, began putting the film together. Normally, structuring a *60 Minutes* story is the most demanding part of the process. In this instance, it was relatively easy. We decided to use Thornwell's therapy session three times within the piece, filling in with the other interviews as needed and letting Rather's standups move the story forward. Baldo had done a masterful job of dealing with the end, staying on Thornwell's face until the last possible frame, then cutting to an earlier picture of his hands circling in the air as they "reached for his brain," and finally cutting to the swan that took flight, mixing Thornwell's scream with the swan's honking. It was more powerful than I'd hoped for, making me grateful that Greg Cooke's camera had not stayed on its subject.

The screening with Hewitt, always a nervous time, went well. Outside of a few minor changes in narration, he loved the piece and scheduled it for air the following Sunday. I was on my way back to my office when he caught up to me in the hall. "There's one thing that's been bothering me," he said. "That last shot, the one with the swans. You've cut it so that it looks like they're taking off because of the scream. I don't think we can do that."

"Why not?" I asked. "Don't you think people will understand that they weren't responding directly to Thornwell?"

"I'm not so sure," he said. "The way it's cut doesn't make it look like that. I think you'd better change it."

"I can't," I said, my heart accelerating.

"Sure you can. Stay on Thornwell. It'll be just as effective."

"I can't stay on Thornwell, Don. The camera isn't on him when he screams."

Hewitt had enough. "Then do something else."

Knowing there was nothing else, I rushed into Rather's office and told him what had just taken place. "Dan, you've got to turn him around," I pleaded. This isn't just another story; it's a great story!" Rather, who had glowed when Hewitt complimented him on the standups he'd balked at doing, got suddenly fired up and called Don.

"Rather here," he said, in his formal manner. "Don, I like the ending . . . Yes, I understand where you're coming from, but I think we're on solid ground. With your permission, I'd like to leave it as it is. If you catch any flak, direct the phone calls to me." Rather paused to listen. "Okay. Thanks, Don." He hung up the phone. "You can relax, Harry. The ending stays."

"You're my hero, Dan," I said, almost meaning it.

More than fifty million viewers tuned in to watch *60 Minutes* the night "The Thornwell File" aired. Among them was Fritz Hollings, the Democratic senator from South Carolina, Thornwell's home state. Hollings was so outraged by what he'd seen that he drafted a bill to compensate Thornwell for his treatment by the Army. It passed and Thornwell was awarded $625,000, some of which he used to purchase a modest house and swimming pool in Oakland.

About six months after moving in, Thornwell was in the pool when he was struck by one of the seizures he'd been having since the army gave him LSD. The cause of death was listed as drowning, which was accurate, if not altogether true.

CHAPTER 14

PLAYING GOD POORLY

After six years at *60 Minutes,* I had got into my head the dumb idea that what I really wanted to do was to direct—meaning to make narrative films with actors. My ticket to Hollywood appeared in the form of the Thornwell story. What happened to Jim was so unjust, his tale so powerful, I was certain it would spark interest there. So, a couple of days before the story aired, I paid Thornwell $1,000 in option money, getting around this violation of CBS News standards by having my wife write the check. This meant that she controlled the dramatic rights to his life; and if someone wished to turn it into a movie, they'd have to hire her husband as the director. Amazingly, it all happened exactly as planned. I flew out to Los Angeles to research my next story and to winnow down the list of the seventeen Hollywood producers who had watched Thornwell's saga, called *60 Minutes,* and were transferred to me. Most told me

I could coproduce with them—an endeavor they said would make me lots of money—but insisted that no studio would accept me as a director. However, MTM Productions, which did the majority of its business with CBS, decided it could sell me and the movie to the network, particularly since my *60 Minutes* story had been seen by more than fifty million people. They did, and after Hewitt gave me a leave of absence, I was off and running; or, more appropriately, taking baby steps. Directing a movie requires a different skill set than directing a documentary, which reacts to unstaged events as they occur. In movies everything is scripted, which gives the director total control over everything that happens. This includes the actors, whom you can move around like chess pieces. For someone coming from the world of documentaries, it takes some getting used to; at least it did for me. Then there's the lighting, which takes a lot longer than the static interviews on *60 Minutes.* Before a scene is shot, it needs to be blocked, which means telling the actors where to start, where to move, and where to stop. This enables the director of photography to light the scene properly. The actors retreat to their trailers to get made up while their stand-ins go through the motions for the DP and his lighting crew. Eventually the actors reappear on the set. But as you're ready to film, one of them says there's a better way for him to do the scene: if he moved from the kitchen table to the trash compactor instead of to the stove, it would feel more natural. Letting him follow his whim often means that the scene will need to be relit for the unplanned deviation. And *that* means more time lost—time that doesn't exist when you're fighting the clock to film the seven pages of script you must complete each day, or risk being shut down. All of these problems are laid at the foot of the director, who is the closest thing on the set to God. I discovered very quickly that (a) I was not comfortable being God, and (b) that certain actors like to test God all the time, particularly if they sense that He is anxious. This seldom happens to a road-tested God, who in these situations understands that rational discourse is ineffective and ends the bullshit. Lacking God's two thousand or so years of on-the-job training, I tolerated it.

Thornwell, the movie, got off to the worst possible start imaginable. The first scene we filmed showed a handcuffed Thornwell being led away by his superiors for stealing military secrets. Simple enough, right? Except that the actor CBS approved for Thornwell somehow decided to play the scene as if he was tripping on LSD, ignoring that the drug wasn't given to him until considerably later in the script. To compound matters, I had a lot of heavy hitters watching from the sidelines; people who normally wouldn't have been there but for the allure of an all-expense paid frolic to France. In attendance was the CBS executive in charge of the movie; the CBS executive's assistant; the MTM executive in charge of the movie; the producer of the movie, who was pissed that he wasn't the director, and so on. Naturally I froze—long enough to convince everybody watching that I had no idea what I was doing, which was more or less true. Recovering from the shock of the actor's unexpected interpretation, I jogged over to him and suggested that because Thornwell's encounter with the drug was some forty pages down the road, he might be overplaying the scene. "No," he said, "the man has just been handcuffed, he's under stress, he's the only Black in the unit. And," he continued, glaring at my pale complexion, "*I* know how he feels." He had me there.

"Then do me a favor," I said. "Give me a little less on the next take, so I have something to choose from."

The actor, of course, had heard this before. "How much less?"

"Fifty percent," I said, running out of camera range and yelling "Action!" to avoid further discussion.

Things only got a little better after that. Although I never settled into being God, and the actor never settled into being Thornwell, we managed to finish the movie and get it on the air—to less-than-rapturous reviews.

Sensing that Hollywood was not in my future, I headed back to CBS News—but in an unexpected capacity. Struck by the dazzling success of *60 Minutes,* now the highest-rated show on television, the network suits decided to double down by giving Mike Wallace, its star correspondent, an additional prime time series, *The Mike Wallace Profiles,* scheduled to appear monthly starting in the fall. Mike surprised me by calling while I was editing *Thornwell* in California to say he'd like me to be the executive producer. With it came a significant boost in salary, a small staff, a designated suite of offices, and the enmity of Don Hewitt, who wanted 100 percent of Mike's time and now would have to settle for less. The show was based on an old Mike Wallace series called *Biography,* which was still running in syndication. *Biography* was what it sounds like: film clips of the celebrities it profiled strung together with narration from Wallace. Unlike that series, ours would be limited to "deads," Mike's term for the panoply of deceased politicians, performers, and other personae who were either famous or notorious. The list of candidates was endless: Aristotle Onassis, Pope Pious XII, Babe Ruth, Adolf Eichmann, Edward R. Murrow, et al.; a mixed bag that appealed to Mike and me for its variety and the opportunity to supplement their histories through investigative reporting. We began with the little-known story of Jean Seberg, a movie actress who in 1965 at the age of seventeen won a worldwide talent competition held by director Otto Preminger. Seberg would star in a new motion picture, *Saint Joan,* based on the life of Joan of Arc, the teenage girl who led France in a rebellion against the English and for her trouble was burned at the stake. Seberg's talent wasn't towering, but her intelligence was keen, her beauty sublime, and her story the stuff of which documentaries are made.

Jean Seberg's all-too-brief life was extraordinarily gripping. After Preminger's movie burst upon the scene, Seberg became an international star. She also became involved with the revolutionary Black

Panther Party, whose top management was remarkably successful at tapping the wallets of Hollywood's white liberal community. Although actors like Marlon Brando, Vanessa Redgrave, and Jane Fonda gave big, no one gave bigger than Jean Seberg, whose $150,000 donation to the Panthers made her the target of an FBI probe, which monitored her activity and recorded her phone calls. One of the conversations resulted in a *Newsweek* story reporting that Seberg was pregnant by a "Black activist" she met in California. The story wasn't true, but it destroyed her reputation, ended her career, and eventually led to her suicide.

It took us months to put the pieces of the Seberg story together. In a production assistant's garage, we located the sole remaining copy of Seberg's screen test for Preminger. We also found the FBI audio tape of that phone conversation and we played it to a woman who confirmed that she, not Seberg, was the pregnant person referred to on the tape. Finally, we got Seberg's father to give his first and only interview. As he told Mike, "I have this [American] flag here in the corner of the house here that I used to put out every morning. I haven't put it out since."

The techniques we used in the Seberg story were put to even better use in a historically significant half hour we did on Robert Kennedy and his remarkable conversion from a hard-nosed pragmatist with little interest in civil rights to a symbol of hope for Black Americans. The turning point came in a 1963 meeting that took place between Kennedy, then the attorney general, and a group of prominent African Americans who wanted him to get a Black perspective on the anger and frustration those inside the civil rights movement were feeling. I decided to hold the same meeting eighteen years later with as many original participants as I could get. Among them were James Baldwin, Harry Belafonte, and Martin Luther King Jr.'s attorney, Clarence Jones.

CLARENCE JONES
And as I think back, the dominant recollection I have is that [Robert Kennedy] the chief law enforcement officer of the United States government was surprised and shocked to hear what a cross section of Black Americans were saying about the condition of Black Americans in the South and in the North.

JAMES BALDWIN
I had just come out of Birmingham, and I wanted to talk to him . . . about the FBI in the Deep South.

MIKE WALLACE
What about the FBI in the Deep South?

JAMES BALDWIN
We called them the blood counters . . . That meant the FBI stood there and watched this man bleed to death, and then reported in to Washington saying: "This man bled thirty-nine thousand drops of blood and we find no violation of his civil rights." That's why we called them the blood counters, and that's what I wanted to talk to Bobby Kennedy about.

CLARENCE JONES
And we now know that the bureau had informants placed there, informants who themselves encouraged hostile activities against civil rights workers.

HARRY BELAFONTE
I agree with that, but why would Bobby Kennedy, who had all of our phones tapped, who knew all of

the conversations that went on between Dr. King and a host of his supporters, including myself...

MIKE WALLACE
Wait a second, Harry, what did you just say? Bobby Kennedy had your conversations bugged?

JAMES BALDWIN
Of course.

CLARENCE JONES
I know as a fact... from information obtained under the Freedom of Information Act... that every telephone conversation that Martin King made to me was tapped. I know that every telephone conversation that he made to Harry Belafonte was tapped.

MIKE WALLACE
Well, that's the question that I want to ask. Is that J. Edgar Hoover? Or is it...

CLARENCE JONES
No tap could have been done without the approval of the attorney general of the United States, which was Robert Kennedy.

I first learned of this meeting in historian Arthur Schlesinger's lengthy book, *Robert Kennedy and His Times.* Although Schlesinger's account was powerful, it could not match the present-tense electricity of a documentary. Prompted by Mike, who was almost psychic in his ability to jog memories and summon emotions, Baldwin, Jones, and Belafonte plunged the audience into the anguish of the civil rights movement and created living history.

Sadly (for me, anyway), *The Mike Wallace Profiles* made its own kind of history when it became the rare television series that was not canceled by the network but was cut loose by its star. The morning after the Seberg show aired, I arrived at the office early to get the overnight ratings. I was beaten to the punch by Hewitt, who had them in his hand as I walked in. They were solid, but nothing like the numbers *60 Minutes* was racking up on a weekly basis. Hewitt's glee turned strident when Mike appeared. "Why do you want to waste your time with this?" he asked, showing him the overnights. Mike didn't take the bait, but it made a huge impact. Shortly after we finished our next two stories, the one on RFK and another on Noël Coward, Mike came to me and said he was giving up the show. I was crushed. We'd done great work, and I didn't want to go back to *60 Minutes* where I'd be just another foot soldier. Mike, who for one of the few times in his life actually felt guilty, had come up with a solution to appease me. In addition to his duties on *60 Minutes,* he was going to sign on as the investigative correspondent for the *CBS Evening News*—if I would agree to be his producer. Because he'd be on the show infrequently, it would allow him to keep a normal schedule on *60 Minutes* while letting me dig my teeth into significant stories.

"How long will these stories be?" I asked.

"If the story merits it, they'll give us up to four minutes." This was wildly generous for a thirty-minute newscast (actually twenty-two minutes if you subtract the commercials), but compared to the stories I'd been producing for *The Mike Wallace Profiles,* it was a drop in the bucket. Nonetheless, I took the job. Immediately thereafter, Hewitt appeared in my office to let me know he wanted me back at *60 Minutes,* doubtless so he could have Mike's undivided attention. Stupidly I turned him down. Mike and I did a couple of middling pieces together, but his heart was not in it. In truth, neither was mine. After six months Mike called it quits and I returned to *60 Minutes,* although this time with a different kind of deal. No longer wishing to be the chattel of one correspondent, I asked Hewitt to let me rotate between Wallace, Rather, and Bradley. Don agreed, and because no one owned me, I spent the next two years doing exactly what I wanted with whomever I wanted. As television goes, it was a wonderful gig; but the same combination of impatience and ambition that sent me to Hollywood was now telling me to take the next step up the corporate ladder: become an executive producer in on ongoing series and run my own unit. I was an excellent producer, a first-rate critic of my own and other people's work, and I liked the idea of helping others to shape their stories. My problem was that I lacked the interpersonal skills needed for the next level. Undaunted, I set out to acquire them by politicking every heavy hitter in the news division, something that did not come easily. I met with Howard Stringer, the executive producer of *The CBS Evening News,* and asked for his support. I did likewise with Dan Rather, now the show's anchor. And I was able—finally—to finagle a lunch with Van Gordon Sauter and Ed Joyce, respectively the president and senior vice president of CBS News. At that time, it was rumored that Andy Lack, the executive producer of *CBS Reports,* the CBS News documentary series, would be leaving it to run a new magazine series aimed at a more youthful audience, so I pitched Sauter and Joyce for Lack's soon-to-be vacant job. I was on my best behavior and must have done okay, because Sauter—after remarking that he didn't understand why so many people found me difficult—offered me half the job. Of the fourteen CBS reports being done each year, seven would be under my aegis. I wanted all of them, of course, and told Sauter so, not having the insight to grasp that I was being put on trial to see how well I did. In the end it made no difference. In one of *CBS News'* periodic budget cutbacks, *CBS Reports* was unexpectedly canceled. A few weeks later, Sauter was fired and Ed Joyce took over the reins of CBS News. Because Joyce had liked my work, and because there was a slot open for a senior producer on a new weekly show, I decided to enlist the aid of Mike Wallace, a man who had never questioned my ability and whom I still considered a mentor and friend. I'd made an appointment with Joyce to pitch myself for the show and I asked Mike to see him before then and sing my praises. "Mike," I said, "I want you to do this *in person,* not by phone."

"What's the difference?" he asked.

"The *difference,*" I said, "is that he will realize it's important to you and therefore in the best interest of CBS News. A word from you around here is like the Good Housekeeping Seal of Approval."

"Fine," Mike said. "When's your appointment?"

"Ten a.m. on Wednesday."

"Consider it done."

Wednesday came, or rather late Tuesday afternoon, when I showed up at Mike's office to see how his conversation with Joyce had gone. "Good," he said. "I told him you were a first-class talent."

"Did he say anything negative?" I asked.

"It was a brief conversation. We were discussing other things and then he had to get off the phone."

"You did this on the *phone*?" I said. "You didn't walk across the street and see him as I asked you to?"

"Joyce called me," he said. "So I brought it up that way. I thought it was more natural."

"Mike, you knew how important this was to me!"

"Harry, I did it. It's over." Mike glanced at his watch. "Got to go." He picked up his briefcase and sailed past me, leaving me standing in the now vacant office. My meeting with Joyce was a non-event. He made no commitments and I did not get the job.

According to the book he wrote about his time at CBS News, Ed Joyce's biggest problem was Bill Moyers, who had arrived from Public Broadcasting Service with a head full of ideas and a driving ambition to do serious, long-form documentaries—which was not where Joyce wanted to go. I had known Moyers from his days at PBS. I was a freelance producer on the second season of his series *Bill Moyers Journal,* where I'd exited under less-than-pleasant circumstances to take the job with *60 Minutes.* I had persuaded Moyers to do a story on the two most successful writers of television drama in Hollywood, Richard Levinson and William Link, who had created *Columbo,* did television's first original movie, and were card-carrying liberals. They were an oddly matched couple. Levinson, the primary writer of dialogue, was tall, aristocratic, and clean-shaven, while Link, the master of plot, was half a foot shorter and had a goatee that made him a dead ringer for Lenin. Old friends of mine, they had agreed to let me follow them through the production of *Tenafly,* their new pilot for NBC. I had also persuaded Larry White, NBC's vice president of programming, to let me inside the process in which NBC would decide whether to order the show as a series. What interested Moyers—and me—was that *Tenafly,* which was the last name of a Black detective named Harry Tenafly, would be the first dramatic series on television to star an African American.

I had only completed a day's worth of filming when the job offer came in from *60 Minutes,* which after agonizing for all of five seconds I accepted. Moyers did not take the news well, even though I told him I would complete the story for him without further payment. "Let's look at what you've shot," he said grudgingly. Since production on the *Tenafly* pilot hadn't started, what I had in the can was a story meeting on another Levinson and Link detective series in which they were leading several Universal TV executives through the twists and turns of their complicated plot. I had filmed the sequence to introduce the boys, as everyone called them, in full action mode, but I soon realized that clarifying the plot and its half dozen characters would not only take too long; it was beyond the attention span of even PBS's postdoctoral audience. So, I cut it to illustrate how the creative process works in television, with a line of narration at the top telling viewers that if they couldn't follow what was going on, well, neither could we. The sequence, which was fast and funny, accomplished its task. Although I had taken pains to explain all this to Moyers, he was not amused. "What I've seen doesn't have anything to do with our subject matter."

"Bill," I said, "The sequence is meant to show Levinson and Link in their milieu before we get to *Tenafly*. It's the setup, not the story."

"You pitched me on a documentary about why television has ignored the problem of race," he said, "not a film about two Jewish writers from Hollywood."

"They're from Philadelphia," I said, "and only one of them is Jewish." I glanced at Moyers, who seemed annoyed that he'd been overly inclusive. "Fine," he said. "It's the short one that's Jewish."

"The short one is Link and he's a gentile," I said. "The tall one is Levinson. He's the Jew."

"I don't care *who* the Jew is," Moyers said. "You're going to *60 Minutes* and I'm no longer interested in the subject matter. Let's leave it at that."

Years later, Moyers himself left PBS for CBS News and a job that would supposedly allow him to make quality documentaries on a permanent basis. I had given myself one last try to advance within the corporation, so I hitched my star to Bill—who by now had kind of forgiven me—and persuaded him that working together to create a viable series might get him what he was yearning for. The effort resulted in my being named executive producer of a summer replacement show cohosted by Moyers and Charles Kuralt, in which Andy Lack, who was the senior executive producer, quickly poisoned my relationship with Moyers and cut me loose from the broadcast. Having nothing to do and nowhere else to go, I returned to *60 Minutes,* where I decided to produce stories that were interesting, though not especially taxing, as I plotted my exit from CBS News.

CHAPTER 15

CONVERSATIONS WITH ANIMALS

I had recently read an article in *Rolling Stone* about man's attempt to communicate with animals. There was Koko the gorilla, who understood sixty different words; the Yerkes Primate Center in Georgia, where scientists had taught chimpanzees to count. And best of all, Nim, a home-raised chimpanzee adopted by a Columbia University professor of psychology, who was teaching Nim sign language. Although the print piece was fascinating, it didn't do justice to an obviously visual story. Don was an easy sell and it appealed to Morley Safer's offbeat sensibility, so I was off and running. First stop was Dr. Herb Terrace, the psychology professor who had somehow convinced Columbia to install him and Nim in an 1870-something mansion outside of Manhattan that was owned by the university and had fallen into disrepair. Terrace, who had hired a series of graduate students to teach Nim to sign, was quite picky about the actual filming. "Nim needs to focus on his lesson," Terrace said, as we drove to the location, my cameraman following us. "He is easily distracted, and if he sees a camera, the lesson is lost. I can't afford to let that happen." We pulled up to the decaying mansion, which in the August heat reminded me of the steamy tropical hotel in *Night of the Iguana* where Richard Burton and Ava Gardner perspired, drank tequila, and engaged in heavy flirting. The cameraman and I stepped gingerly on to the rotting floorboards of the porch where Nim has his daily tutorials. Terrace explained that a student holds up various objects for Nim—a hat, an orange, a child's stuffed animal—and signs the words for them to Nim. The drill is repeated over and over until Nim recognizes each object and signs the proper word back. You won't need sound," Terrace told me. "Think of it as a silent movie."

"What's the payoff?" I asked. "Since we don't have Charlie Chaplin twirling his cane and strolling off into the sunset."

"The payoff," said Terrace, "is that a chimpanzee in Oklahoma is also being taught sign language. He's being brought here in six weeks."

"And . . .?" I asked.

Terrace smiled. "*And* . . . you will be there to record the world's first encounter between two animals using language to communicate with each other."

"What do you think they'll talk about?" I asked the eminent psychologist.

"I don't know," he said. "It's unlikely they'll be discussing Kierkegaard, but it should be interesting."

When the cameraman arrived, Terrace pointed at the field in front of us, an uninviting expanse of weeds that had not been mowed in years. "Walk straight out for twenty-five yards and set up your camera. You'll have to lie down so Nim won't see you." It was a hot August day and the field was swarming with insects. We found a spot that gave us a good view of the porch, cleared away an ancient pile of cow dung, and assumed the prone position. It reminded me of the World War II movies I'd seen as a boy. Dana Andrews, sitting in a foxhole with a wise-guy kid called Brooklyn, waiting for the Japs to come over the rise so they could take them out with their machine gun—and if they ran out of ammo—their bayonets. A poke in the ribs from the cameraman ended my reverie.

"They're here," he said. "I'm rolling." I looked up. Holding Nim's hand, Terrace led him to a spot on the right side of the porch. On the left side, Nim's teacher was already in place. He held up a ball and made the sign for it. Nim responded with his own sign. The teacher shook his head and held up the ball again. Nim responded once again. He must have nailed it, because the teacher showed him another object—a hat. Nim seemed puzzled. Or at least I think he was. My experience with chimpanzees was confined to the early days of *The Today Show*, when its host, Dave Garroway, shared credit with a chimp named J. Fred Muggs. Mr. Muggs's skill set did not include interviewing, but he made up for it with a wide variety of facial expressions and an ability to roller skate.

Meanwhile, back at the mansion, Nim was signing with increased enthusiasm, or so it seemed. We filmed for another thirty minutes and tiptoed out of there. "That was interesting," the cameraman said, his voice tinged with what some might construe as sarcasm.

A week later, Morley and I were about to leave for the airport and a flight to California, where Koko the gorilla and her owner/trainer, Dr. Penny Patterson, lived, when my phone rang. It was Dr. Penny. "Glad I caught you," she said. "You'll have to postpone your trip a couple of weeks. Koko is in estrus."

"In estrus?" I asked, sounding puzzled. Penny was prepared to explain. "She has her period." I took this in as best I could. Was Penny referring to the, well, mess this might create?

"That's not a problem," I told her. "We're on a very tight schedule and we'd really like to come out. I'm sure we could shoot around it."

"It's not that," she said. "It affects her mood. She won't be as cooperative as you want."

"And how does that exhibit itself?"

Dr. P. thought for a second. "Well, for instance, remember the tickling thing I told you about?" I did indeed remember. Koko likes to tickle visitors and be tickled in return. I had convinced Morley to participate in the game. It would be a brief sequence in the film, but it would be colorful—and a way for the correspondent to have more camera time.

"So, we'd have to forget about the tickling?"

"I wouldn't recommend it," Penny said.

"Why not?"

Penny paused for dramatic emphasis. "She might tear Mr. Safer apart."

The thought of a four-hundred-pound gorilla dismembering my correspondent on camera had definite appeal. But sensing it might harm my career, I agreed to postpone the shoot. Now I had to break the news to Morley, who I knew would not be pleased with the sudden cancelation. I found him waiting on line at the coffee wagon, along with a bunch of people from the office. "We'll have to postpone the trip for a couple of weeks," I told him. He asked why. "Koko might behave badly," I replied. "She's in estrus."

Morley rummaged around in his brain for the meaning of the word, just as I had. "What the fuck does that mean?" he finally asked.

I looked around. There were several women on the line, some of whom appeared to be listening. A vulgar phrase from adolescence popped into my head. "It means," I said, sotto voce, "that Koko has the rag on."

This did not sit any better with Safer. Morley was from Canada, too far north for the euphemism to have traveled. "She has the rag on?" he said, louder than before. People on line were now giggling.

"It's slang for having your period," the young woman next to him offered.

"I see," said Morley, who had yet to grasp the full import of her explanation.

"Therefore," the woman added helpfully, "Koko may be irritable, whoever this Koko is."

"She's a gorilla," I announced, grabbing our coffee and hustling Morley out of there to avoid further dialogue. Two weeks later, with Koko's estrus a thing of the past, we left for California.

Koko lived in a large barn on the outskirts of Stanford University, where Penny Patterson taught. She greeted us as we got out of our car. "Koko's been napping," she said, "but she's looking forward to seeing you. I'll go get her." We looked around as the crew set up. Koko shared the space with an assortment of barnyard animals, which seemed to spur Morley's creative juices. For someone who was about to get in the ring with a gorilla, he was in awfully good humor. "We might do a standup about Koko's friends," he joked. Morley gazed down at a pig that was rubbing against his trouser leg. "Geoffrey, here, does television repair," he announced, "while over there, Maria the goat enjoys reading romance novels and listening to Puccini." The impromptu riff was interrupted by Penny leading Koko into the barn. I signaled the cameraman to roll.

"Koko," Penny said, "this is Mr. Safer."

"She can call me Morley," he replied. I stared at Koko, who even in her gorilla crouch stood taller than my five-foot seven-inch correspondent and outweighed him by hundreds of pounds.

"We have a busy day," said Penny, "so let's get going." She reached into her pocket and pulled out an apple. "Koko want apple?" she asked. Koko lumbered over to a keyboard that I hadn't noticed, extended a finger, and daintily pressed one of the keys.

"No," it replied in a robotic monotone that startled everyone, including Geoffrey, the TV repair pig, who scurried out of the barn.

"What Koko want?" Penny asked.

Koko didn't hesitate. She pressed another key. "Koko want banana," announced the keyboard. Penny dug into her other pocket and produced a banana, handing it to Koko.

"What Koko say?" she prompted.

Koko, who had already peeled the banana and stuffed it in her mouth, reached over and pressed a third key. "Thank you," the voice intoned. The interview with Penny proceeded from there, with Koko responding perfectly to all of her teacher's verbal cues. I then took pity on my correspondent, saying we had so much good material the tickling sequence wasn't really necessary. Morley was having none of it.

"Let's go," he said, moving to the center of the barn.

"Better take off your jacket," Penny said. "She likes to grab articles of clothing."

"And do what?" Morley said.

"You know, rip them up."

Morley gave me his Saville Row jacket, looking a bit less confident than before. "Now what?" he asked. Penny took Koko's hand and led her to Morley.

"Tickle her."

"Where?"

"In the ribs," Penny advised. Morley did so. Koko extended a finger and poked Morley in the midsection as she emitted some deep chuffing noises.

"What are those sounds?" Morley asked.

"Probably pleasure," Penny said, "although it's hard to say."

"Probably?" Morley sounded concerned. I didn't blame him. In every Tarzan movie I had seen, Cheeta—Tarzan's boon chimpanzee companion—had emitted the same excited chuffing to warn Johnny Weissmuller, the actor playing Tarzan, of danger ahead. Since Weissmuller survived to star in twelve jungle epics, it must have worked.

I'm going to move around and get another angle," said our cameraman. "Keep tickling, Morley."

"Easy for you to say," Morley grumbled. The tickling went on for several minutes, with much forced laughter from my correspondent and increasingly louder chuffing from his opponent.

"Just ran out of film," announced the cameraman. "It'll take me a second to reload."

"I think we have it," I said. "I don't want to miss our flight." I thanked Penny, handed Morley his jacket, blew Koko a kiss, and got the hell out of there, my correspondent safely intact for his next stop: the Yerkes National Primate Research Center in Atlanta, Georgia.

The chimpanzees at Yerkes were undoubtedly smart; not only smarter than your average ape but smarter than your average human at solving puzzles put in front of them. First, the chimps had to figure out how to open a plexiglass box in which a scientist had placed anywhere from one to six M&Ms. They did this by counting how many of the candies were in the box and tapping the appropriately numbered key to open it. When we arrived at Yerkes, I was dubious that chimpanzees could do math. After my visit, I was convinced that chimps could become champion clog dancers, paint like Vermeer, and play third base for the Mets—as long as the supply of M&Ms didn't run out. The chimps combined their talent with breathtaking speed. On a given signal they would dash to the box, tally the M&Ms inside it, and punch the key that unlocked the box. All in a matter of seconds.

The Yerkes scientists had also taught the chimps to communicate with each other. In one experiment, a chimpanzee named Austin was shown a large pile of M&Ms locked in a box, while his buddy Sherman was shown the keyboard symbol that opened the box. Austin, chosen because his appetite for M&Ms was extreme, quickly learned to press a symbol meaning "Ask for help," which simultaneously announced the word "Help!" Hearing this, Sherman would come running and press the correct key for Austin, opening the box so the two pals could gorge themselves on M&Ms. When I was there, the experiment was performed perfectly every time. But once the box popped open, it was every chimp for himself. (Note to any behavioral scientists reading this account: Chimps play well with others, but do not like sharing.)

I left Yerkes with an addiction to M&Ms, a new respect for chimpanzees, and the possibility that Nim and Washoe might actually use sign language to communicate when they met at Columbia University's mansion in the Bronx, saying God knows what to each other while history awaited.

I was back at CBS when I got a phone call from Herb Terrace. "We have a problem," he said. "Washoe can't come to us. I just finished speaking to her trainer, Roger Fouts. He says she won't fly."

"She *told* him that?"

Terrace laughed. "Not exactly. She's under the weather and Roger is afraid that the plane trip from Oklahoma would do her in."

"No problem," I said. "We'll do the shoot there."

"Exactly," said Terrace. "Except I can't get Nim to Oklahoma. The airlines won't let him sit with me in the cabin, and if I sedate him and put him in a crate, he won't be in any shape to sign with Washoe."

"So, what do you suggest, Herb?"

Long pause. "The only solution is to fly privately." Terrace went on to explain that his grant money from Columbia did not include chartering a plane, but he hoped that *60 Minutes*, the most popular and prestigious show in all of television, would recognize the significance of the ape-to-ape encounter and spring for the flight. Furthermore, he had a friend who owned a plane that we could use to transport Nim for a nominal fee.

"What's nominal?" I asked.

Longer pause. "Five thousand dollars."

"Herb, I . . ."

"To Oklahoma and back," he said. "You can come along. No extra charge."

I somehow was able to persuade Don Hewitt that such a trip (about $40,000 today) was not only in the interest of the show but in the interest of science, which is how I found myself aboard a noisy propeller-driven DC-3 that I had last ridden as an airsick child. The trip, as the expression goes, was uneventful. Nim slept. Terrace read. I threw up over Omaha. After a surprisingly smooth landing at the Norman, Oklahoma, airport we went our separate ways, agreeing to meet at a pre-arranged location at eight the next morning.

And so we did. Herb Terrace, Nim, the film crew, and I arrived early. We sat under an oak tree, watching the sun make its way across eastern Oklahoma and over our bucolic setting, a meadow covered with green grass and wildflowers that led to a gently sloping hill. As a distant church bell tolled eight times, two figures appeared on the hilltop. Holding hands, they made their way down. Then Roger Fouts, who knew the value of a dramatic entrance, released Washoe from his grip. Seeing Nim, she bounded toward him. Seeing Washoe, Nim leapt from Terrace's lap and began to hoot excitedly. Washoe, who was ten years older than Nim, did not return the compliment. Was she put off by Nim's boyish enthusiasm? Did he fail to comprehend the gravity of their meeting? What would be their first words to each other? Then, a blur of hand signals. They moved closer. Another blur. Was it dialogue or disappointment? Would they sit and chat or merely circle each other warily? Would it be the Neil Armstrong moment I had hoped for? "One small step for an ape. One giant step for apehood?" Spoken in sign language, of course. Then I thought of the famous program intro from Edward R. Murrow, icon of journalism: "It was a day like all other days, filled with events that alter and illuminate our time, and *you* are there." Although I was merely a Murrow wannabe, I too would remember this day. A frisson of something or other traveled down my spine as Roger Fouts joined Herb Terrace underneath the tree.

"Dr. Fouts, I presume," Terrace said, extending his hand. I had not anticipated the Stanley and Livingstone moment, nor had my film crew, which was busy documenting the interchange between Washoe and Nim. "What do you think?" Terrace asked Fouts. "Are they signing?"

"Hard to say," Fouts replied, "but they seem to be getting along."

"Let's stir up the pot," said Terrace, taking the hat from his head and hurling it at his young charge. Nim jammed the hat on his head and made a series of faces that immediately reminded me of Crazy Guggenheim, the fedora-wearing drunk on the old *Jackie Gleason Show*. Terrace yelled at Nim to get his attention and signed the word for hat. Would Nim sign back? Would Washoe notice the hat and want it? Would she convey that to Nim? I remembered what Terrace had told me weeks ago: Whatever they were going to talk about didn't include Kierkegaard.

Back in New York, I began putting the story together with my editor Richard Manichello.

The Koko and Yerkes segments were easy to deal with, but Nim's was a nightmare. He and Washoe were moving their hands so quickly that what they were signing—if they were signing at all—was impossible to conclude. Manichello's solution was to look at everything we shot of Nim and Washoe in slow motion, which since the story was done on film would cost a fortune in lab work. I was dubious, but Manichello, who somewhere along the way had become convinced the two chimpanzees were communicating and he was their designated translator, went ahead. The slow-motion footage earned us a visit from the show's senior producer, a CBS News lifer named Palmer Williams, whose job was to ride herd over the budget and deliver bad news with the kindness it only occasionally deserved. "I just saw the lab bill for the slow-motion work," he said calmly. "Was this really necessary?"

Manichello leapt into the fray. "It was crucial, Palmer. We're close to a breakthrough here. Let me show you." He put on the first slo-mo reel, which I had yet to watch. We all looked silently for thirty seconds. The chimps' hand signals had certainly slowed down, but they were still much faster than the sign language that we're used to seeing on TV during important political speeches. Manichello stopped the film to show us a closeup of Nim's hand. "See that," he said. "*That* is the sign for hat."

"How do you know?" Palmer asked. I was thinking the same thing. Manichello picked up a paperback I hadn't noticed before. Its title was *Basics of American Sign Language*. He turned to a heavily earmarked page with a drawing of a hand.

"Look at the placement of the thumb and forefinger," Manichello said. "Now look at the screen." Palmer complied. "Look at Nim's fingers. Same placement."

"Could be," Palmer said. "I'm not sure. And anyway, signing the word 'hat' doesn't make a conversation." He glanced at his watch. "I have a lunch date. Just finish the story, will you?"

I waited until Palmer left the room. "Rich, you didn't tell me you'd been studying sign language."

"All in the name of science," he said. "We're going to win an Emmy for this!"

Three days later, he showed me a cut that was at an even slower speed than before. "I put a sequence together and had each frame triple printed, so you can really see what's going on," he said.

"Jesus, Rich!" I exploded. "You should have asked me before you did that. We are absurdly over budget."

Rich seemed offended by my remark. "Harry, just look at it, will you please?"

I did. "So?"

"*So*? It's a conversation! When we add subtitles, it will be clear."

"Rich," I implored. "Just tell me what the fuck they're saying."

"Sure." He ran the film again. "Here's Nim signing 'hat.' Washoe then signs 'hat' back to Nim." He paused for effect. "Now it gets exciting. Washoe signs 'Give me hat.' Nim says 'No.' Then Washoe grabs the hat, puts it on her head, and runs away. Rich stopped the film and looked at me in triumph. "Pretty cool, huh?"

I looked at him in disbelief. "We need to get someone to see the film who actually signs."

Rich was crestfallen. "I was very careful," he said, holding up his *Basics of American Sign Language* paperback, now dog-eared beyond recognition.

"I'll find somebody, "I told him. "In the meantime, don't do anything."

Twenty-four hours later I was back with an American Sign Language interpreter, a pale, prim woman in her twenties who was raised by deaf parents and had been signing since the age of two. "Let's start with the slo-mo reel," I told Rich. "The one where each frame is triple printed." The woman, whose name was Shirley, watched silently for twenty minutes, arms folded, saying nothing. "Want to see it again?" I asked. Shirley shook her head from side to side. The silence was making me nervous. "Okay, Rich. Put on the hat sequence." He did. Shirley watched. I watched Shirley. There was no tell. Shirley would have made a great poker player. "So, Shirley," I said. "Tell me what you think."

Shirley rose from her chair put on her coat and walked to the door. Her first words were her last. "Whatever it is," she said, pausing for emphasis, "it isn't sign language."

Somehow, we got the story on, leaving the question of animal-to-animal communication for the viewer to figure out. A year later, Herb Terrace sided with Shirley. In a front-page article in *The New York Times,* Terrace admitted that he was a victim of wishful thinking and that Nim and Washoe and all the other animals who were judged to be learning language, were not. My thoughts turned to Geoffrey the pig, who after reading the *Times* article must have been relieved that he had a backup in television repair.

CHAPTER 16

DANCING WITH THE STARS

I never worked with anyone who attracted attention like Dan Rather. In the '70s and '80s, being on the road with Dan was like traveling with Robert Redford. Rather had an aura that made men stare, grandmas ask for autographs, and women swoon. It's undeniable that his on-air arrival at *60 Minutes* on December 7, 1975, which coincided with the show's move from 6 p.m. to 7 p.m. on Sunday, helped kick ratings into the stratosphere. But as every producer assigned to Rather knew, there were factors at work that turned almost every road trip into an adventure—although not necessarily the kind you'd write home about.

Dan's peculiar side has been written about frequently: Forcing CBS to air six and a half minutes of a black screen because he refused to come to the studio after a tennis match delayed his newscast; an eight-hour ride in a Chicago taxi whose driver had kidnapped him;

being assaulted on Park Avenue by a stranger who asked him, "Kenneth, what is your frequency?" My own experiences add to this catalog of weirdness. A few chapters ago, I wrote about Dan and me being briefly jailed in France, but equally memorable was a segment I produced about an event that took place in 1950 at the height of the Cold War, amid fears that the Russians might resort to biological warfare against us. To find out if such an attack might be effective, the US Navy dispatched a gunship to the middle of San Francisco Bay and loaded its cannons with a supposedly benign bacteria called *Serratia marcescens*. Navy personnel stood on rooftops all over the city, holding pieces of litmus paper that changed color when the bacteria touched it. The idea was to fire the cannons and see how far *Serratia marcescens* would travel. The top-secret experiment worked perfectly, turning litmus papers red from Pacific Heights in the north to Bernal Heights in the south and all points in between. The wind also carried the bacterial spray through the open window of a large hospital room where seven patients were recuperating. Hospital records revealed that six of the seven were made ill by the bacteria, but survived. The seventh patient's outcome was different. Edward Nevin was recovering from pneumonia and due to be discharged. Instead, his condition worsened and he died. Some thirty years later, a lawyer named Edward Nevin II read a story in the *San Francisco Chronicle* about the secret biological experiment and sued the US government for having caused his grandfather's demise. Nevin, who happened to be a medical malpractice attorney, had done his homework. He found the world's leading expert on *Serratia marcescens,* who testified that the supposedly benign spray was not quite as benign as the navy had presumed. There was a reasonable probability, the expert said, of it causing someone with diminished lung capacity to stop breathing and die. I thought it was a terrific story and decided that the most compelling way to tell it was to have my intrepid correspondent, Dan Rather, talk the viewer through it in real time. The idea was to put Dan on the deck of a warship in the middle of San Francisco Bay as he explained how its cannons had fired canisters loaded with *Serratia marcescens* into the air, spritzing the city. Our primary camera crew would film Dan's standup from the ship. A second camera would be in a helicopter that hovered overhead. At a prearranged part of the standup, Dan would turn to the second camera for a brief line of dialogue to set up the rooftop sequence. Pointing to the sky, he would tell viewers that the windblown bacteria blanketed San Francisco—a signal for the helicopter pilot to soar rapidly upward. Dan and his ship would get smaller and smaller in the frame until the chopper disappeared into a bank of clouds. The next shot in the film, also taken from the helicopter, saw Dan standing on a rooftop, holding a coffee filter (it photographed better than a piece of litmus paper) up to the heavens as he explained how the navy collected the windblown bacteria. (I had wanted the coffee filter to turn red; a snap with today's digital technology, virtually impossible back then.) The shot would finally pull back to reveal the rooftop, and then the city of San Francisco, while Dan told how *Serratia marcescens* had traveled through the open window of the hospital where Edward Nevin was resting three decades ago, very possibly killing him.

It was an insanely ambitious setup. In order for the sequence of shots to work, we needed a cloudy day and a launch to speed Dan from the boat to the pier. There, he would get in a waiting limo, which would spirit him to the building whose reluctant landlord had agreed—for an unreasonable amount of money—to let *60 Minutes* borrow his rooftop. Dan would race up five flights of stairs (the building had no elevator) and wait for the helicopter to descend from the clouds so he could complete the second part of his standup, which when edited would look like one piece. To complicate matters further, the helicopter couldn't get close enough to Dan in either location for the shot I wanted: The sound of its engine would drown out what he was saying and the wind created by its whirring blades would probably blow Dan off the roof, where unlike the deck of the ship there was nothing to hold on to. The solution today would be a drone; back then it was equipping the chopper with a Tyler mount, a metal platform that is bolted to its exterior and has a small perch for the camera operator to sit on. Feet dangling in midair, the operator films his subject—the image stabilized by a special gyroscope. The Tyler mount takes four hours to install and can only be done by a certified Tyler technician. A careless mistake can result in the occupant plunging to his death, which explains why few cameramen are willing to film from a Tyler mount and why they are compensated so highly for doing so.

To add to all this, I realized that we couldn't take any old boat into the middle of San Francisco Bay; it had to be a military gunship with the requisite flags and cannons. Fortunately, my San Francisco-based soundman, Paul Oppenheim, a man of infinite resources, had a friend who knew a friend who had purchased a mothballed World War II light cruiser, restored it to perfect shape, and rented it out complete with uniformed crew for parties and special occasions. Luckily it was available the day we wanted to film. The whole deal—the cruiser, the chopper, the launch, the limo, the Tyler mount, the second cameraman, the rooftop rental—was pricey: $20,000 in 1980, more than three times that today. Since this was way beyond the scope of a normal *60 Minutes* budget, I had to clear it with Don Hewitt. Don loved the idea, but bucked it up to Robert Chandler, the CBS News vice president in charge of the show and a notorious tightwad. Perhaps because *60 Minutes* had reached stratospheric heights (it would finish the season as television's highest-rated broadcast), Chandler reluctantly approved the cost, sending me a cryptic message that it had better be worth it. All that remained was making certain my correspondent was going to arrive in San Francisco the next morning on his scheduled 7 a.m. flight from JFK. Since I had reviewed the entire procedure by phone with Dan a few hours beforehand, I assumed there would be no problem. I was in my hotel room when

Dan's assistant called, telling me that something had come up and Dan couldn't make it until the day *after* tomorrow. Since everyone had insisted on money up front, all charged to my CBS credit card, and since the weather forecast for the day Dan would now be arriving was terrible—rain, fog, and wind—I blew up. "He's got to come! He has no choice!" I told the assistant. The assistant, whose job was to protect Dan from people like me, said that he was out of the office and couldn't be reached and to adjust my plans accordingly. After many hurried phone calls, I learned that the helicopter, the helicopter pilot, the Tyler mount, the Tyler mount's technician, the dangling cameraman, and the launch to take Dan from ship to shore were all available, but that I would have to pay each of them for two days, not one, since I was inside the twenty-four-hour cancellation window. The landlord whose rooftop we were using added to my agita by charging me triple the price for the second day. That left the cruiser, whose owner said he would rent it to me for a second day if I would reimburse him for the party rental he had to cancel, the food he had ordered, and would agree to give his company a credit on the show. This brought us to $45,000—about $144,000 in today's dollars—with no guarantee that the dicey weather forecast would allow us to get the shots we needed. Adding to my woes was that I was already in the hole for the cancellation fees, with nothing to show for them except the certain wrath of Robert Chandler.

I called Hewitt, explained the problem, and told him that Rather was missing in action. "He's not missing," Don said. He's having dinner tomorrow with Roone Arledge. (Arledge, the president of ABC News, was trying to get Dan to anchor their broadcast when his CBS contract expired.) "Dan loves being courted."

"What do you want me to do?" I asked. "If we check with Chandler, he'll say no."

"Who said anything about checking with Chandler?" Don replied, forgetting that he'd told me to go to Chandler in the first place. "Shoot the standup. We'll figure out a way to bury the cost."

"Thank you," I said, "but there's one other thing. The weather forecast is for wind and rain. We might not be able to pull it off."

"You'll pull it off," Don said, clearly getting bored with the conversation. "We didn't get to where we are by being chickenshit."

As it turned out, the weather was okay and everything went exactly as planned. Dan's standup looked smashing and the rest of the story was equally good. Because Ed Nevin was part of a large Irish clan, many of whom remembered his grandfather, Ed decided to throw a party to celebrate his recent victories in the lower courts and the upcoming *60 Minutes* segment. Sixty-five members of the extended Nevin family gathered to cheer Ed on and raise a glass to his not-so-recently-departed grandfather. It was a great end to the story, but I knew that adding some music to the scene would heighten the emotion. This, I also knew, was a problem. CBS News standards did not allow the use of music unless the source was visible, a show-and-tell rule that was better suited for kindergarten classrooms. "Visible" meant that either live musicians would have to be playing at the event in question or the story would have to include several frames of a needle dropping onto a record. Since the Nevin gathering did not include music, I chose plan B, hoping I could get away without using the shot of the needle drop I had recorded for posterity. I sailed through the first screening with Hewitt, who complimented Dan on his terrific standup, approved the story, and said nothing about my use of music at the end—a Celtic tune that played under Dan's final narration and, over close-ups of wonderful Irish faces, swelled to its conclusion.

Next up was the Robert Chandler screening, normally pro forma for this kind of story, as Chandler's corporate role was to ensure the accuracy and fairness of controversial reports, which mine was not. Chandler, who in his tough-guy role never smiled, was in grimace mode as the story ended. Remembering how upset he was at the cost of the standup—and knowing that Don would abandon me the moment Chandler questioned it—I was prepared for the worst. "Where did that come from?" Chandler asked, looking directly at me.

"Where did what come from, Bob?" I said, stalling for time.

"The *music*, where did it come from?"

I relaxed, sort of. Chandler had bypassed the deadliest sin—the money—and landed on something less threatening. "I, uh, put it there, Bob."

"I know you put it there, damn it! What's the source? Is it a record?"

"Yes," I acknowledged, not yet having to lie.

"Did you film the record being played?"

I paused to collect my thoughts. If I answered truthfully, Chandler would insist on including the shot, which I knew would wreck the rhythm of the ending. (The reader will have to trust me on this. Editing is about timing and pace. An out-of-place shot—even a few frames of it—can bring down an otherwise splendid sequence.) But if I lied, Chandler would tell me to eliminate the music, which I didn't want to do either.

"Yes, Bob," I replied, "it's on film. But putting the shot in would ruin the scene." As soon as I said the words, I wanted to take them back. Chandler, who had the soul of an accountant, didn't like being challenged.

"Show me the shot of the record player," he said, clearly not believing I had taken it. Before I could answer I heard a rumbling from behind me. It was my correspondent, who until now had been silent. Dan straightened in his chair and glared at Chandler.

"Bob," he said. "I have known Harry Moses for years and he is as trustworthy a person as I have ever met. If he says he has the shot, he has it."

"I'm not saying he doesn't have it," Chandler replied, somewhat taken aback by the unexpected challenge to his authority. "I just want to see it."

"Harry," Dan said sternly, "I forbid you to show him the shot."

I looked around the room. Everyone seemed as shocked by Dan's outburst as I was.

"I want to see the shot," said Chandler.

"You don't need to see it," Dan answered.

"Don't tell me what I need to see," said Chandler.

"That's exactly what I am telling you," Dan replied. "I've seen the shot myself. It's there. It's a fact." This startled me even more. Dan and I had not discussed the shot. Dan had not seen the shot. Dan had no idea if the shot even existed. "Furthermore," Dan said, "I don't like having my producer's honesty challenged."

"I'm not challenging his honesty," Chandler said.

"Yes, you are," Dan said, raising his voice and standing upright. "And his integrity!"

"But . . ."

Rather, now in full fury, wouldn't let Chandler complete the sentence. "Don," he said, addressing our mutual executive producer, "either the story goes the way it is, or I go." Dan looked slowly around the hushed screening room, glared at Chandler one more time, and exited, slamming the door behind him. I wasn't sure what had prompted Dan's bizarre reaction. Was it his attempt to apologize to me for his costly tardiness? I didn't think so. Was it his dislike of Chandler? Although none of us really cared for Bob, I doubted it. Or was it a not-so-subtle reminder that Dan was being aggressively wooed by ABC, and if CBS wanted him to stay, it had better make nice? I'm pretty sure that Chandler was going through the same calculations and concluded that he didn't want to shoulder the blame for losing the shiniest star in the CBS News firmament.

"Fuck it!" Chandler said, breaking the silence. "Air the goddamn story!" Chandler left the room, my honor and integrity intact until the next time around.

I had known Lesley Stahl for a while when I was asked by Don Hewitt to do a story with her.

Our relationship was superficial. Lesley knew who I was, I obviously knew who she was. That was it. The pitch meeting in her office was brief. I described the story I wanted to do. Lesley told me that she liked it and was on board. We agreed to start taping as soon as she returned from her summer vacation, during which time I would do the research and send her background notes and questions. As I left her office, she gave me her phone number in Nantucket and told me to call her anytime I needed to discuss something. So far, so good.

I then began researching the story, which focused on Lt. Colonel Scotty Rogers, a brilliant US Air Force fighter pilot on the fast track for general. Rogers had been denied a promotion and relieved of command because he had been accused of sexually harassing Julie Clemm, a female lieutenant in his unit. The accuser, however, was not Clemm but Rogers's second in command, Major Michael Cloutier. The kicker to the story was Clemm's sworn statement that although she *had* been sexually harassed, the perpetrator wasn't Rogers but Cloutier, who was bucking for (and eventually got) Rogers's job.

Scotty Rogers was now stationed in Shreveport, Louisiana, where the air force had banished him to a position that required him to do virtually nothing. I flew there and found him earnest and highly credible. However, Rogers had a cleft lip, which was prominent enough to be disconcerting in an interview. After observing him discreetly from various angles, I realized we could get around the problem by photographing him head on, which would make the deformity less distracting. It also meant that we would have to change Lesley's usual camera angle and lighting, which—considering the circumstances—I assumed would be no problem.

During the course of research, I decided to check in with Lesley, whose phone number I had misplaced. When I asked her assistant Ethan for it, he wouldn't give it to me. "She's in Nantucket," he said. "She can't be disturbed."

"Ethan," I said. "Lesley gave me the number herself. She told me to call anytime. Okay?" Reluctantly, he handed it over.

"I wouldn't do this if I were you," he said. "She doesn't like to be bothered on vacation."

"Ethan, the woman's a human being. She puts her pants on one leg at a time, just like the rest of us. She doesn't need special treatment." At which point I called her.

Lesley picked up the phone. "Hi, it's Harry," I said.

The voice on the other end did not sound altogether pleased. "Harry who?"

"Harry Moses. We're doing the Scotty Rogers story together."

"I can't talk now," she said. "I've got a lot of people here. Call some other time." At which point she hung up. I put the receiver down and stared into the middle distance. Although this was not a good omen, I decided to give her the benefit of the doubt. A week later, with the research complete, I called again.

"It's Harry *Moses*," I said, emphasizing the last name in case there were several Harrys in her life.

"How did you get this number?" she asked.

"Lesley, you gave it to me. If this is a good time, I'd like to discuss the story."

"It's not a good time," she said. "Send me the research and questions and the travel schedule."

"When will we talk?" I asked.

"When I get off the plane," she said, hanging up on me again.

It was a balmy ninety-eight degrees when I picked up Lesley at the Shreveport airport. As the first words out of her mouth made it apparent, she was not in a good mood. "You got the story wrong," she said. "Have you seen this week's *New Yorker*?" I told her that I had. "Did you read the article on military spending? That's the story we should be doing."

"Lesley, our story is on the military but it's about sexual harassment," I said. "Did you look at the research?"

"Of course I looked at it. What I'm saying is that you chose the wrong story."

"Lesley," I said. "I'm here, you're here, the story's here. Why don't we do the interview and discuss this later. Any questions about the material?" Lesley shook her head. "Good. Then let me tell you about Scotty Rogers." I went on to explain in detail about his cleft lip and the necessity of adjusting the camera angle and the lighting to minimize it. "In order for your shot to match his shot, I had to do the same with you."

"I'll look at it," she said, proceeding to make cell phone calls until we arrived at the hotel, where the interview was taking place and where a giant Louisiana cockroach had fallen from the ceiling onto my head the night before, a sure sign of bad luck.

I walked into the room, trailed by Lesley. She sat down opposite Scotty Rogers and I introduced them. "Before we start," she said, not wanting to engage in small talk, "let me see the shot on the monitor." A small TV monitor was brought out for her. The screen had a close-up of Rogers. "Not him," she said. "Me." I pressed a button on the monitor and Lesley's image popped on the screen. She studied herself intently. "It's too straight on," she said. "Change the camera angle. Change the lighting. Make it the way I like it."

"Lesley," I said, speaking before the camera crews could make the changes. "Remember the conversation we had in the car?" I paused to choose my words carefully as Rogers was facing her. "The one about how we needed to make certain adjustments from the norm and how if we didn't, uh, certain consequences would result that would make the, uh, interview you're going to have with Colonel Rogers somewhat, uh, unwieldy to use." Lesley glared at me and said nothing. "I want you to have the full picture," I said. "It's your decision."

I waited for her answer. And waited. And waited. The wait, in fact, was so long that I found myself reminded of the famous Jack Benny story in which a robber points a gun at him and says, "Your money or your life." Benny, who was known for his cheapskate image, was silent for thirty seconds, an eternity on radio. "Mister, your money or your life," the robber says again.

"I'm thinking," Benny answers. "*I'm thinking*!"

I awoke from my reverie to find Lesley still mulling things over. Another fifteen seconds went by before she spoke. "All right," she said grudgingly.

"Roll tape," I announced to the crew before she could change her mind. The first thirty minutes of the interview were not a triumph. Because Rogers and Lesley had exchanged barely ten words, he was quite nervous. Lesley should have been aware of this, but she did nothing to make him feel more comfortable. Furthermore, as was obvious to both Rogers and me, her knowledge of the story was spotty. She had read the information on Rogers, but she had not looked at the research on the other participants, even though I had told her that doing so would further her understanding. As a result, Lesley was confused about the chronology of events and the names of the characters. When we changed tapes, I drew her aside. "I think we have to start over."

"Why? I thought it was fine," she said.

"I think we can do better. The two of you weren't communicating very well and some of the information was unclear. Michael *Cloutier* is the guy who blew the whistle on Rogers for sexually harassing Julie *Clemm*. Clemm said it was *Cloutier* who harassed her, not Rogers."

"I know that," Lesley answered testily, although she'd mixed up the names twice during the interview and had to be corrected by Rogers. "Let's just get on with it. I don't want to miss my plane."

"I promise you won't miss your plane," I said, whereupon the power failed and all the lights in the room went out.

We eventually managed to get through the interview and the rest of the story. Although I found Lesley imperious, some of the interview subjects were so taken with her celebrity that they asked her to pose for snapshots with them, which she seemed to enjoy greatly. Our final interview was with a Northwest Airlines pilot who had previously served with Rogers and was functioning as a character witness for him.

We did it at a Northwest conference room in the Detroit airport, which didn't look like much but was convenient for Lesley, who wanted to get back to New York by dinnertime. Lesley instructed the Northwest PR woman assisting us to notify her when the plane was boarding. In the middle of taping, the woman entered and told Lesley it was time for her flight. Although there was another one an hour later and we were only halfway through the interview, Lesley removed her mic and dashed through the doorway. "I've never seen *that* before," said my well-traveled cameraman. I hadn't either. Nor, I'm sure, had our bewildered interview subject, who had changed his schedule and sacrificed a weekend with his family to accommodate us and help Rogers.

Back in New York, matters proceeded to get worse. I had completed a rough cut of the story and called Lesley to come and look at it. "I don't want to look at it," she said, "I want to see the script."

"Lesley, the script won't tell you anything about the impact of characters, or about the pace and flow of the story. Why don't you watch what we've got, see what needs changing, and then we'll work on the script."

"No," she said. "Bring me the script."

Ten minutes after I had given it to her, she called back. "I want to see the interview transcripts. Bring them to me now." This was not good news. Correspondents do not normally look through transcripts unless the story is so full of flaws that you need to search through the original material for better stuff. And this story, although by no means perfect, was not a candidate for radical surgery. I dropped the interview transcripts on her desk. She barely looked up at me. "Come back in an hour," she said.

An hour later, I reappeared. Lesley handed me a pile of pages that she had pulled out of the transcript books. "Look at the first page," she said, which was a Q&A sequence with Lesley and Rogers that she had circled. "Why didn't you use this?" she said.

I read the circled passage, which was ancillary to the point of the story. "Because Rogers's answer didn't go anywhere."

"But I was so *good* there," she said. "Use it."

This was too much. Conscious of my anger, I lowered my voice and spoke calmly. "Lesley, if we can't do this in a collegial manner, then we shouldn't do it all."

"What did you say?" she asked. It sounded like a threat.

I lowered my voice another notch. "That if we can't work together collegially, we shouldn't work together at all."

"Are you yelling at me?"

"I am not yelling at you," I said. "I am merely saying that we need to do this collegially."

"Don't you yell at me," she yelled.

"Lesley," I said, reducing my voice to a whisper, "go through the transcripts, mark up what you want, and I'll look at it. If I've missed something important, I'll find a place for it. If we still disagree, we'll duke it out." I got up and left.

I would like to report that the process got easier after this, but it didn't. Lesley and I eventually (and painfully) arrived at a script we both could live with. Now it was time to show the finished product to Hewitt, whom I pulled aside as people were filing into the screening room. "Don, I need a favor," I said. "Please don't ask for a lot of changes. I just don't have the energy to spend another week making revisions with that lady."

"I hear you," he laughed. "How's the story?"

"Essentially fine. It's too long and the writing sucks, but . . ."

"She rewrote you, right?" he said.

"Uh huh."

"Figures. She can't write. Don't worry. We'll keep it simple."

As it turned out, I didn't have to worry. Don liked the story and wanted only minor changes. That was it until a couple of days before air. The show for that week was running long, so I was asked to cut thirty seconds from my story. I looked at the script and realized that if I eliminated the last two Q&As with the Northwest Airlines pilot—the guy whose interview Lesley had walked out on—I would have my thirty seconds. (Because the pilot's interview ended up not advancing the story, I had fought Lesley about including him to begin with—one of the many battles I lost.)

I walked into Lesley's office, script in hand. "The show's long. We need to lose thirty seconds. This is what I think we should do," I said, showing her my cut.

Lesley looked at it and erupted. "I *told* you I wanted this in. This is the most important sound bite in the piece. You're not taking it out."

"Fine," I said, knowing this was another battle I wasn't going to win. "What do you suggest?"

"Leave me the script," she said. "Come back in half an hour." I did. When I looked at her cuts I was appalled. She had taken out two seconds here, three seconds there—a total of seven itty-bitty deletions that chopped up the flow of the story. She had also eliminated one crucial ten-second sound bite of Julie Clemm defending Scotty Rogers that really made you care about him. (The Clemm bite, I couldn't help but notice, was not preceded by an on-camera question from Lesley, so it could be removed without affecting Lesley's face time.)

Not wishing to have anything more to do with Lesley than necessary, I showed Lesley's cuts to senior producer Phil Scheffler. He agreed they didn't work. I then showed him my solution, which he liked. "Will you please deal with her?" I asked him. Phil marked up a new copy of the script with my cuts, took a Post-it stamped with "From the desk of Philip Scheffler," affixed it to the script, and wrote on it, "Lesley, I think these cuts are much better."

"Here," he said, handing me the script. "Give this to her."

I backed away from the offending document. "Phil, you have to talk to her about it in person. Not me. You."

Scheffler looked at me and laughed. "Are you nuts?" he said.

Having lost the battle of the cuts, I now had to deal with the battle of the studio intro, the piece of copy at the head of each story, which the correspondent reads in front of the cover page. Lesley had rewritten the intro without bothering to show it to me. I learned this when Hewitt called me into his office to review it. "This doesn't frame the story properly," he said. "What's wrong with what you had originally?"

"Don," I said after I'd read it, "this is the first time I've seen this. I didn't write it. And it doesn't work."

"So, change it back to what you had," he said.

"Happily," I said. "Will you tell Lesley, so she doesn't have a fit when she records it?"

"Yeah, yeah, sure," he said, as I breathed a sigh of relief and headed across the street to the studio.

I watched Lesley on a bank of monitors from the studio control room as she rehearsed reading the intro, which was on teleprompter. "This isn't what I wrote," she announced. "Is Harry there?"

I pressed a button on a nearby mic to speak to her. "Lesley, Don didn't like what you wrote, so he changed it back. Didn't he call you?"

"No, he didn't."

"Sorry," I said, "but this is what he wants."

"I don't care what he wants," she said, "I won't read it."

Merri Lieberthal, who produced the studio portion of the show, intervened. "Lesley, Don approved it. Please read it."

"No," said Lesley. "It's not what I wrote."

Merri then called Don, who was conveniently out to lunch. "Don's not around," she said to Lesley. "Why don't you record it and we'll discuss it with him later?"

"I'm making some changes," Lesley said, which she proceeded to do.

"Are they okay?" Merri asked me, concerned about their accuracy. Although they were not elegantly written, they did not do great damage to the intro.

"I think it's the best you're going to get," I told her.

"Roll tape," Merri said, wanting to get out of there as much as I did.

Once the intro was recorded, I found myself walking across Fifty-Seventh Streetstreet with Lesley. She was still fuming.

"I told you what I wanted," she snapped, "and you changed it."

"Lesley," I said, stopping in the middle of the street. "A, you didn't tell me anything. B, I didn't change it, Don did. And C, why are you so angry?"

"Because my orders were disregarded," she said. Lesley shifted into high gear and headed toward the other side, oblivious to the oncoming traffic that was doing its best to avoid her.

In the spring of 1986, Diane Sawyer and I were searching for our next *60 Minutes* story. (At the time, I was one of five producers assigned to Diane.) "You know who I'd like to do," she said, "James Baldwin."

"Any particular reason?" I asked.

Diane shot me one of her soulful looks. "He's such a wonderful writer. I think we should just do him. Don't you?"

"He *is* a wonderful writer," I said. "But I'm not sure what the story is."

"Harry, there's *always* a story," she cooed. "Just think about it."

I knew Diane, so I knew that thinking about it was only going to delay the inevitable. Also, I had no real objection to doing something with Baldwin. On the plus side, he lived in the South of France, which I find preferable to, say, the south of Iowa. On the minus side, he hadn't written much lately, which made it difficult to envision a segment. In addition, Baldwin had a serious drinking problem. (I learned this firsthand several years earlier when Jimmy, as everybody called him, participated in a story Mike Wallace and I did about Bobby Kennedy.)

Then I came up with what I thought was a workable idea. A political scientist named Charles Murray had just written a book called *Losing Ground,* which was getting a lot of press. Its thesis was that Lyndon Johnson's Great Society program had actually encouraged Blacks to stay on welfare because they made more money *that* way than working. It was an argument I knew Baldwin would take issue with. Also, because we would be focusing on Murray as well, it would take the heat off me to deliver an entire story on Baldwin . . . whom I didn't think could carry the burden alone.

Diane—who didn't care how she got Baldwin as long as she got him—bought the concept, so I flew down to Washington to meet Murray. Charlie, as he likes to be called, lived in a pleasant townhouse in the Adams Morgan section of the city—a former blue-collar neighborhood then in the throes of yuppiedom. Although very far right on most issues, Murray didn't foam at the mouth. He happily agreed to the interview and seemed disappointed when I explained that he would not actually meet James Baldwin,(who was one of his favorite writers) but that the debate would be channeled through Diane. A week later we filmed the interview, which I had scheduled first so we could read some of Murray's quotes to Baldwin.

Back at *60 Minutes*, I learned that Baldwin had come to New York. Swallowing my disappointment at missing spring in St. Paul de Vence, I met him for lunch, handed him Murray's book, which I had no confidence he would look at and watched as he consumed a prodigious amount of scotch. We made plans to film in two weeks.

The morning of the shoot, Diane and I swung by in a car to pick up Baldwin. He was twenty minutes late, but thankfully sober. Jimmy and Diane chatted as we headed for Harlem and the block where Baldwin grew up. I needed some shots of the two together and we'd decided it would be interesting to take him back to his old neighborhood. We got out of the car and the soundman began putting wireless microphones on them. Cameraman Greg Andracke took me aside. "Harry, how am I going to keep them in the same frame?" he asked. Looking at Sawyer and Baldwin, I saw immediately what Andracke was talking about. Diane, who with her high heels was more than six feet tall, towered over the diminutive writer.

"The only way it will work," I said, "is if he walks on the sidewalk and she walks in the gutter."

"What about the automobiles?" Andracke said. I looked again. The street was lined with cars parked up against the curb, leaving Diane no room to stay next to Baldwin.

"At the end of the block there's a fire hydrant where there's a few feet between vehicles," I said. "They can walk there, go out of frame and we can pick them up again on the stoop of Baldwin's old house. If Diane stays at the bottom and we put him a couple of steps higher, it ought to be fine."

"Which house?" Andracke asked me. I pointed to it.

"Won't work," he said. "They'll be in shadow. Their eyes will look like olive pits." I peered up at the sky. Right again. The sun was perched behind Baldwin's former home and was shining brightly on the other side of the street.

"What a pain in the ass you are," I said to Andracke. "We'll do it across the street. We don't have to say it's his house."

We filmed the walk and set up on the stoop of a ratty-looking tenement. "You want to see the shot?" asked Andracke. I peered through the viewfinder of his camera. They were, to put it mildly, an odd couple. Diane, a platinum-tressed Valkyrie in a brilliant red Armani silk dress; Baldwin, a dark-skinned, gnomic Wotan in a worn tweed jacket and off-the-rack khakis.

"So," Diane began, "what was it like growing up here?"

"What do you think it was like?" Baldwin inquired. A good question, I thought, since I was pretty sure Diane hadn't spent much time in this part of New York. A slight breeze rustled her Armani and blew a few strands of blonde hair across her face. She pushed them gracefully aside and pressed on.

"What I wondered," she asked, "was how aware you were of the white world."

"I was like any other Negro child my age," Baldwin said. "I played with my Negro friends, went to my Negro school, and came home to my Negro mother and father. My world was circumscribed."

"Do you remember the first time you encountered prejudice?" asked Diane.

Baldwin straightened himself to his full height, climbed up a step, and peered down at Diane. "My dear lady, of course I do. I was eight years old. My mother sent me to the store to pick up a pair of gloves for her. The store owner, a white man, patted me on my kinky-haired head and remarked to his white salesperson what an ugly, pop-eyed little nigger I was."

"How awful," Diane gasped.

"It was commonplace," Baldwin said. "It was no different than the experience of any Negro child anywhere in this country."

Diane mounted two steps and reclaimed her height advantage. "Then you must be pleased," she said, "at the progress that has been made."

"What progress is that?" Baldwin wanted to know.

"Surely you won't deny that Blacks are in a much better position now than they were thirty years ago," Diane protested.

"By your standards, perhaps," said Baldwin.

"By anybody's standards," Diane countered.

"That is not the way I look at it," Baldwin said, moving up another step. "This society, this *white* society, is no respecter of my rights. What you call progress, I consider rightfully mine. And until I possess what is rightfully mine, what has been *taken* from me, what has been *denied* me, there can *be* no progress. Never, never, never!"

Baldwin's unexpected outburst had rendered Diane temporarily speechless. We broke for lunch, where I managed to keep liquor away from Jimmy, and resumed the interview in a private room at the restaurant. As I suspected, Baldwin hadn't read Murray's book; but in the hour-long interview with Diane he airily dismissed it, insisting that the issues it raised were irrelevant until the greater issue of racial equality had been fulfilled. (At one point, Diane became so frustrated at Baldwin's refusal to see her side of things that she asked him if he was a communist. His response was far more measured than mine would have been.)

Although I knew Baldwin's truculence would give me trouble in the cutting room, I found the interview fascinating. Listening to him speak, I understood why he had achieved literary prominence. Like all great artists, he had an original voice, which I believed was still worth hearing.

The editing of the story was indeed difficult. Diane's interview with Murray was peppered with quotes from Baldwin's essays and Murray had responded to them all. So, Baldwin's refusal to respond to Murray was frustrating. In the end, I decided to tell the viewer what had taken place and make a virtue of Baldwin's extraordinary passion. Diane agreed. We recorded her narration and prepared to show the rough cut to Hewitt.

Waiting in the screening room, editor Hank Greenberg and I watched the troops stream in: senior producer Phil Scheffler, senior editor Esther Kartiganer, show producer Merri Lieberthal, Diane, and executive producer Don Hewitt. I was not looking forward to the process. I never did. Don was a decisive and often brilliant critic, but occasionally he could be destructive. I had long stopped trying to anticipate his reaction to a story. As Hewitt's rear end hit his seat, I hit the button on the speaker box. "Roll it," I told the projectionist. The lights dimmed and Diane's voice—which was laid over black since she would later record the words in the studio—filled the room.

"This is a story about the state of race relations in America as seen through the prism of two writers. The first, Charles Murray, says the social welfare programs of Lyndon Johnson's Great Society actually made things worse for Blacks by paying them more to stay home than to seek work." The walking shot of Diane and Baldwin popped on the screen as Diane continued. "The second, author James Baldwin, says the problem is more profound. Baldwin claims that Murray is not only wrong but that what he says is irrelevant."

Baldwin and Diane were now standing on the stoop. Baldwin was speaking. "This white society is no respecter of my rights. What you call progress, I consider rightfully mine." Andracke's camera closed in on Baldwin, who continued to berate Diane. "And until I possess what is rightfully mine, what has been *taken* from me, what has been *denied* me, there can *be* no progress. Never, never, never!"

I peered through the flickering light at Hewitt. He shifted uncomfortably in his chair and scribbled something on his yellow notepad—a bad sign so early in the game. The film ran its course and I prepared myself for the onslaught I sensed would follow. I was not disappointed. "How can he say that?" Don shouted, as the lights came up in the room. "How can he say there's been no progress? Blacks in this country have never been better off. Any Black high school graduate can apply to Harvard or Stanford and they'll be happy to accept him. They're *looking* for minorities." I tried to respond but Don rolled right over me. "It's the same thing at corporations," he went on. "They're dying for Blacks. Same thing at CBS News. If a Black kid with credentials applies for a job, he'll get hired before a white kid will."

"Don, I think you're missing the point," I said. "Baldwin isn't talking about opportunity, he's talking about equality."

Hewitt glared at me. "What else did he say?"

"The interview lasted an hour," I said. "There was nothing substantially different." Diane swiveled around in her chair and looked at Don.

"I pressed him very hard," she offered. "I think you've seen the best of it."

"I'll tell you how hard Diane pressed him," I laughed. "She accused him of being a communist."

"Why didn't you put that in?" Hewitt said. "Maybe he is."

"Don, James Baldwin is not a communist," I replied. "And his answer didn't go anywhere."

"Let me see the transcript," Don said. I handed him the binder containing the Baldwin interview. He leafed through the pages for several minutes as we all sat there silently. Finally, he spoke. "You can't tell anything from these fucking transcripts. Hank, put the interview up in your room so I can take a look at it." My editor left as I contemplated my next move. When Hewitt has real problems with a segment, he sometimes screens the "outs"—the material that was shot but wasn't included in the piece. The producer stays in the room to note his changes and to resist them if he doesn't agree. I chose a different tack.

"Don, let me ask you something," I said. "I want to make sure I understand your difficulty with the piece. Did you find it boring? Did you find Baldwin's refusal to respond directly to Murray troublesome? Or is it something else?"

"What it is," said Hewitt, "is that what he's saying just ain't so. That's why I want to look at the outs."

"Got it," I said, as evenly as I could manage. "I'm going to lunch."

An hour later I walked into Hank Greenberg's cutting room. "You just missed Don," Hank said. "He looked at every frame. I've never seen him do *that* before."

"Did he find anything useful?" I asked.

"If he did, he didn't tell me," Hank answered. "What's next?"

"I'll go find out," I said.

I went to Hewitt's office and he waved me inside. "I screened the entire interview," he said. "There's nothing there."

"Fine," I said, knowing it would be impossible to turn him around. But he wasn't through with me.

"Harry," he said, "this is one of the dumbest ideas for a story I've ever seen. Do yourself a favor, will you? Lay off the liberal bullshit and do stories that are about something."

This was more than I could bear. "Don, whose idea do you think Baldwin was anyway?"

"Yours, of course," he snapped.

"Nope," I said. "It was Diane's."

Hewitt looked at me incredulously. Sawyer, who had spent six years working for Nixon, most of which were *after* he resigned in disgrace, was not exactly a flaming left-winger.

"Jesus Christ," he exploded, "that takes the fucking cake! I'm gonna talk to her right now! She can't do things like that around here!" Don stormed out of his office and down the hall to Diane's. I walked back to Hank's cutting room.

"At least you're not bleeding," he said.

"I *am* bleeding. It's just inside where you can't see it. I'm probably hemorrhaging as we speak."

Hank spoke as a father would to a stubborn child. "Give it up, Harry. It's just a story."

"No," I said. "It's more than that."

In the early '80s I was producing an Ed Bradley story on an ABC movie for television called *The Day After,* which focused on a town in Kansas that had been devastated by a nuclear explosion. The reason for doing the story was the discovery that the nuclear freeze movement had so heavily influenced ABC through the writing of the script and the making of the movie that the final product was a virtual infomercial for the movement's point of view. Because ABC could not resist the idea of having *The Day After* plugged on *60 Minutes,* no matter what we said about it, the network agreed to offer up its president of entertainment, Brandon Stoddard, for an interview, with the full understanding that we would be going after him for caving to special interests.

After a couple of days of filming in Lawrence, Kansas, where *The Day After* was shot, we were ready to take a morning flight to Los Angeles where Stoddard was located. When I met Ed Bradley for breakfast, he had a long face. "What's wrong?" I asked him.

Ed told me that the NBC newscaster Jessica Savitch, an old and close friend of his, had died in an automobile accident last night. "The funeral's in Philadelphia tomorrow. If I go to LA, I can't make it." I thought about this for a minute. Since the interview couldn't be postponed, Ed's absence would mean that I would have to interview Stoddard. And because Stoddard's interview was the centerpiece of the story, and contentious to boot, it would be impossible to keep me out of it. You'd have to hear my voice, see my face, and identify me as the interviewer. I pointed this out to Ed, who mulled it over for a while. "Jesus," he sighed, "I don't know what to do."

"If you're asking me," I said, "I'd go to the funeral. She was your friend. Life is more important than television."

"That's okay with you?" he asked, looking greatly relieved.

"Sure. Just remember that I'm going to have to be visible in the interview."

"I understand," Ed replied, starting to leave. I stopped him.

"Ed, I want to make absolutely sure we're on the same page here. Because I will be challenging Stoddard throughout the interview, I will not be able to edit myself out of it."

"Fine with me," he said, squeezing my shoulder as he got up from the table. "Thanks, Harry. This is the right thing to do."

I called Hewitt to tell him what happened and to ask if he was okay with me doing the Stoddard interview. He was, so I went to Los Angeles, interviewed Stoddard, and after a lot of poking and prodding, got him to admit that ABC was probably snookered by the nuclear freeze people. I then returned to New York and was editing the story when I got a call from my agent, Richard Leibner, who also represented Ed. "I just want you to know," Leibner told me, "that Bradley thinks you're the greatest thing since sliced bread."

"How so?" I asked.

"Because you made him go to the funeral. Because you told him that life was more important than television. He said he'll never forget that."

A few weeks later, I'd finished editing and brought Ed in to screen the cut. When the story ended, he seemed unusually somber. "It's good," he said, "but it's too long."

"Fine," I said. "Tell me what doesn't play."

"The interview with that ABC guy, Brandon Stoddard. You don't need it. Take it out. It does nothing for the story."

"Ed," I said, raising my voice perhaps more than was necessary. "It *is* the story."

"No, it's not," he said. "It doesn't add a thing to it. Take it out."

"Ed, the story is about ABC being co-opted by the nuclear freeze movement. Stoddard all but admitted it happened. Without him, you've got a lot of charges and countercharges and no conclusion."

"I don't see it that way," he said.

Since I'm a slow learner, it only then occurred to me that Ed's problem wasn't with the interview but with the fact that someone else had done it. Someone who you heard and saw. Someone who wasn't Ed Bradley. "Ed, I can't take myself out of it," I said. "I tried, but there are too many exchanges."

"I don't want you to take yourself out of it," he answered. "I want you to get rid of it."

"I think we're at an impasse," I said. "Let's show it to Hewitt. Whatever he wants, I'll do. Okay?"

"Maybe," Ed replied. "Let's see what he says.

An hour later, Don Hewitt arrived. He sat impassively screening the story. "There are some changes you need to make," he said when it had ended, "but nothing major. It's pretty good."

"Don, what do you think about the interview with Stoddard?" Ed asked.

"It was fine," Don answered.

"I don't think it's necessary," Ed said. "It doesn't help the story."

Don, who has an explosive temper, exploded. "Are you nuts?" he yelled. "It *is* the story. Furthermore, you can't take Harry out of it. There are too many Q&As."

"Who said anything about taking Harry out of it?" Bradley said. "Harry's not the issue. The interview doesn't go anywhere."

Don, who has the attention span of a gnat, got up and left. "Ed, if you don't want to run the story, we won't run it. If you do, the interview stays."

Ed pushed his glasses down the bridge of his nose, just like he does on TV, and looked over them at me. "Did you talk to Don before the screening about the way I felt?" he asked.

"Nope," I said. "So, are we running it or not?"

"I'll think about it," he answered.

He did. It ran. And I got my fifteen minutes. Which I think is overrated, although my mother loved it.

CHAPTER 17

LEAVING *60 MINUTES*

At CBS, the knock on me—accurate enough, as it turned out—was not my ability but that I was deficient in "people skills." This was understandable, since it's hard to instill confidence in others when anxiety perches on your shoulder and won't crawl back in its cage. But what I lacked in human relations I made up for in advance planning. A man named Bob Clampitt, whom I knew socially, was running an organization called Children's Express, which taught print journalism to children ages nine to thirteen. I immediately realized that seeing the kids working on stories would not only be an interesting segment for *60 Minutes* but might induce Public Broadcasting—which had money back then—to air it as a series. I did the story and showed it to PBS, who liked it enough to give me a $200,000 grant for a half-hour pilot. If I made it efficiently, the money would be enough to carry me for a while, even if the pilot wasn't picked up. Then came the matter of resigning. Because my contract was up in two weeks, CBS could not stop me from walking. It could, however, make life exceedingly difficult for me in ways that I did not anticipate. I first told Diane Sawyer, who took the news well. I then told Hewitt that I had something to prove to myself and, having recently turned fifty, I needed to give myself that shot. Don said he understood but asked me to do one more story with Diane before exiting—a profile of the NBA's shiniest new star, Michael Jordan. "Don, I just can't do it," I told him. "I've made this commitment to myself and I need to go through with it." I then went back to my office to begin the slow process of packing up fourteen years of stuff. I'd barely opened the first file drawer when the phone rang. On the other end was my agent, Richard Leibner.

"Harry," he said, "I don't know what happened between you and Hewitt, but I just got a call from Eric Ober saying that you were in breach of contract and he wants you out of the office by 5 p.m." (Ober was the CBS News vice president for long-form news programming.) Since *CBS Reports* had recently been canceled, this meant that Ober's job consisted of being in charge of *60 Minutes,* which to be generous took no more than two or three hours a week. This left Ober with a lot of time on his hands to justify the fat corporate salary he was being paid and may explain why he sprang into action so quickly when Hewitt told him of my insubordination. In short, the two weeks I had given myself to pack up, say goodbye to my colleagues, and move out had been reduced to less than an hour. It was not the way I wanted to leave, which was further sullied by Hewitt claiming he had fired me. The good news was that I had a pilot to make and—should it pass muster with PBS—I would be the executive producer in charge of my very own series.

As it happened, the pilot turned out well and I was off and running; setting out to prove to myself, CBS News, and the world at large that I had the right stuff. What I hadn't taken into account were the three hundred or so PBS affiliates, who from the Great Plains to Guam had decided that *CE News Magazine,* as we had decided to call it, was such a thoroughly rotten idea that its first season would be its last season, even though no one except a few PBS executives had seen the pilot or even knew what it was about. I was told this just minutes before I stood up to describe the show at the PBS annual convention in San Francisco. Knowing that whatever I said would be meaningless, I shortened my presentation and got off the stage as quickly as possible. Although it was demoralizing to learn that my little series had been voted least likely to succeed, I rented office space, hired a staff, and started pre-production.

Making *CE News Magazine* was in certain ways a nightmare. The oldest reporter was thirteen, the youngest nine. All required adult supervision, which meant that I needed to hire associate producers who were not only gifted researchers and ace schedulers but also willing to nursemaid the kids as they traveled to various locations without parents in tow. This was challenging enough for stateside assignments, but when you tossed in stories from exotic locations like the Middle East and Africa, the degree of difficulty multiplied. Then there was the preparation of the diminutive correspondents. I decided to treat them pretty much the same as I did Mike, Morley, or Dan: writing a description of the story, giving them questions, discussing each interview in detail. Still, once the interview began, the kids were on their own.

In the process, we discovered that a couple of them were unusually gifted at confronting adults. Our star correspondent was Jonathan Zachary, a cherubic-looking twelve-year-old whose mop of blond hair and easygoing manner concealed a killer instinct. My favorite Jonathan story was an investigation into the warehousing of children by parents who had grown weary of living with their difficult offspring and had the means to send them to one of these facilities. And because children are minors with few discernable rights, it didn't take much to legally lock them up. Among the worst offenders was a facility named Charter Oaks, which was located on the outskirts of Miami, Florida. Enter Jonathan Zachary and his physician mom, whom we sent down to Charter Oaks to see if it would admit

Jonathan because his grades had slipped and his mother had caught him drinking a beer. (Both true.) Over Jonathan's protests, Charter Oaks agreed to take him in for an initial six months. Jonathan and his mother left, promising to return the next day with Jonathan's bags packed, a check made out to Charter Oaks, and the agreed-upon six month's stay. Because we had previously arranged with Charter Oaks headquarters to bring a camera crew to tour the facility (they jumped at the chance for free advertising), we showed up the next day and were able to film what took place.

ADMISSIONS DIRECTOR
Hello, Jonathan. I know you must be apprehensive, but I'm sure you'll like it here.

JONATHAN
I don't want to go.

ADMISSIONS DIRECTOR
We admitted you yesterday, Jonathan. Your mom wants you to go, and . . .

JONATHAN'S MOM
I've changed my mind.

ADMISSIONS DIRECTOR
But yesterday you said that he had problems.

JONATHAN'S MOM
That's correct. And I described them to you.

JONATHAN
You were going to keep me for six months because my grades had gone down and I had a beer.

ADMISSIONS DIRECTOR
I'm sure there are underlying psychological problems your mom is aware of. That's what we're here for.

JONATHAN'S MOM
I'm also a physician. If Jonathan has underlying psychological problems, I'm *not* aware of them.
Nor did I refer to anything like that yesterday.

JONATHAN
If you did this to me, how many other kids are you doing it to?

ADMISSIONS DIRECTOR
Every child we admit has a reason for being here.

JONATHAN
Yeah. Because their parents want to get rid of them!

What happened at Charter Oaks went to the heart of the series. We were giving children permission to confront adults by virtue of their being journalists. No question was out of bounds. No answer was automatically accepted because it was uttered by a grown-up. It was empowering, and it was great television.

Buoyed by the reaction to the Charter Oaks piece, we set out to do an investigative story every week. We went to Israel to interview Palestinian children who were taking part in the intifada by risking their lives to throw rocks at armed Israeli troops. And with the permission of her parents, we sent a fifteen-year-old girl and recent graduate of *Children's Express* into a supposed abortion clinic in Ohio run by evangelicals. Her cover story was that she was four weeks pregnant, was afraid to tell her parents, and that neither she nor her boyfriend wanted the baby. But she soon learned that the clinic's reason for existing was to convince every pregnant person who came there that abortion was akin to murder. It started by showing them a film, complete with a bogus but terrifying soundtrack, of a fetus being torn apart as it was pulled from the womb. A female "counselor" then told her visitor that God wanted her to give birth to the baby, an oft-rehearsed sales pitch that was captured by our reporter's hidden camera. There had been several television stories on fake abortion clinics dotting the Midwest, but until we blew our whistle, there had been no video of what actually happened to the vulnerable young women once they stepped inside them.

Because we were doing tough stories, the media began paying attention to us. There was a full-page article about the show in *Time* magazine, and a grant from the United Nations to travel to Zambia and report on the affect its struggling economy was having on school children. Finally, we dispatched our three best reporters—Jonathan Zachary, twelve-year-old Suki Chong, and ten-year-old Laurel Barkley—on the presidential campaign trail, where George H. W. Bush was running against the hapless Democratic nominee Michael Dukakis. In California, Jonathan interviewed Bush's campaign manager, Craig Fuller, who boasted about the positive campaign they were running. Jonathan then acted out a word-for-word replay of the infamous black-and-white Willie Horton commercial, in which viewers were reminded that Dukakis had released Horton, a convicted rapist and murderer, from prison, to see him promptly rape again. Fuller's open-jawed response, a wordless "Who *is* this kid?" look, was memorable. From there we went to Ohio, where Dukakis was seated in a diner having lunch with some local citizens while a dozen or so camera crews recorded the strained conversation. As the meal ended, our ten-year-old correspondent Laurel, who had never seen so many cameras in one place, shouted out a question.

> LAUREL
> Governor Dukakis, this looks like acting. Are you acting?

DUKAKIS
Certainly not. This isn't acting. This is real.

LAUREL
Then why are all these cameras here?

DUKAKIS (to the adult reporters in the room) Next question, please.

Observing that Laurel was spooked by Dukakis's curt response, our producer introduced his young reporter to famous "take no prisoners" correspondent Sam Donaldson, who was covering Dukakis for ABC News.

LAUREL
Do you think I did something wrong by asking Mr. Dukakis if he was acting? He didn't seem to like my question.

DONALDSON
Who cares? You were doing your job. He *was* acting, and everybody there knew it.

LAUREL
Then what I did was okay?

DONALDSON
Absolutely. But if you ask tough questions, you've got to be prepared to take the heat.

From there, the story cut to California, where we had been able to snag an interview with Bush's nominee for vice president, Dan Quayle. Quayle had recently taken a lot of criticism for avoiding the draft in Vietnam by joining the National Guard, for his misspelling of potato (he put an *e* on the end), and for his uncompromising stand on abortion. After Jonathan took him to task for these relatively minor sins, twelve-year-old Suki Chong took over.

SUKI
You've said that abortion is murder. Why do you believe that?

QUAYLE
Because you're taking the life of a child.

SUKI
But suppose the mother doesn't want to have the child?

QUAYLE
It doesn't matter. A life is a life.

SUKI
Let's say my father molested me and I became pregnant. Would you change your mind?

QUAYLE
No, I wouldn't.

SUKI
But I'm twelve years old and I'm too young to take care of a child, and I'm pregnant because of my own father, and you'd *still* want me to have the baby?

QUAYLE
It's a very hard decision to make. But taking everything into account, yes, I'd want you to have the child.

As soon as I screened the videotape of the interview, I realized I had something that would make news. Clutching the tape, I jumped in a cab, sped to CBS, and hunted down Dan Rather, who had replaced Walter Cronkite as anchor of the *CBS Evening News*. I persuaded Dan and his executive producer, Tom Bettag, to look at the interview now. They found it equally stunning and decided to put it on the air that evening. Bettag asked me how much money I wanted for it. "Nothing," I said. "Just credit *CE News Magazine* on the air and tell your viewers they can see the full broadcast on PBS." Then, because Bettag knew there'd be blowback from the Quayle campaign saying we had taken the vice-presidential candidate out of context, he decided to air the entire six minutes we had shot—unedited. Among those watching was the host of NBC's *The Tonight Show*, Johnny Carson, who promptly invited one of our young reporters to be a guest on his program. The attendant publicity helped us win an Emmy and a Peabody Award for "significant and meritorious achievement in broadcasting."

Ordinarily, this would have made me feel pretty good, but problems I was having with the founder of *Children's Express* were beginning to overwhelm me. Bob Clampitt created his organization to teach print journalism to kids, letting them do their own reporting on simple, straightforward stories. But after seeing the first few episodes of the television version, Bob decided that the show was untrue to his original concept. He wanted the nine- to thirteen-year-old reporters to find their own stories, do their own research, write their own questions, write the narration, and have final say in the editing; things that do not happen even with the highly experienced fifty-to seventy-five-year-old correspondents on *60 Minutes*. I did my very best to involve our kid reporters in the process, but since they were all in grammar school, following Clampitt's directive would have meant yanking them from their classrooms and giving them a crash course in television production. Although I made sure that every single story reflected their sensibilities and point of view, it was impossible to do what Clampitt wanted and get a show on the air. I tried to explain this to him, but Bob refused to back off. He phoned me every day until I stopped taking his calls. He finally wrote me an angry letter that said if the show lived past its first season, it would be produced his way,or he would withdraw the television rights. With the finish line upon us and the PBS affiliates having ruled us a failure before we entered the starting gate, Clampitt's threats were a non-issue. There was no other place for us to go. Then Steven Spielberg called.

It wasn't Spielberg himself, of course, but one of his "people"; a female program executive named Dawn, who told me how much Steven loved the show and how much he wanted to keep it on the air. I explained that PBS was not a candidate, and I didn't know who else might carry it. "That's easy," she said. "It's a Steven-to-Barry call." (Then, as now, everyone in Hollywood uses first names. If you have to ask whom they're referring to, you're not a player.) Although I wasn't even close to being a player, I understood the reference. "Barry" was Barry Diller, who then ran the Fox network. I was certain that our show wouldn't find a home on Fox, whose idea of a program that had kid appeal was the hormone-driven teenage drama *Beverly Hills 90210.* But thinking that the Spielberg connection could prove useful in the future, I told Dawn to have Steven pitch Barry. "Great," she said. "I'll keep you posted." A week later, she called me back. "Barry loved the concept," she said, "but he doesn't have a slot for it. What about CBS?"

"What *about* CBS?" I asked, being pretty sure it wasn't going to dump *Captain Kangaroo* for *CE News Magazine.*

"They're in big trouble," she said. "They're getting killed in prime time. It's worth a try."

In for a penny, in for a pound, I thought. "What the hell. Go ahead."

A day later, Dawn called me back. "CBS is interested," she said. They're thinking about an 8 p.m. Tuesday slot."

"That's prime time," I gasped.

"I know," she said. "We need to do a budget. How much do you want per episode?"

"I'll call you back," I said.

My amusing peccadillo had suddenly become a problem. Going into business with Steven Spielberg was certainly alluring. I imagined myself at Hollywood cocktail parties saying things like, "As I was saying to Steven the other day," or "Steven and I are working on something that will make *Jaws* look like sushi." But I knew that Clampitt's issues with the show were not going away, and I didn't know if he was enough of a Spielberg starfucker to let me run it without interfering. As it turns out, he was. Sort of. Clampitt wanted a threefold increase in the $5,000-per-episode fee I was paying him for the television rights as well as the title of co-executive producer. I had no problem with the money, or the title, but I couldn't see myself working side by side with a decision maker of equal authority who had less understanding of the way television works than his youngest reporter. Stalling for time, I called Dawn again, naming a figure so high that Spielberg's company would back away from the project. Which of course they did not.

"That works for us," she said. "We'll give you that for every program and whatever else we get from CBS we keep." I suddenly realized that the figure I named—double the PBS budget—was chicken feed and that Dawn had already negotiated a fee with CBS for twice that amount, maybe more. Then it occurred to me that with our current production winding down and people going their separate ways, I would need two months' lead time to get the first new episode on the air—with no guarantee that Jonathan and Suki, my duo of star reporters, would be available.

"When does CBS want to start?" I asked.

"ASAP," Dawn said.

"How soon is that?"

"Three weeks," she answered.

If it's possible to breathe a sigh of relief while groaning, I did it. There was no way I could turn out new programs that fast. But Dawn was not giving up. "You know Howard Stringer, don't you?" Indeed, I did know Howard. We were colleagues at CBS News, except that Howard, a tall, charming Welshman who had no visible anxieties, was on a much faster track. When I first met Howard, he was in charge of *CBS Reports*. Then Howard was promoted to executive producer of *The CBS Evening News*. And after that, president of CBS Entertainment.

"Yes, I know Howard," I told Dawn. Why do you ask?"

"Call him. He's excited about doing something with Steven. Maybe you can work things out."

I hung up the phone and called Howard Stringer, hoping his battalion of secretaries wouldn't put me through—which they did immediately. The conversation was brief.

ME
Are you sure you want to do this, Howard?

HOWARD
Yeah. Our 8 p.m. Tuesday slot is getting killed. Actually, our entire lineup is getting killed. So why not try something new?

ME
That's the thing. I can't deliver new shows for two months. We're winding down here and I . . .

HOWARD
Not a problem. We'll air the shows you did for PBS until you get back up to speed.

ME
But people have already seen them.

HOWARD
No one watches PBS, chum. They're barely watching us. Got to go now. Good luck!

This was not what I expected to hear, which put me in a place I did not expect to be: choosing between a ton of money and an equal amount of personal discomfort. Anxiety inevitably leads you down the wrong path, but the prospect of doing battle with Clampitt every day for the next year was too much to bear. So, I chose the road less traveled; the one with so many potholes that no one in his right mind would take it. In brief, I opted out: pissing off CBS, pissing off one of Spielberg's people, and bewildering my accountant, who was the guardian of my shaky finances. But life, as they say, goes on, and in this instance it did in the nick of time.

CHAPTER 18

THE SUBWAY SHOOTER

If you're a tiny independent, producing quality television is a really tough business; mainly because it's really hard to find someone to pay for your project. For example, a 2018 documentary I made on Louisiana's criminal justice system took me four years from the day I had the idea, to persuading someone (in this case the Kellogg Foundation) to come up with the $650,000 it would cost to make. That's the rule, not the exception. However, there have been just enough instances in my life where the idea hits the buyer at exactly the right time to keep me from selling dental insurance. In fact, there's something undeniably appealing about a profession in which you can wake up one morning with an idea, make a phone call, and have the person on the other end say yes. Sometimes it's just dumb luck; more often it's a confluence of circumstances.

In the '80s, for example, the New York that I lived in and loved was an unsafe place to reside. Times Square, now Disneyfied to the point of being close to squeaky clean, was a polluted stream of addicts, hookers, corrupt cops, porno movies, sex shops, and other venues so forbidding that anyone possessing a microgram of sanity would avoid. Then there was the mob, which had its fingers everywhere: sanitation, construction, narcotics, and an assortment of other businesses, each affecting the wants and needs of New York's victimized denizens. No one living in the city was immune to this mishigas. Organized groups of vandals, many of them still in high school, roamed the streets after dark, breaking into cars, pilfering their contents and, if feasible, spiriting the vehicles away. My own vehicle, a ten-year-old Volkswagen that I parked on the street, was repeatedly assaulted for its Blaupunkt radio, a status symbol I was unaware of until its two replacements were also snatched. The technique used by the Blaupunkt bandits lacked elegance. The radio was wrenched from its dashboard with a crowbar, leaving a jagged hole where WQXR was playing Brahms only hours before. Taped to the windows of every German-made car in every neighborhood, were signs proclaiming "No Radio." I placed one on my VW, along with a pricey contraption to protect the vehicle itself from being stolen. "The Club" was a Darth Vader–like device that fit over the steering wheel like a giant clamp, immobilizing it, unless you knew the six-digit code to its combination lock. Impervious to anything short of a nuclear event, "The Club" so irritated the last group of thieves they slashed all four of my tires.

It was the subway system, though, that epitomized the city's fall from grace: stations foul and rat-infested, with the omnipresent smell of urine; cars ablaze with unremovable graffiti; hustlers of every color and ethnicity demanding cash for their concocted horror stories; passengers undistracted by cell phones, staring into space and praying their stop will come soon.

Into this hellhole an incident occurred that seized the imagination of the country. A bespectacled young man riding on the number 2 train was menaced by four Black youths demanding money. The man, who had been mugged a few months before, now carried a gun that he used to great effect: paralyzing one youth, wounding another, and sending the third running. The owner of the weapon was Bernhard Goetz, immediately characterized by the tabloids as "The Subway Shooter." Depending on the paper's politics, the nerdy Goetz was characterized as a folk hero or a vigilante; the press breathlessly tracking his flight from the city to a tiny town in New Hampshire. Weary of the chase, Goetz surrendered to the local gendarmerie and confessed all on grainy black-and-white video.

Three years later, the Subway Shooter—as Bernhard Goetz was now universally referred to—stood trial for manslaughter and attempted murder. His exploits had not been forgotten by New York, now joined by the rest of the planet. Journalists from Tehran to Tel Aviv crowded the courthouse, brought there by the fears of their own citizenry. The Goetz trial was a story of them versus us, with everybody understanding who "them" was—the Shiites, the Palestinians, and in America the Blacks—whatever "Other" was seen as a threat.

It suddenly occurred to me that an awful lot of people would like to see the Goetz trial, which was impossible because cameras were not allowed in the courtroom. It also struck me that there was a way for the world to tune in—even though it would be after the fact. So, I picked up the phone (which was the way things were done back in the day) and called Lindsay Law, who was in charge of a new PBS dramatic series, *American Playhouse.* I suggested that he let me dramatize the Goetz trial. "It's a sensational event," I said. "We'll simply edit the trial transcripts to an appropriate length and use actors to play the various parts."

"We're doing it," Lindsay said, startling me with the rapid response to my ten-second pitch. "If we can get two hours out of it, I can give you $1 million to produce it." I made an instant calculation in my head, realizing that if we paid the actor's scale and turned a PBS studio into a courtroom, I could probably pull it off.

"Onward!" I said.

Unlike the movie *Thornwell*, which was a nightmare from beginning to end, *The Trial of Bernhard Goetz* went smoothly, even though I decided to direct it myself. This time I was able to surround myself with people I had worked with before, including Greg Andracke, who had shot a bunch of stories for me at *60 Minutes* and was widely considered to be the best documentary cameraman in the business. Although Greg had a flair for the dramatic when problems occurred (his favorite expression was "I'm surrounded by assassins"), I never had to worry about the framing, the lighting, the camera moves, or the multitude of other things that can go wrong when you're making a movie. My relationship with the performers was also worry-free, mainly because there were no stars. The movie was filled with faces you would recognize but whose names you would not. In the trade they're called character actors: talented professionals who do their jobs without complaint, know their lines, and don't stiffen their backs when the director suggests a different way to play the scene. The schedule called for us to film the trial in seventeen days. We did it in sixteen, finishing under budget and sending everyone home happy. That even included the critics, who were uniformly praiseworthy, including John O'Connor of *The New York Times*. O'Connor had taken me to task for the *60 Minutes* story I did on nuclear energy, but redeemed himself (in my eyes anyway) by calling *The Trial of Bernhard Goetz* "the year's best docudrama . . . as fresh, painful, and provocative as if it all happened yesterday."

Another fast "yes" resulted in yet another movie. This one came from Showtime, whose program director, Steve Hewitt, Don's son, asked if

I could come up with a documentary that was a new way to look at the Rodney King story. Rodney King, as many will recall, was a Black citizen whose brutal assault by the Los Angeles police was captured on video and made headlines everywhere. I thought about it for a while and concluded that nothing really groundbreaking could be done on Mr. King, whose troubles were still dominating the media. Instead, I sent Steve a proposal I had written seven years before on another African American, Johnson Whittaker, who was the second Black cadet to attend the US Military Academy at West Point. Even though Whittaker's story took place in 1881, more than one hundred years before the King incident, there were obvious parallels. Whittaker was about to graduate and receive his officer's commission in the army when he was blindfolded and badly beaten by six white cadets. He was then charged by West Point for assaulting himself to avoid taking a final exam in philosophy, which the Military Academy claimed he was sure to fail. Remarkably, a complete transcript of Whittaker's court-martial, some twelve thousand handwritten pages, resided in the National Archives in Washington, DC. Steve read the proposal immediately, asked me to lunch, and was waiting at the restaurant to tell me that Showtime was making the movie. In addition to producing it, he also agreed to let me direct it and write the script.

The script itself was a challenge. Whittaker's court-martial was always intended to be the centerpiece of the movie, but unlike the Goetz trial, it was not sufficient unto itself. The relationship between his two lawyers, for example, had to be a central part of the story. The court-appointed lead attorney, Daniel Chamberlain, was the former governor of South Carolina and, as the court transcripts made evident, a racist. His assistant, chosen by Whittaker, was Richard Greener, the first Black graduate of Harvard Law School. Their relationship must have been antagonistic, but I had to imagine what took place between them outside the courtroom. Johnson Whittaker was pretty much a blank slate. The trial transcript revealed little about him other than the subservient posture he took while testifying under the advice—one can only assume—of his white lead attorney.

I began by putting together a script, which meant having the National Archives copy those twelve thousand pages of handwritten transcripts so I could begin the editing process. In reading them I learned that racism during Reconstruction, the period immediately following the Civil War, was far more blatant than anything I could have imagined. In the middle of Whittaker's court martial, for example, the trial was moved to a local theater so the prosecution could demonstrate the intellectual and moral superiority of whites to Negroes and, by extension, West Point's corps of cadets to Johnson Whittaker. The curtain was duly raised to reveal a chimpanzee, several Black dwarfs arranged in order of height, and finally Whittaker himself—barefoot, dressed in ragged clothes, and obviously forced to participate. Although the arguments that buttressed this bizarre tableau were not included in the transcripts, one can easily determine their intent: the distance between apehood and Whittaker was slight.

I considered putting this tableau in the movie, but the thought of finding the requisite Black dwarfs and a chimpanzee that would behave itself on stage persuaded me to stay inside the courtroom. (In retrospect, I probably should have tried.) The final script was 50 percent trial and 50 percent my creation, the latter being an educated guess about Whittaker's state of mind and the conflict between Black attorney Greener and his white counterpart Chamberlain. Showtime made it clear that as much as it wanted to make the movie, it would require two name actors to play these parts. Anything over $300,000 for the two roles needed their approval, which would not come easily. I discovered that in the Hollywood of the '90s, such a paltry amount did not get you far, even with actors having a known social conscience. This was equally true of their agents, who when weighing their liberal clients' publicly professed interest in making movies that actually were about something, always opted for the money. This led me to try various management companies, whose role was to guide their clients' careers rather than procure employment. Back then, the list of Black actors who were genuine stars was slim; basically Denzel Washington—as pricey back then as he is today—and a cadre of talented but relatively unknown performers. Then a convenient article in the Sunday Arts & Leisure section of *The New York Times* surfaced, calling my attention to Samuel L. Jackson and his featured roles in two of Spike Lee's most noteworthy films: Mister Señor Love Daddy in *Do The Right Thing*, and a terrifying crack addict in *Jungle Fever*. I called Steve Hewitt to see if Jackson's rapid ascent qualified him for stardom, at least by Showtime standards. It did, so I put in a call to Jackson's manager, who liked the project, said his client was available to play Whittaker's lawyer, Richard Greener, and agreed to the fee. The manager then suggested another client, Sam Waterston, as Daniel Chamberlain, Whittaker's lead attorney. Waterston, already a film and television notable, was immediately acceptable to Showtime and also signed on. The rest of the ensemble, all character actors, were relatively easy to cast and I was off and running—temporarily.

The first step was meeting the two principals. Waterston lived thirty minutes from my home in Connecticut. I told him I'd be happy to come his way, but he insisted on coming to me. Waterston arrived and after proclaiming that he was not a writer, gave me sixteen pages of handwritten dialogue that he said I should consider adding to his role as the racist governor. It was pleasantly done, but I sensed trouble—which when we started filming proved correct. I was directing a scene in which a group of cynical journalists were shouting questions at Whittaker during a break in the courtroom proceedings. Waterston, who was not in the scene, sidled over to me and suggested—not once, but three times—that I might consider another approach to the scene, which (a) it did not need, and (b) was none of his business. His manner was polite, and remained so throughout filming, but I could sense that he was getting an enormous amount of pleasure in pulling me aside and saying if I'd only done it his way, the scene would be better.

Waterston's outward affability hid a very large ego. Showtime had paid for a documentary crew to memorialize the project and promote it on air, part of which contained interviews with the two stars. On the afternoon the crew was to film Waterston, we received word that his father was gravely ill and that Waterston needed to come home before the old man died. We ordered a private plane to pick up Waterston at the local airport (we were filming in rural Virginia) and spirit him to Washington, DC, where he would catch a commercial flight that would take him the rest of the way. Waterston's interview had just ended when we got word that the private plane had landed and was ready for him. We had a car and driver standing by to bring Waterston to the airport, but he seemed in no hurry to reach his father's bedside. Instead, Waterston launched into a prolonged conversation with the producer of the documentary about the parts of the interview he wanted her to use and the parts he did not, over which he had no control to begin with. The discussion lasted for fifteen minutes and was still going strong when our unit production manager interrupted it, telling Waterston that if he wanted to say goodbye to his father he had to leave *now*. Waterston continued arguing for several minutes more before making his way to the car, an act of filial indifference that deserved its own Emmy. At the end of the production, Waterston left me a handwritten note saying that he hoped the movie would turn out well and that with a little more experience under my belt, the next one would be better.

This brings me to Sam Jackson, who did not arrive until the night before his first day of shooting, which coincidentally began with the climactic scene in the movie. At dinner, Jackson surprised me by quickly turning the conversation to the Goetz film, asking if I remembered him auditioning for the role of a police detective. I told him I did not, saying that we had looked at almost one hundred actors for the various roles and hoped he wouldn't hold it against me. Jackson smiled and said of course not. Although I wanted to take his assurance at face value, I had a gnawing feeling in my gut there would be problems. Cut to the following day, in which Jackson's and Waterston's characters, Greener and Chamberlain, have just been informed that their client, Johnson Whittaker, had been found guilty of all charges, thus denying him his officer's commission in the army. Alone in the now empty courtroom, Greener proceeds to lecture Chamberlain about his tepid defense of Whittaker. Chamberlain attempts to leave but is physically blocked by Greener, who ends his angry tirade by calling Chamberlain a racist. That speech, as well as the directions for playing it, had been in Jackson's possession for three months. We had blocked the scene and were ready to roll when Jackson told me that he couldn't perform it as written. "It's 1881," he said. "Back then, a Black man wouldn't dare make physical contact with a white man."

"Normally you'd be right," I told him, "but considering Chamberlain's failure to offer any defense for his client, and that he and Greener were the only two people in the courtroom, I think it's justified."

Jackson looked at me with something close to contempt. "I don't," he said, leaving unsaid that he, a Black man, would know better than I.

I swallowed nervously. This was not the way I wanted to start. "I'll tell you what, Sam. Do it the way it's written and then do it your way. If your version is better than mine, I'll use it. Fair enough?"

I meant every word, but Jackson clearly didn't believe me. "Let's go," he said. Waterston, who didn't hide his amusement at my discomfort, got in position and the two actors performed the scene exactly as written. Furthermore, the take was excellent.

"That's a keeper," I said to Jackson. "Now let's do it your way. "

"No," he answered. "Let's move on."

"Sam, I meant what I said. I could be wrong about this. If you have something else in mind, I'd like to do it."

"Uh, uh," he said, walking away. I stood there, realizing I had just lost control of the movie.

The next seventeen shooting days were one of the most unpleasant and anxious times of my life. Waterston continued giving me unwanted advice and Jackson was no longer speaking to me. Although he always knew his lines and his performance was professional, the one time I proposed a slightly different way to play a scene, he mugged his way through it, intentionally exaggerating what I'd suggested. Normally I would not have tolerated this, but I was worried that Jackson might exit at any time, leaving me—as the picture's producer—obligated to make up the difference in a $2 million movie that would be wildly over budget as a result. At the end of the movie, with budget intact but with the ulcer that Mike Wallace had given me resurfacing after a fifteen-year hiatus, I asked Jackson why he had decided to stop speaking with me. "Your idea and my idea of who Greener was were so different, it was the only way I could hold on to the part," he said. Then Jackson looked at me and smiled. "You thought I was going to walk, didn't you?"

"Actually, yes," I said.

"Oh, I never would have done that," he replied. "That would have been completely unprofessional."

Assault at West Point is the last television movie Jackson made, and the last movie I will make with actors . . . not that anyone is beating down my door to make another one. Truth is, I'm a pretty good documentary filmmaker, but I'm merely competent at directing narrative films—a lesson that expended way too much energy and took me way too long to learn. There is, however, a happy postscript to the story. During the writing of the script and the making of the movie, I began calling the Defense Department of the Army to ask that Whittaker's commission be awarded to him posthumously. After a year of lobbying, it was. At a White House ceremony, President Bill Clinton made a moving speech about racial injustice and presented the framed certificate of Whittaker's commission to his granddaughter, now in her seventies. It was a satisfying end to an otherwise trying experience.

CHAPTER 19

MIKE REDUX

My second and final tour of duty with *60 Minutes* began in 1997 when I got an unexpected call from Don Hewitt. Although we had not parted on the best of terms, he surprised me by asking if I would like to do an update of a story I had produced twenty years earlier about child beauty pageants. What prompted the query was a six-year-old beauty contestant, JonBenét Ramsey, whose recent murder had gone viral when her parents became the main suspects. (They were not charged and the killer was never found.) Don had zero interest in doing the Ramsey story but didn't mind capitalizing on the publicity surrounding it. The idea was to revisit the contestants of my piece, now adults, to see if the experience had scarred them. (They were all doing fine, thank you, including my personal favorite: a twelve-year-old twirler of flaming batons who was now the thirty-two-year-old executive producer of Minneapolis's top-rated newscast.)

Hewitt's call came at a good time for me. After eleven years on my own, I had grown weary of the constant struggle to raise money for the next project and needed a break. The gig was meant to be a one-off, but it turned into four more stories and eventually a permanent producing job with *60 Minutes II,* a Wednesday night version of the original. Before I could start, I was obligated to produce the last story I had brought to Hewitt. It centered on a US Marine pilot who had flown his jet over a mountain resort in Italy, mistakenly clipping a cable and sending a gondola filled with twenty skiers to their deaths. Although every news organization had been after him, the pilot had not spoken to the media until I persuaded his attorney, Frank Spinner—with whom I had worked on another story—to give *60 Minutes* an exclusive. The correspondent assigned to the story was Mike Wallace.

At sixty-three, I was a different person than the young producer Wallace had brought to CBS News. I had learned much since then, both in making films and starting a business from scratch. Somewhere along the way, I had been liberated from the ambition that drove me from *60 Minutes* to the world beyond. Whatever I needed to prove had, for better or worse, been proven. Still, I had mixed feelings about teaming up with Mike again. I had not forgotten his casual abandonment of *The Mike Wallace Profiles,* nor was I able to forgive his failure to walk across the street and say some words on my behalf to the president of CBS News, especially when Mike had walked so much further to get me there. The answer, I had come to conclude, was this: Mike was generous when he perceived it was in his interest; indifferent when the circumstance was otherwise. For that and other reasons, we had not spoken for almost fifteen years.

Our initial dialogue was strained. "You may have noticed that I've been somewhat cool to you," Mike said, referring that I'd been back at *60 Minutes* for a year and a half and though we'd passed each other in the hallway, we hadn't exchanged a word.

"I've noticed," I smiled, not wishing to make it easy for him. An uncomfortable silence followed.

"Do you want to know why?" he finally asked.

"If you want to tell me," I said.

"It was because of the trial."

I knew immediately what Mike was talking about. In 1982, a CBS News producer named George Crile had done a documentary on the steady increase of troops during the Vietnam war. It's thrust was that General William Westmoreland had falsely overestimated the enemy's strength to justify sending more American soldiers to Vietnam. Crile's correspondent was Mike. In 1985, three years later, Westmoreland sued CBS News, George Crile, and Mike Wallace for their reporting, which the general claimed was biased and untrue. Mike was sensitive about the issue. Testifying under oath, he would have been forced to admit that all of the spadework for the hour—the research, the finding of characters, the questions, the script—had been done by Crile; that Wallace, television's premier investigative reporter, had almost nothing to do with it. The potential of a public unmasking sent Mike into an emotional tailspin and a trip to the hospital the night before he was scheduled to testify. He was still there when Westmoreland unexpectedly settled his suit out of court the next morning and Mike was saved from taking the stand.

"What about the trial?" I asked.

"You didn't come to the courthouse. You weren't there to support me."

I was dumbfounded. In 1985, I was back at *60 Minutes* working full-time with Diane Sawyer, who was busy making a mark for herself on the show. Mike and I were cordial when we saw each other then, but the relationship had changed and we both knew it. I began saying words to that effect, when Mike changed strategy. "Never mind," he said, opening his arms to me. "I forgive you." I let myself fall into the embrace, relieved that the conversation was over. Grinning, Mike closed the door to his office, where I spent the next half hour telling him about the story. It was as though I'd never left.

Mishap Valley, the title of the *60 Minutes* piece, remains one of the strongest investigative pieces I produced. At first glance, the evidence against the Marine pilot, Captain Richard Ashby, seemed overwhelming. The gondola cable that he clipped was 363 feet above the ground and Ashby's flight plan restricted him from flying his jet below a thousand feet. In a press conference, a Marine Corps major general announced that "the gondola cable system was marked on the US map as an aerial cable way. If a detailed map study had been done by the air crew as it should have, the crew would have been able to determine there were obstructions in the area. . . . The cause of this accident was not the weather, or aircraft malfunctions, or equipment failure, but the actions of the air crew."

As I eventually was able to confirm, everything in the above statement was false. The map that Ashby had been given did not have an aerial cable on it and Ashby's radar altimeter failed to alert him that he was flying too low. Plain and simple, the Marine Corps was using Ashby as a scapegoat for an accident that had strained relations to the breaking point between the United States and Italy, whose prime minister was threatening to kick the Marines out of the country and shut down the only NATO air base in the region. The saying "Military justice is to justice as military music is to music" came to mind throughout filming.

Fast-forward to the final day of editing. Now eighty years old, Mike had begun to slow down. It was both a function of age and the depression that had affected him for much of his life, with which he had recently gone public. The change was most visible in his interviews. Although he eventually got to the point, Mike's mastery of the material was not what it used to be. Also missing was the electricity that made Mike so special and made everyone he talked to more responsive. Mike was simply operating at a lower wattage. His participation in the process also had lessened. I wrote the script and had him record it without first showing him the rough cut, which he seemed fine about. With the story scheduled to air next week, and a Hewitt screening scheduled for tomorrow, I asked Mike to come to the office on Sunday to look at the cut. In the edit suite with me was my associate producer, Yvonne Miller, and our film editor, Joe Murania. Both had worked on stories with Mike before and both knew how difficult he could be when he didn't like what he saw. This time—double negative notwithstanding—there wasn't much not to like. It was clear that Ashby was being used as a scapegoat by the Marines and equally clear that the slashing of the cable was due to a confluence of circumstances, none of which were Rich Ashby's fault. Mike, however, didn't like the way the piece was structured, an opinion to which he was certainly entitled. But the way he wanted to change it completely stopped the film's momentum. I said so. He disagreed. I fought back. He disagreed more vehemently. "I'll tell you what," I said. "We'll cut it your way, but we'll need to change the narration to make it work. Give me fifteen minutes to write the new lines and we'll record you. Then Joe will lay in the new track and add the picture to it."

"How long are we talking about?" Mike asked.

"Probably an hour," I said, glancing at Joe Murania, who looked pained. "Maybe a little more. Go back to your office. We'll call you when we're ready."

It took us almost two hours to make the changes, with Mike calling every fifteen minutes to ask when he could see it. Joe, Yvonne, and I looked at it before we sent for Mike. It was obvious it didn't work. Then Mike looked at it. "It's perfect," he said, clapping his hands for emphasis. "I'm going home."

"Mike, it isn't perfect and you know it. The story's still there, but the film goes off the tracks at the exact point the changes were made."

"I don't know what you're talking about, Harry." It was not said nicely.

I looked at Joe, who clearly wanted to be elsewhere. Like many of the editors, he was afraid of Mike. "Joe, go backward about a minute before the new cut," I said. Joe complied. "Now roll it from there." We watched in silence. A few seconds after Mike's version popped on the screen, I reached over and hit the Stop button. "It doesn't want to go where you're taking it, Mike."

Mike rose from his chair to look down at me. "Jesus Christ! You're worse than Bill McClure," he said testily, referring to a producer in the London office who was known for his intransigence. Mike had never seen me like this. I had never seen myself like this either.

"Mike, give us thirty minutes to show you the first cut again. It isn't perfect either, but we can make whatever narrative changes we need tomorrow morning. They're easy fixes."

"Thirty minutes," Mike said, exiting. "That's it."

I looked at Joe and Yvonne, who thus far had not said a word. "Here's what's going to happen," I said. "Mike's going to look at the cut and then he's going to ask you which version you prefer."

"How do you know that?" Yvonne asked.

"Trust me," I said

"What do you want us to do?"

Joe looked up from the editing table, where he was working furiously to restore the cut. "I was going to ask the same thing," he said.

"Tell him whatever you think."

"Suppose I disagree with him?" said Yvonne.

"Fine with me," I said.

"Suppose I disagree with you?" Joe asked.

"Also, fine. Just tell the truth. Finish it up. I'm going to take a leak." I went to the men's room, where Mike was at the next urinal. He flushed. I flushed. We both washed our hands. "We're ready," I said. Mike followed me back to the edit room.

"Roll it," he told Joe, as he entered. Mike remained standing, arms folded across his chest, watching silently. The film came to an end. Mike turned to Yvonne. "Which version do you prefer, Ms. Miller?"

"I, uh, like the original cut."

Mike looked down at Joe, for whom I was suddenly feeling sorry. "And you, Mr. Murania?"

"The same," he said, his response so quiet it was hard to hear.

"And why is that?" Mike asked.

"It tells the story more clearly."

"Really?" Mike said, lowering his voice, arching his eye brows and transforming the simple question into a threat. Long pause.

"What do you want us to do?" Joe finally said.

Mike looked at me. I looked back at him. "Show it to Don the way it is," he said, exiting.

The next day, we did. Hewitt made a few changes but kept the structure intact and the story went on that Sunday. The evidence we had compiled was so persuasive that ten days after *Mishap Valley* aired, Captain Ashby was acquitted of involuntary manslaughter and four other charges that could have sent him to prison for the rest of his life. It was exactly the kind of story that drew me to journalism and helped put *60 Minutes* on the map. Like Jim Thornwell and Bob Pollard, Rich Ashby was a team player, sailing along until the team decided he was extra ballast and threw him overboard.

Eventually the same thing happened to Mike, who was given less and less to do until he came to the realization that it was finally over. By then, I had left *60 Minutes* for the second time and decided I should visit him at his apartment on Park Avenue. He seemed glad to see me, but he was angry at his physical condition, which had deteriorated to the point where walking was difficult. More importantly, the lack of meaning in his life had brought on a full-blown depression and the beginning of memory loss. The last time I visited him there, he was sitting in a chair, an unread newspaper in his lap, while a series of attendants looked after him. "I'm not looking forward to the next five years," he told me. I left, knowing I did not want to see him again.

It was some years later that I learned Mike had been moved to an assisted-living facility in Connecticut and was failing badly. When I told this to my wife, she asked how I would feel if I picked up *The New York Times* one morning and found that he had died. "Not good," I admitted.

"Then go there and see him."

"Maybe," I said. But the more I thought about it, the more I realized she was right. So, I called his stepdaughter Pauline and asked if I could visit Mike.

"It's possible," she said, "but he's not in good shape mentally. He enjoys having visitors, but he won't remember you. And he has difficulty carrying a conversation. You'll have to do most of the talking. If you still want to go, I'll arrange it."

Two weeks later, I arrived at the facility, an upscale place whose walls had the primary color cheerfulness of a kindergarten classroom. Because of my talk with Pauline, I brought along a younger friend, Abby Pogrebin, who had been one of Mike's associate producers between my two tours of duty at *60 Minutes*. Abby, who was fond of Mike, agreed to accompany me and share the conversational load. An attendant led us to a sitting area adjacent to Mike's room and said he'd be out shortly, cautioning that he would not know who we were. Minutes passed. Then the door to Mike's room opened and he came out using a walker. He looked at me and broke into a smile. "Harry Moses!" he proclaimed in the deep, forceful baritone I had heard and often feared for so many years. Mike then shifted his gaze to Abby, whom he clearly did not recognize. Then he looked back at me. "Are you fucking her?" he said, smiling. Although I wasn't prepared for this, neither I nor Abby were shocked. It was vintage Mike: outrageous but expected if you knew him; offensive, if you did not. Mike, now ninety-three, had changed physically since the last time I saw him. He was heavier and his once jet-black hair was streaked with gray. We sat down and began the conversation. As I had been warned, it was strained. Mike sat facing a window that looked down on an oval-shaped track where people were jogging. Mike noticed this and asked what they were doing.

"Running," we told him.

"Is that so?" he said. "Why are they running?"

"Exercise," one of us replied. Mike nodded and the conversation began. We asked how he was feeling.

"Pretty good." He looked at Abby. "Do we know each other?"

"We worked together."

"Where was that?"

"At *60 Minutes*, Mike." He nodded. "You were the best," Abby said. "Do you remember those days?"

"Of course," Mike said.

"It was such a good show," I said. "Do you watch it now?"

"Not much." He looked out the window again. "Why are those people running?"

"They're getting exercise, Mike," I said. "Let's talk about the show. What a bunch of correspondents you were. Wallace, Safer, Rather. And later on, Ed Bradley."

"Ed Bradley," Mike mused. "Was he that colored fellow?"

It went on this way for forty-five minutes. Half of my mind was in the room; the rest was thinking about the other Mike, the Mike who brought me to CBS News and taught me so much. Who helped me, tutored me, admired me, bullied me, stopped caring about me, and finally left me. The man who was smarter than anyone I knew, was now spending his days gazing at a running track and wondering why people were going around it.

After forty-five minutes we had run out of things to say. I took a picture of Abby and Mike. She took one of us. In the photo, Mike is in a wheelchair. I am standing next to him. We are holding hands, looking at each other, smiling. Six months later he was gone.

CHAPTER 20

WHO THE #$&% IS JACKSON POLLOCK?

I left the security of *60 Minutes* for good in September of 2004 to make a documentary whose premise was too good to turn down. But now it was November and I was vacationing in Venice and still waiting for the green light. The setting sun was casting a gauzy salmon glow on the canal as my wife and I admired the splendid view. We were seated on the terrace of the five-star Gritti Palace hotel, where we had strolled from our more modest accommodations to have a drink. "I think I'll call them," I said. "It's noon in New York. They ought to be there." I put down my wine glass and reached for my cell phone.

"Are you sure you should be doing that?" she said, reminding me that I had called only three days ago. Actually, I was sure I *shouldn't* be doing that.

"Yes," I lied.

Anxiety has preyed on me my whole life. For a long time, I thought that everybody in the world felt the same way. Tense. Stressed. Insides churning. Then I entered psychotherapy and learned that these feelings were not universally shared. As more than one mental health professional has told me, the most effective way to combat anxious impulses is to be aware of their existence. If you can stop yourself from acting on them immediately, they will fade. As stopping myself from doing almost anything is not my strong suit, I usually give in.

A perfect example was the phone call I was about to make to New Line Cinema, which for the last three months had been considering whether to green-light a feature-length documentary I'd brought them. It was about a woman who purchased a drip painting in a thrift shop for five dollars and became convinced it was a Jackson Pollock. I had come by the story in the usual way; that is to say, by accident. I'd been doing some business with my friend Steve Hewitt, who had since left Showtime. Steve's girlfriend Nancy, a colonic hydrotherapist by trade, had as a client one Tod Volpe, whose persistent diarrhea had brought him to Nancy's office. There, Tod's equally persistent logorrhea had him talking endlessly to Nancy while she spritzed his insides—or whatever colonic hydrotherapists do. Tod, who had wheedled information about Steve's business from Nancy, told her he had this great idea for a documentary series on fraud in the art world. It was a subject Tod had some knowledge of, having spent two years in prison for neglecting to deliver various works of art that Jack Nicholson, Barbra Streisand, and others had paid him for.

Steve thought that Tod's backstory was intriguing enough for the three of us to have lunch. It took most of the meal to discuss the art fraud idea, which we concluded was a tough sell unless Jack and Barbra were to sign on as hosts. While waiting for the check, I asked Tod what he was doing currently. Things then turned interesting. Tod said he was representing a painting that was almost certainly a Jackson Pollock, who except for Leonardo sells for more money than any other artist—alive or dead. Its owner, he told us, was a woman named Teri Horton, who was trying to parlay the painting she'd bought in a thrift shop for five bucks into the considerably larger sum of $50 million, which is what a Pollock that size (four and a half by five feet) would be expected to go for. "What's the lady's background?" I asked. "Is she an art expert?"

"No," Tod said. "She's a long-distance truck driver. Or was. She's seventy-three. Lives in a trailer park in California." I glanced at Tod, who had the casual confidence of a natural-born grifter.

"Do you think it's a Pollock?"

Tod nodded his head affirmatively. "Come over to my apartment," he said, "and I'll prove it."

Steve and I repeated the conversation to Steve's father, Don, the creator and longtime executive producer of *60 Minutes,* until CBS forced him out because of his age. To make up for it, he had been given an enormous office, a full-time assistant, and $300,000 a year. This didn't begin to pacify Hewitt, who had been earning $6 million per annum and yearned to show the world he still had the right stuff. Don liked the story immediately. "Talk to the Horton dame," he said, "and see what Volpe's got. If she's a good character and the painting's legit, I'll make some calls."

"You know, Don, "I said, "it might be a movie."

"Could be," he said. "Stranger things have happened."

I'd always wanted to make a documentary that would play in movie theaters. Part of it was fantasy. Over a drink or two, I would sometimes imagine being a finalist at the Oscars. The fantasy always ended before I sprinted down the aisle to get the statuette and thank all the little people. (I have a fully functioning ego, but it observes the speed limit.) The other part was that I was weary of working with correspondents who asked the questions I had written, didn't know the story as well as I did, and failed to get the best out of the interview subjects. It would be a relief to do the whole thing myself. Could Teri Horton and her wannabe Jackson Pollock take me there? I was about to find out.

Tod Volpe greeted me at the door and introduced me to Paul Biro, a cherubic man with a stage Hungarian accent. Biro resided in Montreal and made a living by determining the legitimacy of various works of art through forensic examination. As Biro explained to me, "A painting is like a crime scene, e xcept I'm not trying to determine who committed the murder. I'm trying to discover who committed the art." I envisioned a game of Clue: Colonel Mustard in the library with a palette knife.

"Is there's something in Teri's painting that points to Pollock?" I asked.

"Yes," he said. "There's a fingerprint on the back of the canvas." Biro handed me a booklet printed on expensive, glossy stock. "This is a close-up of the print."

"Is that Pollock's fingerprint?"

Biro looked at me and smiled.

"Pollock was never fingerprinted, so we can't say for sure. But the evidence points toward it. He painted alone. He had no assistants. He allowed almost no one in his studio. Then, of course, there's this." Biro turned the page. On it was a photograph of a paint can with a fingerprint on it. "I took this in Pollock's studio, which is unchanged since he died fifty years ago."

"Do the prints match?" I asked. Biro's smile widened. He turned the page again. The two prints were now blown up and displayed side by side. To the naked eye, they were identical.

By noon the next day I'd had a phone conversation with Teri Horton, a feisty, profane lady whose irreverent persona reminded me and everyone else of the late actress and singer Elaine Stritch. Teri had accumulated an extraordinary amount of knowledge on Jackson Pollock, whom she hadn't heard of when she bought the painting fourteen years previously. Teri explained that she had found Biro on the internet after every Pollock expert she contacted told her they had no interest in looking at her work of art. She was an eccentric and appealing character, all of which I related to Steve and Don. Don listened intently before delivering his judgment. "What you have here," he said, "is a combination whodunit and David and Goliath story, which is about as good as it gets." He paused briefly. "How's it gonna end?" I explained that Volpe was hoping to sell the painting to a private buyer, but he was also considering putting it on the auction block. "Go with the auction," Don said. "More dramatic. They could do it at Christie's. I know the guy who runs it." He looked at Steve and me. "So, what's the next step?" Anticipating a positive response, we had decided on the movie route. I would write and direct, Steve and I would coproduce, and Don would be the executive producer. "Sounds good," he said. "I'll call Michael Lynne."

Michael Lynne, we knew, was the perfect person to call. He was then the chairman of New Line Cinema, a prestigious division of Warner Brothers, Hollywood's largest and most successful studio. There was more. Lynne had an extensive modern art collection, had just won an Oscar for *Lord of the Rings*, and best of all, could say yes. Steve and I were in the smaller office next to Don's when Don came running in. "I just got off the phone with Michael," he said. "He loves the idea." Don looked at me, beaming. "He wants a proposal. Write something up. And make it sexy, will you?"

"Done and done," I said. "You'll have it tomorrow."

That was September. Now it was November. I finished my phone call to New Line as the sun disappeared from the Venice canal. My wife had been listening to my end of the conversation, which consisted of a string of "uh huhs."

"So?" she asked.

"They need one more person to sign off. They'll know in a week."

"What's the delay?"

"Money. They don't want to spend more than $800,000."

"Can't you do it for $800,000?"

"I can do it for less. But their budget people are nervous. New Line's never made a documentary."

"How much did their last movie cost?"

"One hundred million," I said. "Maybe more."

"You'll be fine," she assured me. "Where do you want to eat?" I glanced at the Gritti Palace bar menu. Its least expensive item, a hamburger, was forty euros, forty-five with cheese. Verdi was playing on the loud speaker and gondolas filled with silent Japanese tourists were floating gently by. It was picture-postcard perfect, but I still didn't have a deal.

"Elsewhere," I said.

Like almost everything else in life, when the green light arrived it was anti-climactic. My wife and I had a brief, celebratory dinner. Then the preparation began. New Line was unfamiliar with the documentary process, so they decided to treat our little film like their usual big budget extravaganza. They wanted to know where we were filming, who we were interviewing, when the interviews would happen. And they wanted all of this information before we started, with a cost report every single week. It sounded reasonable, except that I didn't have the answers to any of these questions in advance. Making a documentary is not like making a movie. There are no actors. There is no script. The cast of characters changes depending on whom you talked to last. People are seldom available when you need them. Locations remain unknown until the last minute. Travel plans switch without notice. But New Line was adamant. It was their way or no way, so throughout filming I sent them weekly schedules that had little basis in reality. This caused problems down the line, especially when the budget reports came in and New Line saw that the interview with Mr. X in Tucson hadn't happened, but an interview with Ms. Y, whom I hadn't told them about because I didn't know she existed at the time, took place in Reno at ruinous expense.

Then there was the scary New Line person I'll call Ilene. (I'm calling her that because it's her name. I've blanked on her last name, or I'd use it too.) Ilene was a forty-something fireplug from Brooklyn, with the accent and attitude to prove it. Somehow, at least the way Ilene told it, she found her way to Oxford where she "read philosophy." This naturally led to a career in the motion picture industry where, according to Ilene, she was Michael Lynne's go-to gal on the continent. I'd been introduced to Ilene in passing before New Line and I were in serious discussions, but there was no clue she was in charge of the project until she called two days before we were to start filming. The conversation went pretty much like this:

ME
Hello.

ILENE
What the fuck do you think you're doing?

ME
Hello. Who's calling, please?

ILENE
Who the fuck do you think you are? You don't take a dump without telling me first.

ME
I'm sorry. Who is this?

ILENE
Ilene. I'm at the Berlin Film Festival and I just found out you're filming in two days. Why the fuck don't I know this?

ME
Oh! Hi, Ilene. I didn't know you were supposed to be in the loop.

ILENE

In the loop? I *am* the fucking loop. You're not filming anything until I get back from Germany, where it's . . .

ME

But . . .

ILENE

. . . two o'clock in the morning and where I'm freezing my fucking ass off because Michael needs me here.

ME

Ilene, I can't postpone the shoot. It'll cost thousands of dollars.

ILENE

Don't you fucking tell me what you can't do, Henry.

ME

Harry.

ILENE

You don't make a move until I fucking say so.

ME

Ilene, I think it would be better if you spoke to Steve.

ILENE

Who the fuck is Steve?

ME

Steve Hewitt. He's the producer.

ILENE

I thought you were the fucking producer.

ME

We're co-producing. But you really should be talking to Steve. I'll have him call you tomorrow.

ILENE

Did you hear what I said, Harold? Are you fucking listening to . . .

ME

I think I'm losing you, Ilene. Steve will straighten everything out.

I hung up, popped a Xanax, poured myself a scotch, and called Steve, explaining that there was this totally insane lady from New Line named Ilene, who insisted she was in charge of the production and if I ever had to talk to her again, there wouldn't be a production. Steve, who is very good about things I am very bad at, told me he would make Ilene his problem, not to worry, and to have a good shoot.

By the time I got to California, Steve had managed to pacify Ilene, who was eventually removed from being in charge of me and, I hope for the sake of humanity, anyone else on the planet. I had put together a great crew for the documentary. The cameraman was Bill Cassara, who happened to be married to Don's daughter but whom I would have chosen absent the quasi-filial relationship. Bill has many virtues, all of which are crucial to a skilled documentary cinematographer. He knows how to light. He is great at handheld. He sets up fast. He is visually creative. He listens to what's being said. He doesn't complain. He gets along with everybody. He has a great sense of humor. He's fun to have dinner with. The thing about making a documentary is that you're in close quarters with a tiny group of people for an extended period of time. Hours are long. Tempers fray. And sometimes things go badly. So, it's important to travel with persons who care about the film as much as you do and share an investment in making it work.

Bill's soundman was Everett Wong. Everett is a smart, sardonic guy who gets his job done without fuss. Taking sound is an unforgiving, largely thankless gig in which perfection is required 100 percent of the time. Anything less can make the most brilliantly filmed sequence unusable. With Everett I never had to worry.

The last person in our crew was Jan Legnitto, a colleague of mine for many years at CBS News. Jan was the coordinating producer, meaning that she handled the schedule, booked the travel, arranged for the locations, made sure releases were signed, dealt with New Line's accounting department, and did a thousand other things to keep our small ship afloat. Jan is a pessimist's pessimist: The glass is always a few drops from empty. I'm not at my best when calamity is hovering around the corner, but Jan performed her job so capably and saved my butt so many times that I mostly managed to look the other way.

Our first interview was with Teri Horton, the star of our production. I had flown to California a month earlier to do a pre-interview with Teri, so I knew pretty much what to expect. My concern was not what she would say but how she would say it. Let me explain. The filmmaker must not only get the information but get it said in an interesting way. This means that the interviewer's job—in this case, my job—is to make sure that people are the best possible versions of themselves. This is easy when they're animated and articulate; less so when they're flat and have difficulty forming complete sentences. In the documentary business, picking the right character is called casting—even though we don't use actors. Boring is out. Animated is in. It's a gross simplification, but you get the idea.

In Teri Horton's case, there could be no casting. Teri *was* the story, so I had to live with her—syntaxes and all. I realized there would be a problem when I first met Teri. She was funny, irreverent, and had great energy. But these qualities did not often coincide. Teri was hours late for everything and was frequently tired when she got there—victimized by too much gin, too little sleep, and a body suffering from too many years of steering twenty-ton vehicles across America and back. Teri was a tough, colorful lady, but almost every memorable thing she said was buried in a paragraph of junk. To make things harder, one of the standard devices used to eliminate unwanted verbiage—covering the sound edit with a reaction shot of the interviewer—was unavailable, as neither New Line nor I wished me to be seen on camera. This meant I had to work hard to dig out information that was concise, coherent, and compelling, a trifecta that Teri rarely hit.

Teri's interview, which we did inside her glorious mess of a trailer—clown paintings on the wall, bric-a-brac that she had salvaged from various trash cans, six mangy cats, and one terrified canary—took two solid hours and drained both of us. Teri had led an interesting life: Raised on a farm in the Ozarks. Stopped school after the eighth grade. Married and divorced three times. Had two sons kidnapped by her first husband and spent years searching for them until the older one found her. One of the nation's first female long-haul truck drivers. Boozer. Gambler. Dumpster diver. And a Jackson Pollock autodidact, about whom she'd accumulated an encyclopedic amount of knowledge even though she hated his art.

Teri acquired her painting at a thrift shop in San Bernardino that had since gone out of business. She'd paid five dollars (bargaining the price down from eight) and planned to give it as a gag present to cheer up a sick friend. But when the painting wouldn't fit through the door of her friend's trailer, Teri took it home. Months later she had a yard sale in which some items—the painting included—were free for anyone willing to cart them off. It was then that a professor of art history at a nearby college saw Teri's purchase and told her she might be the owner of a Jackson Pollock. Teri's response—"Who the fuck is Jackson Pollock?"—explains the title of my documentary.

What followed was Teri's attempt to sell the painting for what an authentic Pollock of that size would have been worth—about $50 million. Teri's perseverance had resulted in a fair amount of attention over the years—a spread in *People,* an appearance on *The Tonight Show,* and the everlasting enmity of the art world, which looked down its collective noses at the ex-trucker's lack of credentials, not to mention her blue-collar bona fides. But Teri was undeterred. Her unswerving belief that Jackson Pollock was the author of her painting caused her to turn down a legitimate offer of $2 million. "I know damn well what his work was worth," she told me, "and I wouldn't do it."

Teri had a long and complicated tale to tell. Considering the pitfalls, I thought we mostly got what we needed. Now I had to focus on the rest of the story. I decided that the documentary should remain neutral on the subject of whether Teri's Pollock was the real thing; that it would be more effective to let the audience make up its own mind. So, I lined up a bunch of experts who agreed to give me their unvarnished opinions about the painting as we filmed them looking at it. First up was Ben Heller, a crusty octogenarian who was an early collector of Pollock and a pallbearer at his funeral. Heller didn't think much of Teri's painting and said so. The same was true with several other art world types. We needed someone to balance the scales, so Jan Legnitto suggested Thomas Hoving, whom she'd met while working on another film. To put it mildly, Hoving was a character. A tall, opinionated patrician, he was in every way the antithesis of Teri Horton. Hoving's father owned Tiffany's. Hoving was a Princeton graduate. Hoving rose to eminence running New York City's Metropolitan Museum of Art. As one might expect, Mr. Hoving thought highly of himself. "There are a lot of second-rate experts in the world," he told me. "I'm not. Now, if I had been a night watchman at the Met instead of a curator and director for eighteen and a half years, then you might say that my expertise is not so good." Hoving paused for dramatic effect. "My expertise is *very* good."

But if Thomas Hoving was the ultimate snob, he was also the ultimate contrarian. In fact, we had reason to believe he might declare Teri's purchase the real thing. Hoving was dismissive of those who had weighed in against it and his initial reaction to an image of the painting was favorable.

Hoving, the film crew, and I convened at the Manhattan warehouse that was storing the painting. I wanted to make the scene as dramatic as possible, so I had cameraman Bill Cassara follow him down the hall and into a darkened room, where the painting was perched on an easel. As they entered, I turned on Bill's lights and watched Hoving assess Teri's find. Hoving stared intently at its brightly colored blobs and squiggles. Next, he bent over until his head was almost touching the floor and stared at it some more. Righting himself, Hoving took a jeweler's loupe from his pocket and peered at various parts of the painting through its lens. This took a while. Hoving removed the loupe, closed his eyes, and ran his fingers lightly over the surface of the painting as he hummed something that sounded like the theme from *Goldfinger*. Visions of Shirley Bassey danced in my head until Hoving cleared his throat and sat down facing Teri's canvas. He placed his hands on his temple. He closed his eyes again. He fell into a trance. Minutes passed. Suddenly, Hoving snapped to. He blew short puffs of air through his mouth, making noises like a miniature steam engine. Finally, Hoving directed his gaze toward Bill's camera. "It's superficial," he declared. "It's frivolous. It has no appeal and I don't believe it's a Jackson Pollock." Hoving again paused for dramatic effect. "It's dead on arrival."

Dead on arrival? If anything was dead on arrival, it was me. The son of a bitch had just killed my movie! Without a single expert willing to endorse Teri's painting as a true and veritable Jackson Pollock, the story had no controversy and was doomed—or so I thought at the time. When I voiced these feelings to Bill Cassara over lunch, he laughed. "I don't know what Hoving was doing out there, but you got something extraordinary, Harry. The contortions. The thing he put in his eye. The humming. The trance. The arrogance. He's a born villain. It's hilarious, and the audience will eat it up." I agreed that Hoving had put on a show, but I knew that one sequence does not a movie make. Furthermore, I didn't see how his performance would advance the story. It wasn't the first time in my career that the premise I had gone in with refused to conform to the facts. Worse, it was also the premise for which New Line had shelled out $800,000.

Disaster, like everything else in life, comes in threes. First there was the phone call from the profane Ms. Ilene. Then there was the pompous Mr. Hoving's venomous review. And now I had to deal with a query from the office of New Line Cinema's powerful chairman, Michael Lynne, wanting to know when the auction of the painting at Christie's was going to occur. By now it was obvious there was not enough expert support for Teri's painting to warrant an auction. Out of caution, my proposal to New Line hadn't promised one, but it was clear that (a) Lynne had not bothered to read the proposal before deciding to pay for the film, and (b) Don had sold Lynne on the basis of the painting being auctioned at Christie's. I discussed this with Steve and we agreed that the best thing to do was tell New Line that no date had been set for the auction, which was accurate as far as it went. This would give us time to fiddle with the film's storyline, which had unexpectedly taken a hard-right turn.

First, we had to tackle the question of provenance, which Teri's painting didn't have—unless you were willing to count a handwritten receipt from Dot's Spot Thrift Shop. Provenance, as art attorney Ron Spencer told me, is the *sine qua non* of authenticity. "If you can trace the possession of the work from the artist to the present owner, that is strong evidence that the artist created the work . . . The *Mona Lisa* was bought by Francis I in 1508 directly from the artist and you can trace it from the artist right up to the point that it's in the Louvre."

Teri had run into the provenance issue before I came into her life; or more to the point, it had run into her. Out of frustration, she came up with a unique solution. No provenance? No problem. She'd make one up. As Teri's story went, she was left the painting by an elderly bartender named Pops, whom she had befriended. Pops was given the painting by Jackson Pollock in return for drinks at Pops's place of employment, an upscale inn in Mt. Baldy, California. In the '40s, the inn was a popular destination for movie stars to have affairs. Pops poured drinks for all of them: Cagney, Bogey, Gable, Grable, and the Duke, which was what everybody called John Wayne. "Then one weekend it snowed big time and they could not get out," Teri told me. "And Jackson had always kept paints with him, so he came up with the idea that they should all paint a picture." According to Teri by way of the fictional Pops, Broderick Crawford, the tough-guy star of *All the King's Men* and later of *Highway Patrol,* only painted in the nude. Joan Crawford (no relation), who brought all her lovers to the inn, posed a different problem. "She was noisy and she was bothering everybody, 'cause she was up at the bar and trying to watch Pollock [as he painted]. And he didn't want anybody watching him, you know? He always made it a point that you couldn't get rid of Joan Crawford. She was such a bitch when he was trying to paint."

We had Teri recount this dizzy tale while sitting at a bar reminiscent of the era, which Bill Cassara lit using blue gels to give it a film noir look. The story's ending was memorable: "Everybody came around with their paintings . . . to show each other, [and] Jackson's painting was all on this mirror behind the bar . . . And all of a sudden he said, 'Oh, wait a minute. I'm not finished yet.' So, he got up on the bar and signed it—with his dick."

In a strange way, it all made sense. Pollock was a drunk and a carouser who once urinated in art collector Peggy Guggenheim's fireplace during a party in his honor. Teri knew that, so she added some movie stars to the mix and took it a step further. Although it's hard to fathom, Teri told me that some art dealers actually fell for it.

"Had they not believed it," she said, "I'm sure some of them would have wrote back [and] said, 'This provenance is bullshit.' Nobody ever did. And then when [one] dealer told me that he knew who Pops was, I thought, 'Well, shit, I'm in like Flynn.'" Teri broke into a grin. "But then I had to tell the truth."

I was beginning to reconfigure the documentary in my head. If I couldn't find a Jackson Pollock connoisseur to take the painting seriously, then what? Paul Biro would handle the science, but was there someone who would speak to the painting's artistry, if not its authenticity? Although I am an admirer of abstract expressionism and was an art history major in college, I'm no Jackson Pollock expert. Still, I knew enough to realize that counterfeit or not, Teri's painting was a vast improvement on your average faux Pollock. Pollock's unique style of flinging paint directly from can to canvas--he was known in art circles as "Jack the Dripper"—is devilishly difficultto imitate well. I wanted my movie to make this point, and I also wanted it to tackle the issue of provenance, or in Teri's case, the lack thereof. So, I flew to England to film John Myatt, the world's preeminent living forger. The idea was to establish Myatt's credentials as a successful practitioner of his craft and to have him tell us if Teri's oeuvre was too skillful to be faked.

There was no money in the budget for a trip to the UK, but I persuaded the New Line bean counters that Myatt was essential to the story and that I would pick up a London film crew, thus avoiding two expensive airfares. I enlisted my friend Norman Langley, a brilliant cinematographer with whom I'd filmed stories from the Arctic Circle to the Middle East. We set out to visit John Myatt at his home in the county of Staffordshire, deep in the English midlands. Myatt's backstory was fascinating. He had gone through a bitter divorce and was struggling to support his two children when a con man named John Drewe walked into his studio. Drewe had mastered the art of fabricating provenances for paintings that didn't exist. Drewe then enlisted Myatt to create the works of art cited in the phony provenances. Myatt was up to the task. He showed us painting after painting in the manner of Picasso, Monet, Dufy, Giacometti et al. These were not copies, Myatt proudly proclaimed. They were original Myatts, depicting the paintings that Drewe described.

Myatt and Drewe were taking huge risks. Although Myatt's paintings looked good, the materials used to create them wouldn't have passed muster in a high school chemistry class. The paint was house emulsion circa 1996, available at any hardware store. This was mixed with the vaginal lubricant K-Y Jelly, which also was not around when the work's alleged author created his masterpiece. But so seductive were Drewe's provenances (Imagine! An undiscovered Cezanne!) that no buyer saw the need to scientifically test the actual paintings. Museums, galleries, and wealthy individuals happily paid Matisse prices for their Myatt knockoffs. Myatt eventually had an attack of conscience, confessed his crimes to the authorities, and served a couple of months in jail. Drewe served considerably longer.

I was more than a little apprehensive when it came time to ask Myatt to comment on Teri's painting. In spite of—or perhaps because of—his brush with the law, I doubted he would bend the truth to suit me or anyone else. I began by asking how he might go about creating a drip painting that would fool connoisseurs of Pollock's work. "[Pollock] had a considerable alcohol problem," Myatt said, "so if I were starting [one], I would get drunk first . . . I don't think you could be sober and do one. That's just one of the pitfalls. And there's hundreds of them. The right kind of paint, the right kind of speed of the throw, the right kind of dynamic in the way the painting moves . . . It's just too much to think about . . . I mean, it could be done, but it wouldn't be a *good* fake . . . It just wouldn't be." I then handed Myatt a photograph of Teri's painting, which he studied for a long time.

"Could you do this?" I finally asked. Myatt looked at me, then looked back at the photograph and sighed wistfully.

"No," he said.

I knew the Myatt sequence would shore up Teri's case, but the real argument for her painting was the forensic one. We began by taking Paul Biro back to Pollock's studio in East Hampton, where he had found a fingerprint that matched the one on Teri's painting. Visiting the studio is like entering a time warp; nothing has changed since Pollock's death in 1956. After donning slippers, you step into a large room whose paint-splattered floor resembles a huge Jackson Pollock. On it the artist would place a canvas, seize a can of paint, and sling the contents across its surface. It was like the jazz Pollock listened to—an improvised riff of blobs and lines, bristling with energy. A Jackson Pollock does not inspire universal awe (like jazz, you either get it or you don't), but his prices are awe-inspiring. While I was making the documentary, a painting half again the size of Teri's sold for $130 million, breaking all known records for a work of art.

Camera in hand, Paul Biro entered the studio. "About a dozen paint cans that Pollock used for painting are exhibited in a showcase," Biro told me. "I have found some of these with the same paintbrush in it in photographs dating back to 1950 when Pollock actually physically worked there. I examined all of them." Biro picked up a can of paint and held it to the camera. "I was looking at a fingerprint on a blue paint can. By this time, I had memorized Teri's painting's fingerprint. I felt this . . . could be the end of the search."

It sounds dramatic, and it was. Biro's next step was comparing the two fingerprints, a process that he illustrated for us with the sophisticated digital technology he had in his studio in Montreal. To verify the results, Biro enlisted the services of André Turcotte, a fingerprint expert with a Maurice Chevalier accent and a Salvador Dali–moustache who had supervised a major crime lab for the Royal Canadian Mounted Police. I asked Biro to project the images of both fingerprints against his studio wall as Turcotte analyzed them. Using a pointer, Turcotte demonstrated that the branches of the ridgelines, called bifurcations in fingerprint lingo, were the same on both prints.

In postproduction, we were able to make things even clearer. The narrator (me) talked you through it: "On the left is the fingerprint from the back of Teri's painting. On the right is the print from the can of paint in Jackson Pollock's studio. The bifurcations described by André Turcotte are outlined in yellow. And when the two prints are brought together," I paused for dramatic effect as they merged, "it is apparent they are one and the same."

Tod Volpe sat in my living room watching Bill Cassara make some last-minute adjustments to the key light. Tod's chronic logorrhea had made him exceptionally difficult to deal with. Every day for the last forty-five days had brought a different message on my voice mail addressing Tod's concerns about the movie, which boiled down to ignoring Tod while filming less important people. Had the messages been concise I wouldn't have minded quite so much. But Tod regularly filled the machine's thirty-minute capacity. This would precipitate a second call and another message summarizing the first one (in case I had missed it), before continuing for fifteen minutes more. Now, primed and ready to go, Tod was eager to tell his story: "One morning, six o'clock, the helicopters are all over the roof of my house," he said. "There's bullet-proof vest guys running all over around me with machine guns . . . I look outside and there's a crowd of FBI agents . . . They pull me into my car and said, 'What do you know about Jack Nicholson? What do you know about [such and such] person?' And I said, 'What are you asking me these questions for?' [And] he said, 'Tomorrow morning your name's gonna be on the cover of every magazine and newspaper in the country . . . for [de]frauding people.' Two minutes before I was ready to go into a courtroom, they offered me a plea agreement and I went to jail for two years."

Why, you might ask, did Teri Horton agree to have a convicted felon represent her painting? "That didn't bother me," she said, "that he went to prison for fraud. Because by this time I knew the whole art world is a bumble-fucking fraud. So why would one person that got caught deter me from following up on it?"

This essentially brought Teri's story to time present. By now, Tod also had abandoned the idea of an auction and was trying to sell Teri's putative Pollock the old-fashioned way. Before I came on the scene, Tod claimed he'd been turned down by Bill Gates, Steve Wynne, and David Geffen—all for lack of a provenance. (I somehow couldn't see Tod in the same room with those folks, or even their supernumeraries, but never mind.) His latest scheme was to pay Teri what she now said she'd be willing to accept for the painting ($25 million) through the sale of shares in the Legends Art Group. Legends would then own the painting (immediately reevaluated to its true worth of $50 million) and would employ Paul Biro's forensic skills to authenticate other lost masterpieces that lacked provenances. It was a dubious business proposition at best, led by an equally dubious cast of characters. Mitch Kemper, the CEO of Legends, was a former professional golf caddy turned stockbroker. Clay Kahler, who was employed by a TV production company, had as his most memorable characteristic a right eye that was brown and a left one that was blue. And Ken Chasser, whom Tod billed as a topflight marketing executive, had met Tod in prison, where Ken's skill in marketing illegal substances had landed him. We filmed a sales pitch Tod made to a wealthy client of Mitch Kemper's, an aging actress named Adrienne Rogers, whose chief claim to fame was that she was almost cast as motorcycle queen Pinky Tuscadero opposite The Fonz in *Happy Days.* Tod, whose email moniker was Mesmerizer, demonstrated why. "As soon as this painting is purchased, it makes worldwide news and it's automatically a win. We can't lose... The money will make it win. But while it sits here with no money attached to it, it's like an orphan without a home. It's like Heathcliff in *Wuthering Heights*... He couldn't get his inheritance until he had a title. As soon as he gets a title, he wins. Do you know what I'm saying?"

Apparently, Rogers did. She plunked down $100,000 to become Legends first and only investor.

We had started filming shortly after the New Year and by the middle of April we were largely done. Knowing that the hoped-for sale of the painting was a pipe dream, I had shot every B-roll sequence of Teri imaginable. (B-roll is film terminology for picture sequences under which narration, the character's own voice, or music can be placed.) We went dumpster diving with Teri. We put her in the driver's seat of a huge eighteen-wheeler and hung on for dear life (she hadn't driven one in ten years) as she zoomed down the highway. We filmed her having drinks with friends at a rundown bar in San Bernardino. We even took her to the beach to illustrate a seriocomic story Teri told us about considering suicide after she had lost her nineteen-year-old daughter Corey to sudden heart failure: "I got the bartender to fill me up a brandy and water, and you could look out the bar and look right out to the ocean. And I proceeded to walk out into the ocean. Colder than hell... And I got my brandy and water up in the air... and I'm sobbing... and the water got up to my bustline and I still got my drink up here. No way am I gonna let that salt water get into it. And I finally said, 'Corey, I cannot do this. There's just no way I'm gonna waste this drink. And besides that, the water is too damn cold.' And so, I... went back up to the beach and quit my crying and... went back into the bar and ordered another drink... and that was the only time I ever tried to kill myself."

Back in New York, I began the editing process, which is where films are made—or, in many instances, mangled. There's no script to guide you, no map to get you from point A to point B; only a mountain of raw footage that you and the editor must fashion into a story. My editor was Jay Freund, a seasoned professional with whom I had worked before. Jay has a great critical sense and fights like a tiger for what he believes, qualities that I need in an editor since I'm often too decisive for my own good.

Day one. Jay asks what interview I want to screen first. "Teri's," I say. "We might as well find out if we have a film." Ten hours later, I was sure we didn't. I came home, downed a scotch, and announced to my wife that I was sitting on a turkey. As I had foreseen, the problem was Teri's twisted syntax, which wandered every conceivable way before occasionally arriving at its point. From two hours of interview, we had pulled barely fifteen minutes of usable material—not a good sign. My wife, who is used to mood swings, both from living with me and from being a psychotherapist, suggested that I screen everything before jumping to conclusions. "Of course, I will," I said, but in my heart of hearts I knew I was in trouble. Teri was the linchpin of a movie supposed to run a minimum of eighty minutes, which at that moment looked like an impossibility to fill.

A month later my mood had lightened. After screening the rest of the material, I realized we had some wonderful stuff. John Myatt was charming and convincing. Tom Hoving, as Bill Cassara had accurately predicted, was haughty and hilarious to watch. And Paul Biro's fingerprint analysis was difficult to dismiss, as was his reaction to Hoving's refusal to acknowledge it: "If this gentleman, in some rage, butchered his wife and was taken to court," Biro said, "and the bloody knife was produced as evidence and put in front of the judge, what would this gentleman say: 'I don't recognize the fingerprint?'" Best of all, through Jay's editing Teri was emerging as an idiosyncratic and likeable character. Because of all the B-roll we'd shot, we were able to make sequences from sentences that Jay had seamlessly patched together. The film's opening, for instance, which never changed from the moment we cut it, showed a seventy-three-year-old, bandy-legged, baseball-capped woman walking by a line of massive trucks, hopping into the last one, and driving away. Nothing memorable, until we put Teri's voice over the pictures:

"Everybody knows that a fairy tale starts out 'Once upon a time.' But a truck driver's tale starts out, 'You ain't gonna believe this shit.'"

Want to know who this woman was and what her shit was all about? That's the point. As Don Hewitt said about the opening of every story: "You gotta get them in the tent."

But getting an audience in the tent and keeping them engaged are entirely different matters. Since there would be no auction, Jay and I had crafted a rough cut that focused on the authenticity of Teri's painting, about which we'd created a decent debate. We'd also developed a subplot about redemption for Tod, who was trying to make a comeback after two years in the slammer. That was what we showed to Michael Lynne and a roomful of New Line executives on a late July morning.

Screenings are a funny thing. Even though people don't offer their critiques until the end, you can tell how the picture is being received by the atmosphere in the room. We started off well. Teri's fairy-tale story got real laughs, and I could feel my anxiety receding. Five minutes later it came creeping back. No one had said a word, but words weren't necessary. I sensed that we were losing our audience even though I wasn't sure why. It was visceral. A tensing of the gut. A clenching of the sphincter. A voice inside my head telling me that I had fucked up; that the film I had worked so hard on to make perfect—with every screw tightened and every nut and bolt in place—had come undone.

Michael Lynne had arrived at the same conclusion. His criticism was polite, but succinct. Because the story we fashioned was about the sale of the painting, we'd spent too much time on the Legends Art Group and their efforts to market it. "Those guys are like the gang that couldn't shoot straight," Lynne said. "Use as little of them as you can."

"What about Tod?" I asked.

"Keep Tod," he said. "Just cut him way down. His backstory's more interesting than his current one."

"And what about the painting? Do you . . ."

Lynne didn't let me finish. "The fact that Teri's painting might be a Jackson Pollock is fascinating, but it's an inanimate object. People don't go to movies starring inanimate objects."

Although Lynne didn't seem upset, I was. I had blown it. And after Jay and I licked our wounds, we realized that we had been telling the wrong story. The film wasn't about the sale of Teri's painting. And although Teri was seeking a big payoff, down deep it wasn't about money either. It was about a woman with an eighth-grade education teaching herself enough about Jackson Pollock to have written a dissertation on him. It was about an ex–truck driver using forensic science to challenge all those Ivy League experts. It was the story of class in America, and it was sitting right under my goddamn nose.

Self-flagellation has it merits, but it doesn't get you very far; so, after kicking ourselves in the butt, Jay and I set out to make the film we—I, really—had somehow mangled in its telling. I can't say it was easy getting it right, but after a lot of arguing and two more screenings we were finally there. We ended the film in an interesting way. Ben Heller, the first Pollock expert we had consulted, suggested that the only real way to understand how removed Teri's painting was from an authentic Pollock was to put it next to one and compare them. The difference between the fake and the real, Heller said, would become immediately apparent. Since we obviously couldn't drag Teri's painting into the Pollock gallery at MOMA, where we'd spent a day filming, we went to plan B. Using digital software, Paul Biro stitched a section of Teri's five-dollar purchase to a section of the Pollock that had recently been sold for $130 million. The result was staggering. It was literally impossible to tell where one painting ended and the other began. We then gave our seventy-three-year-old, blue-collar babe the last word: "It *is* a Pollock. I didn't make this journey for nothing. There is a purpose somewhere at the end of this. And until then, I'm not going to quit. Even if I have to go sell it myself."

I liked it. Jay liked it. Steve and Don liked it. Most important, Michael Lynne liked it. But there was a problem. The Pollock-Krasner Foundation, known in art circles as PKF, had heard about our film through their attorney Ron Spencer, whom we had interviewed on the provenance issue. PKF wanted to see the film before it was released in movie theaters. I didn't see why we should screen it for them until Spencer explained that PKF owned the copyright to every acknowledged Pollock painting in the world. Without its permission, he said, we couldn't show a single Jackson Pollock in our film. What Spencer didn't articulate, but which he and I both knew, is that absent these Pollocks, whose images crammed the documentary, the audience would have no basis of comparing Teri's painting to the real thing. Michael Lynne saw it the same way. "If you can't show some real Jackson Pollocks," he said to me pleasantly but bluntly, "I can't release the movie."

A week later, clutching a DVD of my documentary and carrying a handkerchief to mop my brow, I entered the Park Avenue office of the Pollock-Krasner Foundation. I had grave doubts that any of the powerful men deciding the fate of my film would relate to its trash-talking, blue-collar heroine and her five-dollar thrift shop buy. Charles C. Bergman, PKF's chairman and CEO, was a Harvard grad and a philanthropist. Samuel Sachs II, PFK's president, also went to Harvard and was the great-grandson of the founder of Goldman Sachs. Ronald D. Spencer, PKF's attorney, was a graduate of Brown University and Yale Law School and an expert on modern art authentication. I felt I should make some sort of speech about the movie, but having not the slightest idea of what to say, I didn't. We entered a grim little room whose only furniture was three wooden chairs and a table on which sat a small, twenty-inch monitor and a DVD player. I inserted the DVD and we watched the film. That is to say, they watched as I watched them. Screenings, whose difficulties I mentioned previously, are tough to endure. Still, out of the hundreds I've been through, this one was Mt. Everest. There they sat, my three grand inquisitors, as stone-faced as the statues on Easter Island. Not an upturn of the lips. Not a downturn either. There were no tells. It was like playing poker with three guys in dark glasses who had just raised you the pot.

The movie ended. I looked at them. They looked at me. "You probably need to talk among yourselves," I said. "I'll be outside. Call me when you're ready." I exited and walked around the block, trying to collect my thoughts, which is hard to do when you have none. I circled the block again, went back to PKF, and leafed through an old *National Geographic*. Half an hour, or maybe five minutes later—it's hard to say when every second is an eternity—the door to the screening room opened and they called me inside. "So?" I asked, forcing a smile.

Bergman spoke for the group. "So," he said, "we have a problem with the end of your movie."

"Which part of the end is that?" I said, although I knew what was coming.

"The part where you compare the two paintings," he said. We will let you use all the Jackson Pollock images you want if you eliminate that fraction of the film. If you don't, we must regretfully opt out."

"And that is because . . ."

"Because you've made another Pollock."

"I'm confused," I said, playing for time. "If the authenticity of Teri's painting is a closed issue in the art world, which the movie makes abundantly clear, then how can there be another Pollock?"

Spencer jumped in. "You've constructed a single image from two separate works of art. You've joined an undisputed Pollock with a painting that no one has authenticated, to create a painting that doesn't exist."

"The narration doesn't claim it exists," I said, being careful (as my therapist wife had coached me) to moderate my tone of voice, which when I'm anxious turns me into Émile Zola. I grabbed the script and went to the last page, my hand trembling. "This is what it says: 'When you put these pictures together, what you end up with is an image like this . . . Which is which?' That makes it clear there are two paintings."

"Nobody listens to narration," Spencer said dismissively. "When I look at the image, I see one painting. *Res ipsa loquitur.* The thing speaks for itself."

"Gentlemen," I pleaded, throwing myself at their mercy, "how can I remove the sequence? It captures the difference between what the expert eye perceives and what the untrained eye doesn't." I took a deep breath. "Look, all we're doing is what Ben Heller suggested we do: compare Teri's painting to the real thing." I looked at Bergman, who looked at Spencer, who looked at me.

"As the attorney in the room," he declared, "I would advise against it."

"I think he's right," Bergman said. "Sorry, Mr. Moses, but I have to agree with . . ."

Samuel Sachs II, who thus far had been silent, interrupted him. "Suppose you drew a line down it. Wouldn't that solve it?"

"What do you mean, a line?" Bergman asked.

"You know, a black line showing the demarcation between the two paintings. That way there'd be no uncertainty. What do you think, Harry?"

I've always liked people who call me by my first name. At the moment, I was liking Sachs a lot. "I . . . I think I could live with that, Sam," I said cautiously. "It wouldn't make the point as well as it currently does, but I might be okay with it."

"What do you say, Ron?" Sachs said. "It would answer the basic problem here."

Spencer glanced at Bergman, whose expression seemed to be softening. "Let's see it again," Spencer said, pressing reverse on the DVD player and freezing the image of the blended paintings. Using his finger, Sachs drew a vertical line down the television screen.

"If you put a black line there," he said, "any confusion would be eliminated." Bergman now was nodding in agreement.

"How thick a line?" I asked.

"I don't know," Sachs said. "Maybe an inch. Let's get a black marker and a ruler." Both were brought in and Sachs drew an inch-wide line down the middle of the screen. To me it looked enormous.

"It's awfully big," I said.

"It's the appropriate size," Spencer said. Thinking quickly, I pointed out that in movie theaters, where screens are thousands of times larger than the tiny monitor we were staring at, its thickness would be overwhelming. (Although I made this up on the spot, it sounded convincing.) "How about a quarter of an inch?" I suggested.

"Half an inch," Spencer said.

I let out a long, painful, and completely calculated sigh. "How about splitting the difference?" T. S. Eliot once wrote that life is measured out in coffee spoons. My life had been reduced to a lousy eighth of an inch.

"Mr. Moses," Charles C. Bergman said, extending his hand, "I believe we have a deal."

Six months later the film opened. It got some nice reviews, and when Thomas Hoving appeared on the screen, audiences actually hissed. It then went the way of most documentary features: a brief run in select theaters and nowadays available on Amazon Prime, where you can rent it for $1.98, of which I get about six cents in residuals. The painting, by the way, remains unsold.

CHAPTER 21

SEARCHING FOR NESSIE

I was battling nausea on a boat in the middle of Scotland's windswept Loch Ness, where I was looking for the monster affectionately known as "Nessie." Although I was doubtful about Nessie's existence, Bob Rines, the eighty-year-old subject of a *60 Minutes* segment I had done many years ago, was not. In 1972, Rines had seen Nessie while vacationing here. "I didn't want to stop looking at what I could not believe," he said. "It was at least twenty-five feet long and had a back like a giant elephant. And it stayed there in front of me for ten minutes before it lumbered around and submerged."

One could hardly find a more credible witness than Bob Rines, a teetotaling lawyer, inventor, and physicist with a stubborn streak I admired greatly. Bob made a lot of money over the years and spent much of it trying to prove to science that what he saw was real. In 1972, Rines attempted to film Nessie by installing a kind of underwater soundstage where he had watched her surface. Whenever a large object passed, sonar would trigger the lights and start the camera. Nothing happened until 1975, when Rines's camera captured an image of a head, neck, and body swimming by—and it bore an astonishing resemblance to the monster. That clinched it for Rines. It also explains why my film crew and I had tagged along to watch him launch an unmanned miniature submarine from the deck of our boat into the eight-hundred-foot depths of Loch Ness, hoping to locate Nessie—or what might be left of her. The other reason for my being there had less to do with the unlikely occurrence of getting Nessie on camera than with Bob Rines himself, who exemplified the ornery, driven characters I have always been drawn to and doubtlessly identified with. Bob knew that the scientific establishment considered him crazy and his monster a myth, yet he kept plunging ahead. "You know," he said to me, "Christopher Columbus—and I'm nowhere near the great man he was—was told by all the people who knew *everything* about science, *everything* about geography . . ." Bob's voice then broke into a panicky howl . . . "'Don't go, Chris! You're going to drop off the end of the flat Earth!'" Bob poked me in the chest with his finger to make sure I was getting the point. His voice softening, he continued. "Sometimes, *too much* knowledge prevents you from even looking."

As a thunderstorm threatened above, the film crew, Bob, and I moved below deck. We stood in front of a monitor that had live pictures of the sub's descent, its operator using a joystick to maneuver the depths of Loch Ness. It was like playing a sophisticated video game, except the pictures on the screen were like nothing I, or anyone else in the world until this moment, had seen. The loch was thick with peat, which swayed back and forth in undulating clumps as the sub knifed its way through the dark, its lights revealing an underwater lunar landscape: craggy cliffs, soaring walls of pockmarked stone in muted greens and purples and only the occasional salmon swimming by to remind you this was still planet Earth. The sub leveled off at 376 feet. Directly below it, on the floor of the loch, was a strange shape. "Do you see *that*?" I said excitedly. "It looks like some sort of animal hide."

Rines was cautious. "It fits the description that paleontologists have told us we might expect to see after years of rotting. Let's get a closer look." The sub's jets blew away the debris that was obscuring our vision. A cloud of peat swirled by the camera. Now we could see the shape much more clearly. I was unable to suspend my disbelief any longer.

"Jesus," I said, "it *is* a hide! There's the head, the body, the long neck."

"Let's try to bring it up," Bob ordered, which was easier said than done. The sub was great at taking pictures, less so at bringing objects to the surface. Angling downward, it extended a claw and tried to catch hold of whatever it was we were looking at.

"Can't do it," the operator said, after fifteen minutes of trying. "There's nothing to grab onto. We need something to slide under it and pry it off the bottom."

"I know what'll work," Bob said. "Bring it back to the surface." Bob exited as the sub made the long upward journey to the mother ship. As crew members hauled it onto the deck, Bob reappeared from the bowels of the boat clutching a garden rake with a long handle. He attached it to the claw with a metal clamp, turning the screws tightly to make sure it would hold. The crew gently lowered the sub back into the murky waters of the loch as we scurried below deck and gathered 'round the monitor again. "Position the sub directly above the edge of the carcass," Bob told the operator, bestowing an actual name to my uninformed hunch and giving me goose bumps. The operator fiddled with his joystick. "Now lower the rake and slide it underneath." Sweat pouring down his face, the operator tried to follow Bob's instructions.

"I can't get the angle right," he said.

"Keep trying," Bob said calmly. "You can do it." Minutes passed. On his sixth attempt, the operator managed to poke the rake underneath the carcass. Everyone burst into applause. "Careful bringing it up," Bob said. The operator turned on the sub's thrusters, creating a giant glob of peat. When the water cleared, the carcass was still on the bottom. Alongside it was the broken handle of the rake.

Had I been Rines, a moment like this would have shattered me. The real Bob Rines took it in stride. "The hide isn't going to move," he said. "We'll come back tomorrow with a claw that can grasp it."

"How are you going to find it again?" I asked.

"We have the coordinates of every place we search, so we'll be able to locate it."

Unbeknownst to Rines, the thunderstorm hovering over his craft had interfered with the radio transmission of the coordinates to the recordkeeper on shore. Although the skipper of the ship could return to the general area in which he had previously dropped anchor, that wasn't nearly good enough. Without the exact location, finding the strange shape that lay somewhere on the bottom of Loch Ness was like looking for a needle in a haystack—except in the choppy, unmarked waters of the loch, one first had to find the haystack.

It would be nice to report that Rines was able to bring up whatever was down there, but although he went back every day for a week, the sub could not locate it. His failure gave further pleasure to Nessie skeptics, who continued to insist that Rines's sighting, and more than a thousand other sightings of the monster over the last fifteen centuries, could be written off as unreliable, wishful, or even delusional. Too dismissive? Perhaps, but there is scant scientific reason to think otherwise. With more peat than fish, Loch Ness is not capable of sustaining a family of huge, aquatic creatures like Nessie. For that, one would need an ocean. But Loch Ness is almost two hundred miles from the nearest sea. Furthermore, it's a *freshwater* lake, formed by the melting of glaciers at the end of the Ice Age twelve thousand years ago. In other words, short of hitching a ride from a passing brontosaurus, there seems no way for an aquatic brood of Nessies to get from the ocean to Loch Ness, and no way to survive in its saltless waters once it got there.

Naturally, this irritated Rines, whose life had been filled with challenges he solved by ignoring conventional wisdom. A graduate of MIT at the age of nineteen, Bob joined an elite scientific unit of the army during World War II and developed its earliest radar systems. His groundbreaking work in sonar was used to locate enemy submarines, then the *Titanic,* and finally to give expectant mothers the first look at their unborn child. Rines then became an eminent patent attorney, founded his own law school, helped draft the Constitution of Bangladesh, and in his spare time wrote the words and music for seven off-Broadway productions. In the course of my earlier *60 Minutes* story, Bob and I had become friends. So when he told me he was going back to Loch Ness the next year, I persuaded HBO to finance a documentary around his efforts to find additional proof that Nessie—at some point in time, if not now—was real.

When my film crew and I arrived in Scotland, Bob had already consulted a renowned glaciologist, Adrian Hall, who told him, and later me on camera, that the existence of Nessie was theoretically possible. Dr. Hall, who had no skin in the game, explained there was a brief window in time *before* the beginning of the glacial melt that formed Loch Ness, when the sea level was high enough for a family of Nessies to live in the same location and gradually adapt to the freshwater deposited by the melting glaciers. To test Hall's theory, Bob decided to bring up core samples from the bottom of Loch Ness. If he could unearth a purely saltwater creature embedded in its muck, it might explain how Nessie got there. On my very last day in Scotland, Rines found his evidence: an oceanic clamshell stuck to the anchor of his boat. This was encouraging, but not nearly enough proof to satisfy Rines. If, for example, a picnicker on the banks of Loch Ness had tossed the clamshell there, its age would be critical. A 1956 clamshell wouldn't cut it. Nor would one hurled at the enemy centuries ago by the legendary Scottish warrior, Robert the Bruce. According to Dr. Hall, the presence of a Nessie in the loch could only be explained if the shell was, give or take, some fourteen thousand years old.

Ever the scientist, Bob sent the shell to the Lawrence Livermore Laboratories in California, which put it in a nuclear accelerator for carbon dating. The accelerator, a whale-shaped hunk of metal about the size of an actual whale, did what accelerators do and eventually spat out its answer: Rines's clamshell was found to be 14,100—confirming Dr. Hall's science and Bob Rines's faith that what he saw surface from the waters of Loch Ness so many years ago was the real thing.

Fast-forward to 2008, when the History Channel was in its second season of a program called *MonsterQuest* (yes, they spelled it that way), whose content still makes me cringe. Employing dubious stock footage, tacky recreations, and pseudoscientists who would have trouble differentiating a test tube from a test pattern, the series explored all manner of monsters, most of which were news to me: *Birdzilla! Swamp Stalker! Skunk Ape!* The featured player in this ghoulish lineup was the mother of them all, Nessie herself. It didn't take the series executive producer long to locate Bob Rines, who was planning one last expedition to Scotland, along with his erstwhile producer—me. I had been searching for the money to make a final film on Bob, who had suffered a stroke and—though determined as ever—was in poor health. So, I swallowed my pride, knowing that except for the Rines portion of the documentary, which was under my control, its remaining content would be, well, fake. In that respect, I was not disappointed. The highlight was a rowboat voyage taken by a tattooed Brit with a shaved skull, who the narrator identified as a cryptozoologist. The Brit propelled his dinghy several hundred feet from shore, baited a fishhook with salmon, and cast it into the waters, hoping to lure Nessie to the surface. After some incoherent musings on the monster lurking beneath, there was a tug on the line. This prompted a grunt-filled struggle to land whatever had impaled itself on the hook. After much sweating and straining, the line broke and the Brit rowed back to shore, a sadder but wiser cryptozoologist.

But never mind. A 2005 Rines expedition that I was not able to attend, had traversed the entire bottom of Loch Ness using the sonar that Bob had helped develop to identify 105 possible targets for the remains of Nessie. To search them all in the week he had given himself, Bob had brought a virtual armada of remotely operated vehicles with him to Loch Ness—four yellow minisubs outfitted to raise anything resembling the carcass-shaped hide that he and I had seen eight years ago. Bob was too weak to descend the stairs from the main ship to its control room, so he sat patiently as various couriers brought him news of what the subs had or had not found. I would like to report that Rines's search had unearthed the proof to confirm his original sighting of Nessie, but I cannot. As Bob, then eighty-six, told me in our final interview, "I know time is not on my side now. It's a race for time. I can't really prove that what I saw is real by holding up some bone and saying, 'See?' I can't." Bob struggled to sit up straighter, his pain visible. "So, all I've got to say is this: 'You're safe in believing Robert Rines. He's a pretty good guy. He's a pretty truthful guy.'"

Bob returned home to Boston, had a second stroke, and died a year later. As I'm writing this—still a working journalist but somewhere in the last act of my own life—I would gladly accept the same epitaph.

EPILOGUE

Soon after turning fifty and having left *60 Minutes* for parts unknown, I attended an exhibition of Edward Hopper paintings at the Whitney Museum in New York. Writ large on the entrance wall was this line from a Robert Frost poem: "I have spent my life in pursuit of the pursuit." The sentence jolted me, so much that I stood there reading it again and again. It referred, of course, to the isolated souls in Hopper's paintings, but it also described me: living not for the moment but the one beyond it; the thing that's just around the corner, until the corner is turned; the prize that always seems attainable but is never quite in reach.

I readily acknowledge that spending one's life in pursuit of the pursuit may not be the healthiest way to live. On the other hand, it has kept me going. At the age of ninety, I am presently fit, disease, free, and can function well enough without the aid of Prevagen. Still, I want to use time wisely, which is to say productively, until it runs out. My brain lacks an on/off switch, meaning that ideas flow more or less constantly. Another book, another screenplay, even another documentary—if it didn't take so long to raise the money and my expiration date was not in view. (As far as I know, it has not been issued, but I'm anticipating its arrival.)

There's another line from a different poem that has also stuck with me; this one by e. e. cummings, whom I have always admired for the refusal to capitalize his name. The subject is a conscientious objector, who when pushed to the brink tells his captors, "I will not kiss your fucking flag." That these words have stayed with me for seventy or so years is, as they say in poker, a significant tell. You can't shove moral outrage to the side in the world we currently inhabit. You can't be a team player when loyalty only runs in one direction. And God knows, these days you can't be a Republican.

Complaints aside, there is much that I am grateful for. To paraphrase the great Sammy Sosa, journalism has been very, very good to me. Likewise, television, which has reached a wide audience for most of the stories I did. As for the stuff that's been swirling around inside me since I was a kid, well, it's still there: anxious, though perhaps not quite as much. Hopeful, because what else is there? Determined to keep going, since even at the age of ninety you never know what's going to happen next.

What you've just finished reading is where this book was supposed to end. But a recent series of tumultuous events have put the future of *60 Minutes* in jeopardy. On June 1, 2026, the new regime at CBS News, headed by conservative print journalist Bari Weiss, fired two of its correspondents, its executive producer, and her three top aides. Weiss's pick for the new person in charge is Nick Bilton, a tech journalist with producing credit on two documentaries but no experience in television news. Bilton's first staff meeting did not go well. In it, longtime *60 Minutes* correspondent Scott Pelley questioned Bilton's "slender" credentials and accused Weiss of "murdering" the show. The next day, Pelley too was fired.

Why Ms. Weiss chose to change the staffing of the most successful news show in television history is inextricably linked to the man who appointed her: David Ellison, the forty-three-year-old head of Paramount Skydance, the new owner of CBS News. Paramount's financing comes from David's father, Larry Ellison, a longtime Trump friend and one of the world's richest men. Paramount Skydance is currently engaged in a $110.9 billion takeover of Warner Bros. Discovery. If successful, a single entity would own not only CBS News, but CNN, HBO, the Discovery Channel, and two of Hollywood's five remaining motion picture studios. Never would so much power and influence be placed in the hands of so few.

The merger's fate rests with the FCC, whose chairman, Brendan Carr, is a Trump appointee. In a remarkable act of fealty, Carr has been known to replace the standard American flag pin on his lapel with a gold-plated effigy of Trump's head. It doesn't take a media expert to see where this is going and why the Ellisons need President Trump's approval to complete their takeover. (Trump's hostility to *60 Minutes* is well known. In 2025, the program's prior owner chose to settle a $16 million law suit Trump had filed against the program, even though it was widely considered to be without merit.)

What's at stake here, the muting of *60 Minutes*, is no small thing. As Scott Pelley writes in his Foreword to this book, "the First Amendment is forty-five words. It contains no asterisks, no exceptions, no fine print. It does not say the press shall be free unless its findings are embarrassing, expensive, or disruptive to the established order. The framers, who had just finished a war with a king, understood something we are in danger of forgetting: a republic without an aggressive, independent press is not a republic at all. It is a stage set."